Native Anthropology

JAPANESE SOCIETY SERIES

General Editor: Yoshio Sugimoto

Lives of Young Koreans in Japan
Yasunori Fukuoka

Globalization and Social Change in Contemporary Japan
J.S. Eades Tom Gill Harumi Befu

Coming Out in Japan: The Story of Satoru and Ryuta
Satoru Ito and Ryuta Yanase

Japan and Its Others:
Globalization, Difference and the Critique of Modernity
John Clammer

Hegemony of Homogeneity:
An Anthropological Analysis of *Nihonjinron*
Harumi Befu

Foreign Migrants in Contemporary Japan
Hiroshi Komai

A Social History of Science and Technology in
Contempory Japan, Volume 1
Shigeru Nakayama

Farewell to Nippon: Japanese Lifestyle Migrants in Australia
Machiko Sato

The Peripheral Centre:
Essays on Japanese History and Civilization
Johann P. Arnason

A Genealogy of 'Japanese' Self-images
Eiji Oguma

Class Structure in Contemporary Japan
Kenji Hashimoto

An Ecological View of History
Tadao Umesao

Nationalism and Gender
Chizuko Ueno

Native Anthropology: The Japanese Challenge
to Western Academic Hegemony
Takami Kuwayama

Native Anthropology

The Japanese Challenge to
Western Academic Hegemony

Takami Kuwayama

Trans Pacific Press

Melbourne

This English edition first published in 2004 by
Trans Pacific Press, PO Box 120, Rosanna, Melbourne, Victoria 3084, Australia
Telephone: +61 3 9459 3021   Fax: +61 3 9457 5923
Email: info@transpacificpress.com
Web: http://www.transpacificpress.com

Copyright © Trans Pacific Press 2004

Designed and set by digital environs Melbourne.
enquiries@digitalenvirons.com

Printed by BPA Print Group, Burwood, Victoria, Australia

Distributors

Australia
Bushbooks
PO Box 1958, Gosford, NSW 2250
Telephone: (02) 4323-3274
Fax: (02) 4323-3223
Email: bushbook@ozemail.com.au

USA and Canada
International Specialized Book
Services (ISBS)
920 NE 58th Avenue, Suite 300
Portland, Oregon 97213-3786
USA
Telephone: (800) 944-6190
Fax: (503) 280-8832
Email: orders@isbs.com
Web: http://www.isbs.com

Japan
Kyoto University Press
Kyodai Kaikan
15-9 Yoshida Kawara-cho
Sakyo-ku, Kyoto 606-8305
Telephone: (075) 761-6182
Fax: (075) 761-6190
Email: sales@kyoto-up.gr.jp
Web: http://www.kyoto-up.gr.jp

UK and Europe
Asian Studies Book Services
Franseweg 55B, 3921 DE Elst,
Utrecht, The Netherlands
Telephone: +31 318 470 030
Fax: +31 318 470 073
Email: info@asianstudiesbooks.com
Web: http://www.asianstudiesbooks.com

All rights reserved. No production of any part of this book may take place without the written permission of Trans Pacific Press.

ISBN 1-8768-4382-9 (Hardback)
ISBN 1-8768-4376-4 (Paperback)

National Library of Australia Cataloging in Publication Data

Kuwayama, Takami.
   Native anthroplogy: the Japanese challenge to Western
academic hegemony.
   Bibliography.
   Includes index.
   ISBN 1 876843 82 9.
   ISBN 1 876843 76 4 (pbk.).
   1. Anthropology – Japan. 2. Anthropology – Philosophy. 3.
Anthropology – Methodology. 4. Ethnocentrism. I. Title.
301.0952

In memory
of my father,
Keiichi Kuwayama
(1922 – 2003)

Contents

Preface	ix
Acknowledgments	xiv
1 'Natives' as Dialogic Partners: Some Thoughts on Native Anthropology	1
2 Native Anthropologists: With Special Reference to Japanese Studies Inside and Outside Japan	15
3 The 'World System' of Anthropology: Japan and Asia in the Global Community of Anthropologists	48
4 'Global' and 'National' Studies of Folklore: Lessons from Kunio Yanagita, an Intellectual Giant of Modern Japan	64
5 Ethnographic Reading in Reverse: *The Chrysanthemum and the Sword* as a Study of the American Character	87
6 Representations of Japan in American Anthropology Textbooks: Focusing on the Use of Photographs	115
Notes	146
References	159
Index	171

Figures

Figure 6.1 Anthropologists' 'world map' 116
Figure 6.2 A typical example of 'photos only' 121
Figure 6.3 Nonverbal communication in Japan 125
Figure 6.4 The duality of Japanese character 128
Figure 6.5 Arranging marriages in Japan 130
Figure 6.6 A modern, nuclear family in Japan 132
Figure 6.7 Another look at the modern, nuclear family in Japan 134

Grateful acknowledgment is made to the following organizations for permission to reproduce material in this book:

- *Figures 6.2, 6.4 and 6.5*: Photo Researchers, Inc.
- *Figure 6.4*: Australian Picture Library
- *Figure 6.7*: Stock, Boston

Tables

Table 6.1 Introductory textbooks on anthropology selected for content analysis 119
Table 6.2 Classification of representations of Japan in 19 American anthropology textbooks used in the early 1990s 120

Preface

The central theme of this book is the position of 'natives' in what I call the 'world system' of anthropology. Since anthropology originally developed in the West mainly as a science of 'primitive' people under colonial rule, scholars used to gather ethnographic data and interpret it in books and articles without seriously considering the reactions of the people they were describing. The situation has changed dramatically in the postcolonial age, when the traditional boundary between the colonizer/researcher and the colonized/researched has become increasingly blurred. Not only do today's 'natives' read what has been written about them, they have also learned to write about their own culture in their own language, from their own perspective. Since their discourse is often associated with native rights movements, or more generally, ethnic nationalism, it has often clashed with the discourses of outsiders, especially those of researchers from former colonizing powers. A major task in contemporary anthropology, then, is the creation of a 'dialogic space' between the describer and the described, as well as among all the people concerned with the culture studied, without privileging one kind of discourse over another.

Seen globally, Japan is placed on the periphery of the academic world system. The Japanese resemble anthropologists' 'natives' because they have long been objects of representation, but their voice hardly reaches the center of the system. This is symbolized by two facts. First, the National Museum of Ethnology in Leiden, one of the oldest museums of its kind in the world, opened in 1837 when it acquired Philipp F. von Siebold's collection of Japanese artifacts. This history shows that Japan was among the first 'exotic' nations to be exhibited in European museums. Second, the Japanese were equally interested in the study of other people and culture. The first professional association was formed when the Anthropological Society of Nippon was founded in 1884, followed by the establishment of the Japanese Society of Ethnology in 1934. With a membership of approximately 2,000 academics, JSE has grown into one of the world's largest organizations of social and cultural anthropology, but its activities are little known outside the country. Some scholars who have been studying Japan for years do not even know of its existence. (JSE has announced that it will change its name to the Japanese Society of Cultural Anthropology in April, 2004). My major objective in this book is to analyze this situation by focusing on the politics involved in the production, dissemination, and consumption of anthropological knowledge on a global scale.

I became interested in this issue when I found that Japan has a voluminous anthropological literature, which has virtually been untapped by non-Japanese scholars, except by the few people, mainly from East Asia, who were educated in Japan. Having received much of my anthropological training in the United States, I had been unaware of the Japanese contribution to the discipline until I returned home in 1993. If anything, I had been influenced by the prejudices against non-Western scholarship that lurk at the back of many American anthropologists' minds. Like racism, these prejudices are often difficult to prove, but through listening to talks given at academic conferences, and from casual conversations I had at social gatherings given at such conferences, it became clear to me that there are deep misgivings about, even hidden contempt for, indigenous (i.e., non-Western) knowledge. This attitude seemed curious to me because, when doing fieldwork, anthropologists patiently listen to the stories their informants tell, even when they do not make much sense in terms of their own world view. Therefore, I have often asked myself why they could not be similarly attentive to the discourses of native intellectuals.

While researching in the United States, living there as a permanent resident for eleven years, I did not think about this question very seriously, but it began to occupy my mind soon after I returned to Japan. It was not long after my return that I noticed that there are many excellent anthropologists in Japan whose important works are little known abroad. Even the thirteen-volume series of cultural anthropology published in 1996–98 by Iwanami Shoten, Japan's leading publisher, have seldom been commented on by Western scholars. Japan does have a degree of influence over its Asian neighbors, where Japanese books are kept at major university libraries, but their impact on local scholars seems limited. That this is not simply due to the language barrier will be clarified later on. Also, I was pleasantly surprised to find that some of the major European works outside the Anglophone community had been translated into Japanese much earlier than in the United States or Great Britain, if they had been translated into English at all. Japanese scholars may not be very creative and original, but they are familiar with the major trends of thought in different parts of the world. To compete internationally, they must constantly upgrade themselves by studying foreign (mainly Western) literature. Conversely, the majority of Americans, including those specializing in Japan, can, it seems, afford to be ignorant of Japanese research, however significant. How can this difference be explained? What are the factors contributing to this 'inequality' in the academic enterprise?

This book is an attempt to answer these questions. The first three chapters, in particular, examine how American, British, and French scholarship has been privileged in the academic world system, rendering equally worthwhile contributions from other countries peripheral to the discipline's central debates. The remaining chapters address more specific issues relating to the anthropology of Japan.

A brief description of the development of my ideas concerning these matters is required to explain how they have come to take their present form. In 1995, two years after my return home, I wrote my first essay on native anthropology. This essay was later revised and published in 1997 in the JSE journal, *Minzokugaku Kenkyū* (*Japanese Journal of Ethnology*), under the title, '*Genchi no Jinruigakusha*' (Native Anthropologists). For non-Japanese readers, I posted an English summary on an Internet mailing list called EASIANTH (East Asian Anthropology). I immediately received responses from many people in different parts of the world. Soon afterwards, Roger Goodman (University of Oxford) invited me to write a more detailed summary for the newsletter of Japan Anthropology Workshop, known as JAWS. My summary eventually appeared with an extensive critique by Jan van Bremen (Leiden University), who had read the Japanese original. Later still, our debate was joined by Pamela Asquith (University of Alberta), who discussed the politics of scholarship by taking the example of Japanese primatology. To further examine the issues, a panel was organized for the 12th JAWS meeting, which was held at the National Museum of Ethnology, Osaka, 1999. In 2000, the results were published in a special issue, entitled 'Japan Scholarship in International Academic Discourse' (Pamela Asquith, guest editor), of *Ritsumeikan Journal of Asia Pacific Studies*. This issue included the article on which Chapter 2 is based. This chapter occupies a central place in my present work.

Chapter 3 is a sort of sequel to Chapter 2. It clarifies my position vis-à-vis that of my critics. It also discusses the relationships between peripheral countries in the academic world system, focusing on Asia. The arguments contained in these chapters are re-presented in Chapter 1, which incorporates some new material from both inside and outside Japan. By relating the Japanese experience to that of other people, it demonstrates the contemporary significance of native anthropology in the wider world. This chapter is a modified version of the article that appeared in *Anthropology Today* (February, 2003), the bimonthly journal of the Royal Anthropological Institute, UK. I met the editor, Gustaaf Houtman, in Washington, D.C. in 2001, when I attended the 100th annual meeting of the American Anthropological Association. He happened to be listening to comments I made from the floor in a session on the internationalization of anthropology. After the session, which was sparsely attended, mostly by non-Americans, he invited me to write for his journal.

Chapter 4 discusses the idea of 'global' and 'national' folkloristics, which was presented in the 1930s by Kunio Yanagita, the founder of Japanese folklore studies. To my knowledge, this is the first essay written in English on that topic. When reading the new *Yanagita Kunio Zenshū* (*Complete Works of Kunio Yanagita*), I discovered by chance that Yanagita had anticipated many of the problems with which native anthropologists are faced today. I gave my first presentation on Yanagita at the 1999 annual meeting of the Folklore Society of Japan. With the encouragement of Michiya Iwamoto (Tokyo University), I wrote a full-length article for the FSJ journal, *Nihon Minzokugaku*. Before it was published, I presented a paper in English on the same subject at an international conference called 'The Human Sciences and the Asian Experience,' held at the Centre for the Study of Culture and Society, Bangalore, India, 2000. Chapter 4 is based on these earlier works. I should add that Yanagita's works are inspiring, but are written in old Japanese, with a distinctive style. I had to repeatedly rewrite this chapter to make it intelligible to non-Japanese readers. At no time in my career had I felt the difficulties of translation more keenly than when trying to complete that task.

Chapter 5 introduces a new concept – 'ethnographic reading in reverse.' The basic idea is that ethnographic accounts of other people can be read as narratives of the author's self using those people as a mirror. I first came across this idea in 1992, when I gave a talk at a workshop held in Tokyo on the American approach to the study of the Japanese *ie* (family). I had to wait some eight years, however, before I was prepared to clarify its theoretical significance for native anthropology. I wish to thank the graduate students at the Department of Social Anthropology, Tokyo Metropolitan University, for having invited me to give a lecture on 'reverse ethnography' at one of their regular meetings in late 2000.

Chapter 6 shows how Japan has been represented in American anthropology textbooks. It is a slightly different version of my earlier work, which appeared as the first of the occasional papers series, Europe Japan Research Centre, Oxford Brookes University, UK. I first met Joy Hendry, directress of this institute, when I visited Oxford in the winter of 1992. In 1998, she kindly invited me to teach a graduate course on Japan while she was on leave. The article included in the occasional papers series was based on an oral presentation I gave at that time. Louella Matsunaga edited my manuscripts for inclusion in the series.

All this makes clear that this book is a product of a dialogue I have had in the past decade with academics in various parts of the world. I occasionally make harsh comments about the Western anthropologists positioned at the center of the academic world system, but I trust these will be received in the spirit of constructive criticism with which they are intended.

Takami Kuwayama
Tokyo, Japan
July, 2003

Acknowledgments

This book has six chapters. Four of them were originally published as journal articles in English or Japanese, but they have been modified or rewritten substantially for inclusion in this book. The article on which Chapter 1 is based appeared under the same title in *Anthropology Today* (February, 2003). Chapter 2 is a revised version of the article that appeared in *Ritsumeikan Journal of Asia Pacific Studies* (Volume 6, December, 2000), published by the Ritsumeikan Center for Asia Pacific Studies, Ritsumeikan Asia Pacific University, Oita, Japan. Chapter 4 represents a major revision of '*Yanagita Kunio no "Sekai Minzokugaku' Saikō*" (A Reconsideration of Kunio Yanagita's 'Global Folkloristics'), which appeared in *Nihon Minzokugaku* (*Bulletin of the Folklore Society of Japan*), volume 222, May, 2000. And Chapter 6 was originally published as the first of the occasional papers series, Europe Japan Research Centre, Oxford Brookes University, UK.

I am indebted to many people in different parts of the world for their support and encouragement in writing this book. My thanks go first to Yoshio Sugimoto, professor at La Trobe University, Australia, who kindly agreed to publish my work through the company he has established. I feel honored to have this book included in the Japanese Society Series, which is recognized as a pioneering project, introducing the international community to Japanese scholarship in the humanities and the social sciences. I also appreciate the professional assistance provided by the staff members at Trans Pacific Press. In particular, I am obliged to Roger Averill for his superb editing and insightful comments and suggestions. Among the people to whom I should like to express my special gratitude are, in alphabetical order, Pamela Asquith (University of Alberta, Canada), Tsuneo Ayabe (emeritus, Tsukuba University, Japan), Harumi Befu (emeritus, Stanford University, USA), Jan van Bremen (University of Leiden, the Netherlands), J. S. Eades (Ritsumeikan Asia Pacific University, Japan), Robert Edgerton (University of California, Los Angeles, USA), Roger

Goodman (University of Oxford, UK), Kyung-Koo Han (Kookmin University, Korea), Joy Hendry (Oxford Brookes University, UK), Gustaaf Houtman (Royal Anthropological Institute, UK), Michiya Iwamoto (Tokyo University, Japan), Nobuo Kazashi (Kobe University, Japan), William Kelly (Yale University, USA), Kwang-Ok Kim (Seoul National University, Korea), Takashi Konami (emeritus, Tokyo University of Foreign Studies, Japan), Takie Sugiyama Lebra (emeritus, University of Hawaii, USA), Gordon Mathews (Chinese University of Hong Kong, China), Louella Matsunaga (independent, UK), Hirochika Nakamaki (National Museum of Ethnology, Japan), Yuji Nakanishi (Fukuoka University, Japan), Ichiro Numazaki (Tohoku University, Japan), Emiko Ohnuki-Tierney (University of Wisconsin-Madison, USA), Hiroki Okada (Kobe University, Japan), James Roberson (Oxford Brookes University, UK), Akitoshi Shimizu (Hitotsubashi University, Japan), Ken'ichi Sudo (Kobe University, Japan), Akira Takeda (emeritus, Ibaraki University, Japan), Yasuko Takezawa (Kyoto University, Japan), Yoshio Watanabe (Tokyo Metropolitan University, Japan), Matori Yamamoto (Hosei University, Japan), Shinji Yamashita (Tokyo University, Japan), and Teigo Yoshida (emeritus, Tokyo University, Japan). I greatly appreciate these people's friendship, advice, and suggestions.

Finally, I should like to thank my wife, Yumi, for having shared with me the joy and sorrow of life since we first met as students. To my children, Takaaki, who was known as Aki among his American teachers and friends, and Satomi, who greatly enjoyed her early years spent in the United States, I am grateful for their emotional support. I also wish to express my appreciation to my parents-in-law, Kunio and Taeko Nakagome, who live with us. For my mother, Teiko Kuwayama, I have no word but *arigatō*.

1 'Natives' as Dialogic Partners: Some Thoughts on Native Anthropology

Native anthropology is one of the major concerns among contemporary anthropologists in Asia and the Pacific region. It is defined here as the attempt by 'natives' (henceforth used without quotation marks) to represent their people, usually in their own language, from native points of view. Native anthropology challenges the existing anthropological practice in two respects. First, it takes objection to the position customarily assigned to natives as objects of representation, which has excluded them as active agents in ethnographic reading and writing. Natives have played important roles in the construction of life histories and ethnographic films, but the final authority usually rests with outside researchers, and natives have at best been acknowledged as collaborators. With some notable exceptions, they have seldom been credited as co-authors.[1] Second, native anthropology represents efforts in many parts of the world to overcome Eurocentrism or Western academic hegemony. In the postcolonial world, the emergence of native anthropologists marks a blurring of the boundary between the colonizer/seer/describer/knower and the colonized/seen/described/known.[2]

Why native anthropology today?

Native anthropology is not a new issue. In 1978, a large symposium entitled 'Indigenous Anthropology in Non-Western Countries' was held in Austria with the sponsorship of the Wenner-Gren Foundation for Anthropological Research (Fahim 1982). At that time, the question of whether or not indigenous social science was possible caught the attention of many scholars in the Third World. In the process of nation-building, new countries in Asia and Africa had encountered a range of problems that could not easily be solved within Western intellectual frameworks, demonstrating a serious gap between Western theory and the reality of the Third World. This gap cast doubt on the 'relevance' of Western thinking in non-Western settings (Alatas 2001). The search for 'alternative discourses' has a long history.

There are, however, two major factors contributing to the current interest in native anthropology. The first has to do with changing relationships between the describer and the described in ethnography. In the past, 'primitives' (natives) were merely objects of representation, but with the spread of literacy, many of them are now able to read ethnography written about their culture and history. As the Mexicans' criticisms of Oscar Lewis's *The Children of Sanchez* (1961) show (Brettell 1993:11–12), they have gained the power to protest against outsiders' representations if they find them objectionable. Native protest is taken seriously today, for it is related to the wider issue of indigenous people's rights. Furthermore, as anthropology has spread to former colonies, native intellectuals have learned to write about their own people from their own viewpoints. Their accounts often conflict with those of outside anthropologists.

The second factor in the current interest in native anthropology is the growing awareness of power inequality between the researcher and the researched. This awareness has been fostered by the works of critical theorists, mostly notably by Edward Said's *Orientalism* (1978), who revealed the close connection between power and knowledge in cultural representation. Since then, anthropologists have increasingly had to concede more influence and control to native voices. However unrefined by Western academic standards, native discourse can no longer be dismissed as mere background 'noise.'

On the concept of native

The English word *native* is derived from the Latin *nativus*, meaning 'born' or 'innate.' In the etymological sense of the word, we may say that everyone is a native of one place or another. During the early colonial period, however, anthropologists tended to use *native* in a pejorative sense. This usage placed natives in the non-Western world in the early stages of social evolution. Among the best known works of social evolution is Lewis H. Morgan's *Ancient Society* (1877), which classified human 'progress' into three successive stages – 'savagery,' 'barbarism,' and 'civilization.' The unequal relationship between the colonizer/civilized and the colonized/primitive is thus inscribed in the word *native*. This explains why the study of one's own culture in Europe or the United States is ordinarily called *insider* research, whereas the same type of study elsewhere is called either *native* or *indigenous*.

The distinction between *native* and *indigenous* is ambiguous and complex. Generally, scholars in the Third World prefer the latter because it is more or less free of the colonial implications of the former. Although it is possible to substitute *local* for *indigenous*, *local* is a neutral word that merely points to a particular place. It therefore conceals important power differences. I have decided to use the term *native* for three reasons. First, it testifies to the 'colonial roots' of anthropology. Second, it draws attention to the 'intrusion' into the academic space of former colonial powers by their subjects. And third, this intrusion signals the radical change taking place in the structure of anthropological knowledge.

Who, then, are natives? By definition, natives are members of the community under study. Since, however, anthropology developed mainly as the study of 'primitive' societies, the term tends to be used to refer to people in peripheral places far removed from the metropolitan centers of the West. In this book, however, natives are broadly understood to be people, especially non-Westerners, who are objects of anthropological research, regardless of their country's level of technological development. Thus, the Japanese can be natives, despite their own colonial past, for they have been, and continue to be, studied and described by Western anthropologists.

The definition of 'native anthropologists' is more complex than that of natives. At the most fundamental level, these are anthropologists who belong to the research community by birth. However, professionally trained researchers are seldom found in the small communities anthropologists have traditionally studied. They ordinarily live outside the immediate research community, and many of them work at educational institutions in the cities. Local anthropologists are, therefore, native only in a secondary sense of the word. Yet, they are part of the larger society under observation, and have common interests with the people being studied. This distinguishes them from non-native researchers, who may maintain a distance or even write about them from detached viewpoints in the name of science.

I must hasten to add that native is a relational concept. Like 'insiders' and 'outsiders,' the category of people defined by this term is not fixed. Rather, it shifts according to the situation in which researchers find themselves. For example, Japanese anthropologists from the cities studying rural communities in Japan are outsiders and non-native to the community they research. They may, however, be considered insiders and native in relation to foreign anthropologists studying Japan. Native is therefore a fluid category whose meaning is dependent on the social context. For a more detailed discussion of this point, see Chapter 2.

Native anthropology: An epistemological issue

In major collections of articles on native anthropology (e.g., Fahim 1982; Messerschmidt 1981), much space has been devoted to discussion of the merits and demerits of native/insider research. It has been argued, for example, that native anthropologists have few language problems and that they can quickly establish a rapport with their informants. It has also been argued that this advantage has its own problems because the cultural proximity between the researcher and the researched makes it difficult to attain objectivity. Another disadvantage of native anthropologists, according to scholars from the Third World, is that they are often mistaken for government agents. There is, therefore, general agreement that native/insider research has both advantages and disadvantages.

The importance of such arguments is obvious; they anticipate the current anthropological discourse on 'anthropology at home.' They relate, however, mainly to fieldwork methods, and the significance of native anthropology would be diminished considerably if the discussion were limited to that of methodology. Because the problems posed by native academics – what we might call the 'professional others' – have the potential to restructure anthropology, it is important to address native anthropology as an epistemological issue, not simply a methodological one.

The ethnographic triad

The place of natives in anthropology may be clarified by applying insights derived from museum studies. Recent studies of ethnological museums have shown the importance of considering the relationship between three parties – the displayer, the displayed, and the viewer. Over the past few decades, the debate on the politics of cultural representation and display has raised awareness that museums are forums for 'dialogue' between the displayer and the displayed, between the displayer and the viewer, and between the displayed and the viewer, rather than 'temples' where sacred objects are enshrined (Yoshida 1999).

This observation may neatly be applied to ethnography as a genre of writing. Like museums, ethnography involves three parties – the writer, the described, and the reader – and they form what may be called the 'ethnographic triad.' Since this simple fact is frequently overlooked, it deserves some clarification. The first party in the triad is the anthropologist who does fieldwork, usually in other cultures, and writes up research results in the form of ethnography. Anthropology is 'homemade,' in the words of Clifford Geertz (1988:145), because many of its activities are carried out at home after returning from the field. The second party in the ethnographic triad consists of natives who have been described in the ethnography. As I have already pointed out, native anthropologists are not usually immediate objects of study, but they are part of the wider society that is being represented.

The third party in the ethnographic triad has received little attention in previous studies. I distinguish four major categories within the ethnographic readership: (1) people who belong to the same linguistic and cultural community as the writer – in most cases, these people are the assumed readers of ethnography, and they consist of both professional scholars and readers at large; (2) natives who have been studied and described – they used to be recognized only as objects of representation, but many of them are now able to read ethnographic accounts of their culture in the original or in translation;[3] (3) native anthropologists, who often work in partnership with outside anthropologists during fieldwork, but tend to be rivals in trade. Many of them have leveled harsh criticisms against Western ethnography, as I will discuss later; (4) people who are neither describers nor the described – anthropologists in third-party countries belong to this category.

Keeping the ethnographic triad in mind, it becomes clear that the recent postmodern critique of ethnography has missed two important points. First, as is symbolically expressed in the title of James Clifford's and George Marcus' canonical text *Writing Culture* (1986), the postmodernists' concern with *reading* and *writing* has led them to pass over the question of what it means to be the subject of those writings. The second party in the ethnographic triad has been virtually ignored. Second, the assumed readership is almost limited to the first category of readers identified above (i.e., people who belong to the same community as the writer). The absence of efforts at writing in the local language to engage in 'dialogue' with the people described clearly attests to this point.

Moreover, little has been said about how to communicate with anthropologists outside the Anglophone world. In *Anthropology as Cultural Critique* (1986), George Marcus and Michael Fischer proposed 'experimental' writing styles suitable for conveying other cultural experience. As they pointed out, new styles such as narratives are useful in stimulating the assumed readers' imagination of other cultures. But the words and expressions used are culturally loaded, and their meanings are not immediately clear to foreign readers from different cultural backgrounds. Experimental writing styles are powerful within the same linguistic community, but they are not the best means of engaging in 'dialogue' with readers from other linguistic communities.

Natives and their discontent

This 'dialogue' is not the dialogue between anthropologists and their informants during fieldwork, as debated among proponents of experimental ethnography. These ethnographers are primarily interested in composing ethnographic texts based on the dialogue they have had with their informants. In other words, their primary interest is in *writing*. By contrast, the dialogue I am proposing occurs *after* the ethnography is written, and it should ideally engage all the people concerned, including the describer and the described.

No one would seriously disagree that anthropology's public mission is to promote cultural understanding among different groups of people. Ironically, people all over the world have accused anthropologists on various occasions of spreading 'misconceptions' of their culture, as the Samoans' persistent criticisms of Margaret Mead's *Coming of Age in Samoa* (1928) illustrate (Yamamoto 1994). In my view, these misconceptions have more to do with the natives' outsider status in the study of their own culture than with factual errors anthropologists may have made. Native discontent stems from the structure of ethnography itself, in which the anthropologists' 'dialogic others' are the readers within their own linguistic and cultural community, many of whom are their professional colleagues. As Johannes Fabian (1983:85) put it, though in a different context, natives are 'posited (predicated),' but are 'not spoken to.' They are, in other words, excluded from the dialogic circle of ethnography and acquire legitimacy only as objects of thought.

Like the Samoans, many people studied by anthropologists have complained about what has been said of their culture because, while they were extensively 'exploited' as sources of information during fieldwork, they are seldom consulted once it is over and the ethnography is written. As the Native American anthropologist Beatrice Medicine contended, it is not unusual that the finished products (i.e., books and articles) are not even shown to them. Medicine had this to say:

> The generations-old complaints by Native people still ring true: 'We never see the books or papers you write about us,' or, 'Are you writing a book about us to make a lot of money?'...Native expectation is that the finished product will be at least shown to them. This expectation is the source of the greatest disaffection in Native groups (Medicine 2001:330).

It would, therefore, be incorrect to suppose that natives are merely contesting the accuracy of outsiders' representations, which almost inevitably include errors and misunderstandings, despite their revelatory values.

Native protest

The controversy between Jocelyn Linnekin and Haunani-Kay Trask about Hawaiian nationalism illuminates this point.[4] In her pioneering work on the invention of tradition, Linnekin (1983) maintained that the resurgence of interest in their history among urban Hawaiians is part of the new movement for cultural revival. In her view, the traditions they admire have been selected arbitrarily and thus 'invented' to suit the present political purposes, rather than having been handed down from their ancestors. Linnekin then cited the example of *aloha 'āina* (love of land), arguing that it has become a convenient slogan in the Hawaiians' demand for the return of Kaho'olawe, where their ancestors are allegedly buried.

Linnekin's constructionist view is theoretically exciting, but she has met strong opposition from Hawaiians who accuse the U.S. Navy of destroying sacred ground for military training. Among her fierce critics is Trask, the author of *From a Native Daughter* (1999), who contended that *aloha 'āina* is an authentic tradition of her people. She argued that *aloha 'āina* has taken on a political meaning because land use is now contested, remarking, 'The Hawaiian cultural motivation reveals the persistence of traditional values, the very thing Linnekin claims modern Hawaiians have "invented"' (Trask 1999:128). Particularly important in our context is her assertion that outsiders' representations have been privileged over those of natives.

> In a colonial world, the work of anthropologists and other Western-trained 'experts' is used to disparage and exploit Natives. Thus, what Linnekin writes about Hawaiians has more potential power than what Hawaiians write. Proof of this rests in the use of Linnekin's argument by the U.S. Navy that Hawaiian nationalists have invented the sacred meaning of Kaho'olawe Island (Trask 1999:129).

Trask further maintained that statements made by white people are accepted as 'facts' with little verification, whereas natives' assertions are subjected to strict examination of evidence. She attributed these different standards of proof to racism. This suggests that anthropology can be used not only to de-legitimize native claims, but also to legitimize possibly coercive relationships by outsiders.

Another example of strong native protest is found in the writings of Molefi Kete Asante, a proponent of Afrocentrism. Criticizing European Africanists for what he calls 'the European project of white domination,' Asante argued that 'in the West, Africans themselves have often remained outside of the standard interpretations of data about Africa or Africans' (Asante 1999: 29). With the emergence of African studies by Africans, however, 'it is no longer possible for Europeans to interpret the African's world for their own interests without the utter involvement of Africans on both sides of the Atlantic' (Asante 1999:29). Although Asante's notion of Afrocentrism contains some extreme ideas that could develop into a blinkered cultural nationalism, his discontent stems from the same source that Trask has criticized.

The 'world system' of anthropology

The discourse of native intellectuals should be distinguished from that of laymen. The internal diversity of a native community should also be noted. Generally, however, native voices have seldom reached the metropolitan West, where much of the esteemed knowledge about them is produced. Even when they are heard, they tend to be stigmatized as 'biased' or simply ignored as 'noise.' I submit that this situation derives from the power inequality in the 'academic world system,' rather than from the alleged lack of sophistication of native discourse.

Every academic field constitutes a 'world system.' Like the economic world system explained by Immanuel Wallerstein (1979), this system consists of two major groups of countries or regions: the 'core' (center) and the 'periphery' (margin). For the sake of simplicity, the group that falls in between – what Wallerstein called 'semi-periphery' – is not discussed here.[5] In anthropology, the United States, Great Britain, and to a lesser extent France, together constitute the core. Even though there are internal differences, their collective power is such that other countries, including those in the rest of Europe, have been relegated to the periphery. As the late Swedish scholar Tomas Gerholm aptly pointed out, the relationship between the core and the periphery may be likened to that between the mainland and remote islands (Gerholm 1995). People on the mainland can go through their life oblivious of what happens on the remote islands, but the opposite is hardly true. Similarly, scholars in the center can safely ignore their counterparts in the periphery without risking their career, whereas the latter will be labeled 'ignorant' or even 'backward' if they are unfamiliar with the former's research. This asymmetrical relationship shows that the core has the power to dictate the dominant modes of academic discourse. The periphery is forced to accept them, for example by adopting the central scholars' theories, methods, and writing styles, if it wishes to be recognized internationally. Under these circumstances, it is difficult for scholars in the periphery to speak as equals with those at the center.

Simply put, the world system of anthropology defines the politics involved in the production, dissemination, and consumption of knowledge about other peoples and cultures. Influential scholars in the core countries are in a position to decide what kinds of knowledge should be given authority and merit attention. The peer-review system at prestigious journals reinforces this structure. Thus, knowledge produced on the periphery, however significant and valuable, is destined to be buried locally unless it meets the standards and expectations of the core – hence the neglect of native discourse in the wider world.

Minority scholars in the United States often complain about their marginal status within American anthropology. The fact is, however, that their voices are communicated to the rest of the world to a much greater degree than that of natives in other regions because they are at least located in the outer reaches of the center of the academic world system.[6]

Skirmishes with 'peripheral' scholars

Let us take up the example of Japan to further clarify this point. Japan is one of the few Asian countries in which anthropology is firmly established as an academic discipline. Internationally, however, its influence is very limited. With some exceptions, Japanese anthropologists are placed on the margin of the world system, and their voices are seldom heard at the center. The account below shows an unusual case in which central and peripheral discourses about Japan clashed on the pages of an international journal.

In 1994, Sandra A. Niessen contributed to *Museum Anthropology* a review article on the permanent exhibition of Ainu culture at Japan's National Museum of Ethnology, known as Minpaku, where she had spent six months as a guest researcher. She presented her article as a reflection on the complexities of representation of indigenous peoples in local and international settings. In Japan, however, the review was received as a severe criticism of local Japanese scholarship. Her arguments may be summarized as follows. (1) Since its opening in 1977, Minpaku has had a close relationship with Shigeru Kayano, the first Ainu to be elected to the Japanese Parliament. Although it was couched in the context of a complex comparative argument, some Japanese scholars objected to what they perceived as Niessen's suggestion that Kayano's view of Ainu culture resembled that of a salvage anthropologist. (2) The ethnographic film made by Minpaku at Kayano's house in Hokkaido was shot in 'sanitized' settings, thus creating 'a fictitious illusion of authenticity.' (3) The politics of cultural representation is seldom discussed among Minpaku staff. The museum has no official policy about what to display and how to display it; exhibitions are programmed on a case-by-case basis. (4) The history of struggle between the Ainu and the dominant Japanese is concealed in Minpaku's exhibition. In North America, similar exhibitions would be criticized as blatant attempts to oppress ethnic minorities. (5) Minpaku's gallery creates an idyllic image of Ainu people. It calls to mind the exhibition *The Spirit Sings*, sponsored by Shell in Canada during the 1988 Calgary Olympic Games, at a time when the First Nation peoples represented in the exhibition were in fact in conflict with Shell over the exploitation of resources on their territory. The exhibition was boycotted by Native Canadian peoples, who gained international attention through their protests. (6) When Niessen asked Tadao Umesao, then Minpaku's director general, if such a reaction could occur in Japan, he 'laughed incredulously,' saying it was 'preposterous.'

Two Japanese anthropologists at Minpaku, Kazuyoshi Ohtsuka and Akitoshi Shimizu, raised strong objections to Niessen's review. Pointing out the trust and friendship Minpaku has assiduously worked to forge with Ainu people, Ohtsuka (1997) objected as follows. (1) Niessen's criticisms of Minpaku are scornful. (2) Her 'surprising misunderstandings' derive from her failure to consult Minpaku's publications, in which the museum's exhibition policies are clearly spelled out. (3) Niessen's article is based on 'superficial impressions.' Had she consulted Minpaku staff before publishing her paper, she could have avoided much trouble and embarrassment. (4) By misrepresenting the cause of Ainu people, Niessen has injured their dignity, and especially Kayano's reputation. (5) The 'illusion of authenticity' she problematized is an example of her quixotic discourse. The depicted Ainu themselves questioned her interpretation. (6) Niessen's claim that Minpaku should highlight the conflict between the dominant Japanese and the Ainu shows how she was intent on 'brainwashing' the Japanese with her own ideas.

Shimizu's objection was more theoretical than Ohtsuka's. He was particularly critical of Niessen's neglect of the Japanese-language literature. According to him, her neglect demoted Minpaku to an 'illiterate' status, 'without history.' In Shimizu's opinion, Niessen innocently assumed that she could understand Minpaku's exhibitions by participant observation only, a method originally developed to study non-literate people. The 'imagined'

Minpaku, said Shimizu, was then judged by the supposedly global standards of North America. Shimizu concluded that Niessen's article is 'a political text which has the effect of establishing the hegemony of the "North American" standards of museums and anthropology over their counterparts in Japan' (Shimizu 1997:120).

In her response to Ohtsuka and Shimizu, Niessen described their views as 'personal and sometimes unprofessional' (Niessen 1997:141). Niessen asserted that she had sent a draft of her article to her Japanese colleagues at Minpaku for feedback before publication, but received no response. Although some of her points are well taken, from my point of view her strategy was that of a detached theorist. For example, she virtually disregarded Ohtsuka's meticulous comments on Ainu history and its display at Minpaku, thereby avoiding a wrangle with Ohtsuka, an Ainu specialist. Instead, she wrote at length – with the benefit of hindsight – about the significance of her article, referring to some of the most recent theories in museum studies in North America. Although Niessen is Canadian and teaches at the University of Alberta, Ohtsuka and Shimizu criticized her for what they felt was too strong an American orientation, involving 'brainwashing' the Japanese and strengthening American 'hegemony.' Her defense was skillful and, insofar as the debate took place in the context of an American academic journal, the Japanese came across as intellectually immature and ideologically motivated. As for the criticism that she did not consult the Japanese-language literature, she ducked it by saying, 'This is an interesting position for museum professionals to take given that the primary goal of the exhibition is to submit its message through objects, and given that, particularly in this case, the museum is an international tourist attraction' (Niessen 1997:141).

I have not taken up this debate with the intention of disparaging Niessen. She reviewed a public exhibition on the strength of her abilities as a specialist on material culture and art without claiming to be an expert on the Ainu or on Japan. However, this case does contain some typical elements in the confrontation between native and outside scholars.[7] First, native texts (i.e., literature written in the local language) are often taken too lightly. Generally, outsiders find it difficult to appreciate the nuances and complexities of native scholarship. Anthropological methods centered on fieldwork do not provide adequate training for an effective use of the local literature. Second, native intellectuals tend to be regarded as 'knowledgeable informants,' rather than as equal research partners. Outside researchers are indebted to them for many things during fieldwork, but in the process of writing up research results, these researchers effectively monopolize the right to interpret the information provided by their 'informants.' Third, native discourse tends to be seen as 'propaganda' promoting a particular political position. This perception keeps natives outside the respectable academic community. Fourth, the researchers' moral responsibility toward the people they study is frequently evaded in the name of scholarship. Native claims that outsiders' representations harm their interests and reputation are often not considered carefully enough. If outside researchers fail to respond to native objections, this can be experienced as hidden, yet deep-seated, contempt for native intelligence.[8]

The danger of cultural nationalism

Having said this, we must remember that native discourse has often supported cultural nationalism, especially when it is connected with native rights movements. Moreover, native discourse tends to generate reverse Orientalism or so-called 'Occidentalism' because it is constructed in opposition to the prevailing discourse in the West. On more than a few occasions, native intellectuals, threatened by overwhelming power, have attempted to gain spiritual independence by eliminating Western influence. Unfortunately, their attempts have largely failed because modernity has been brought about under Western leadership. Its traces are visible in almost every area of everyday life throughout the world. It is safe to say that there is hardly any genuinely indigenous system of thought that is completely free from Western influence, whether positive or negative.

For people in the non-Western world, then, categorically refusing Western ideas is tantamount to depriving themselves of any intellectual power. Indeed, over-emphatic claims to difference have resulted in alienation from the wider world. A case in point is the marginalization of 'African social science' as described by Vineeta Sinha. Sinha (2000a:83) pointed out that although this discipline has merits of its own, it has become increasingly 'exotic' and marginalized because of its adamant rejection of Western intellectual traditions. The study of folklore in Japan may be cited as another example of this kind of marginalization. Founded by a group of ambitious scholars led by Kunio Yanagita (1875–1962), one of the intellectual giants of modern Japan, Japanese folklore studies had the potential to develop into an attractive, stimulating field. Yanagita was well versed with the works of leading European scholars of his time, including James Frazer, and he occasionally expressed his debt to them. His strong cultural nationalism, however, together with his desire to be the indisputable founder of the discipline, led him to intentionally omit bibliographies from his voluminous books. As a result, later generations of Japanese folklorists were unable to trace the origin of Yanagita's thought, and they have been isolated not only from their international colleagues, but also from Japanese specialists in other fields, including anthropology, which has developed under the strong influence of Western scholarship. In Chapter 4, I will examine Yanagita's ideas of 'global' and 'national' folkloristics.

Conclusion

In this opening chapter, I have interpreted the word *native* in its broad sense and discussed the various problems involved in cultural representation from the viewpoint of those being described. To avoid misunderstandings, I must point out that I am not advocating the exclusive right of natives to study their own people. While it is true that the deepest layers of a culture are not easily accessible to outsiders, it is also true that there are many things that escape insiders' attention and others that are best analyzed when seen from the outside. Problems arise, however, when temporary residents like anthropologists assume the superiority of their research skills and excellence of their interpretations while neglecting native reactions. Natives will object when foreign researchers elevate themselves to the status of ultimate judge on their culture. Anthropology has become a global discipline and is practiced today in many parts of the world. The advance of our discipline depends on whether or not we are prepared to accept natives as 'dialogic partners.'

2 Native Anthropologists: With Special Reference to Japanese Studies Inside and Outside Japan

Despite many criticisms of postmodernism, it has shed light on some of the basic problems lurking in anthropology, such as the subjectivity and politics of cultural representation, thereby contributing to a rethinking of the field. In this chapter, I will examine a major issue that has largely been overlooked in the postmodern critique by Western scholars. This issue concerns natives, not as objects of representation, but as readers, even critics, of ethnographies of their culture.

I find it strange that so much has been written concerning ethnographic reading and writing, but that surprisingly little has been written about what it means to be the subject of those writings. It has in fact seldom been asked what happens when natives read what Western anthropologists have written about them.[1] It is not difficult to imagine that things will be very complex when the natives themselves are anthropologists. In Japanese studies, confrontation has indeed occurred, both at academic and personal levels, over the legitimacy of Western analyses and interpretations of Japanese culture. The harsh criticisms leveled against Ruth Benedict's *The Chrysanthemum and the Sword* (1946) by some of the leading Japanese scholars (Kawashima et al. 1950) attest to this point.

Native anthropologists in the non-Western world are a special kind of the Other Westerners encounter in the field. Unlike ordinary informants, they have the professional competence to engage in scholarly dialogue, but they are part of the larger society under study and have common interests with the people being researched. In this regard, native anthropologists may be called 'professional others.' Because many of them were trained in the West or received a Western-style education at home, they can communicate with Western specialists relatively easily. This does not mean, however, that agreement of opinion is easily formed between them. If anything, they tend to be rivals in trade. The situation is particularly complex when native scholars are involved in native rights movements.

People in small-scale, non-literate societies – those people anthropologists used to call 'primitive' – depended on the civilized world for the representation of their history and culture. Even when 'primitives' learned to write, their marginal status made it virtually impossible for them to represent themselves to the outside world. The English word *represent* has three main meanings: 'describe,' 'symbolize,' and 'act as a deputy or spokesman for.' Representation is political, at least potentially, because it is unclear who describes whom or acts for whom, and for what purpose. Since 'primitives' were unable to read outsiders' representations, they had no means to defend themselves from the adverse consequences that the representations might have entailed.

After World War II, the circumstances surrounding 'primitives' changed dramatically as many of their societies were integrated into the Third World. They are no longer self-contained, isolated communities without political power. Nor are they today the exclusive focus of anthropological inquiry. Moreover, many of the peoples anthropologists study are capable of reading what has been written about them either in the original or in translation. They also protest against outsiders' representations if they find them distorted, offensive, or unacceptable. Cases in point are the Mexicans' criticisms of Oscar Lewis' *The Children of Sanchez* (1961) and the anger of Irish people over John Messenger's description of Irish culture in *Inis Beag* (1969) or that of Nancy Scheper-Hughes in *Saints, Scholars, and Schizophrenics* (1979) (Brettell 1993:9–14). Gone is the day when anthropologists freely gathered data in the field and wrote up research results in the office back home without considering how the people they were describing would respond.

In *Argonauts of the Western Pacific* (1922), Bronislaw Malinowski wrote that since tribal people are unable to explain their social organization, ethnographers must collect data, draw general inferences, and formulate abstract statements by themselves (Malinowski 1984:12, 396).

> After all, if natives could furnish us with correct, explicit and consistent accounts of their tribal organization, customs and ideas, there would be

no difficulty in ethnographic work. Unfortunately, the native can neither get outside his tribal atmospheres and see it objectively, nor if he could, would he have intellectual and linguistic means sufficient to express it. And so the Ethnographer has to collect objective data, such as maps, plans, genealogies, lists of possessions, accounts of inheritance, censuses of village communities. He has to study the behavior of the native, to talk with him under all sorts of conditions, and to write down his words. And then, from all these diverse data, to construct his synthesis, the picture of a community and of the individuals in it (Malinowski 1984:454).

Malinowski's view that Western ethnographers must study and write for natives because they cannot do so by themselves reminds us of Karl Marx's statement, 'They cannot represent themselves; they must be represented,' which appeared in the epigraph of Edward Said's *Orientalism* (1978). Putting that aside, I wonder if Western anthropologists' relationship with natives (especially professionally trained people) is as simple as Malinowski thought. Is it really true, as he contended, that if natives could explain themselves, 'there would be no difficulty in ethnographic work'? I doubt it. As the Japanese criticisms of Benedict demonstrate, native intellectuals are often fierce critics of Western analyses and interpretations of their culture. Confrontation has already occurred, and is likely to intensify as we enter the 'postcolonial' age, when no clear dividing line can be drawn between the describer (colonizer/seer/knower) and the described (colonized/seen/known).

Who are natives?

An explanation of the meaning of the word *native* is called for at the outset. A native anthropologist is basically an anthropologist who belongs to the research community by birth. However, just because he shares the same geographic, ethnic, and national background with the people being studied does not automatically make him a native. When their social backgrounds are very different, they consider each other as 'alien' regardless of origin. A case in point is the experience of M. N. Srinivas as described in his book *The Remembered Village* (1976). Born in an urban Brahmin family, Srinivas received his higher education at the University of Oxford, England. Under the guidance of A. R.

Radcliffe-Brown, he carried out research on the social structure of an Indian village called Rampura, Karnataka, located not very far from the village his family had left in his father's generation. In Rampura, Srinivas was treated not as a fellow villager, but as a noble 'guest' who had come all the way from the country of India's former colonizers. Not only did he find it difficult to adapt to rural life, he also felt a sense of alienation from the people with whom he shared his remote ancestors (Srinivas 1976:11–52).

By contrast, anthropologists who are non-native by birth may be considered native when they have fully assimilated into the local community. Frank Hamilton Cushing (1857–1900) is widely considered an archetype of 'going native' for his immersion in Zuni culture.[2] A comparison of Srinivas with Cushing shows that *native* is a subjective, fluid category. It also shows that the researcher's identity is determined not simply by his origin, but also by his relationship with the people he studies. Kirin Narayan (1993a:672) put it well when she remarked, 'Factors such as education, gender, sexual orientation, class, race, or sheer duration of contacts may at different times outweigh the cultural identity we associate with insider or outsider status. Instead, what we must focus our attention on is the quality of relations with the people we seek to represent in our texts.'

Jane Bachnik's analysis of Japan in terms of the paired concept of *uchi* (inside) and *soto* (outside) further clarifies this point. Bachnik (1994) contended that *uchi* and *soto* constitute a 'cline' (continuum), not opposites, on which the two domains are defined in relation to each other in constantly shifting social relations. As she argued, *uchi-soto* is not a fixed social category, but rather an 'index' that depends on the context for generating meaning. Thus, what is *uchi* in one context is *soto* in another, and vice versa, which bears a parallel to E. E. Evans-Pritchard's 'segmentary system' (Evans-Pritchard 1940:144). I would submit that the common assumption that people of the same ethnicity/nationality are insiders (*uchi*) and natives and that, conversely, those of a different ethnicity/nationality are outsiders (*soto*) and non-natives is a misconception. Such a view would merely strengthen cultural essentialism, in which culture is seen as a closed system with fixed boundaries that separate it from other such systems. It would also fan a patriotism that seeks to eliminate or disqualify different people in pursuit of cultural purity.

All this does not mean, however, that the notion of *native* is invalid. It means rather that a more precise definition is necessary in order to make it a useful category. I propose to distinguish between native and non-native by using two principles. The first has three components: (1) the culture used as a point of reference in ethnographic observation; (2) the assumed audience (readers); and (3) the language in which research results are written up. A Japanese anthropologist is a native of Japan not because he is a citizen of Japan, but because he writes in Japanese for Japanese readers from a Japanese viewpoint. (We should note that there is no single native point of view, for cultural experience is multiple). Theoretically, it is possible for the Japanese anthropologist to write in English for American readers, for example, while maintaining his native identity. In actual practice, it is difficult because writing effectively in a foreign language requires not only linguistic competence, but also familiarity with the reader's cultural background. In the process of achieving this familiarity, the writer adopts the perspective of his readers, at least partially.

The second principle by which we can distinguish the native from the non-native concerns the extent to which representations affect the researcher's identity and interests. Having become a Zuni priest, Cushing was unable to write against his tribe, so the story goes, because he had identified with them. Such identification is posited from the very beginning in native research (Jones 1970:255). Natives are often compelled to protest against outsiders' representations because they *live* the culture being studied, not simply observing it at a distance. We must remember, however, that few anthropologists are completely indifferent to the fate of the people they have studied. Given the intense interaction in the field, it would be more realistic to say that natives and non-natives are only different in the degree to which they are committed to the welfare of the research community. Differences are also found in the process by which they gain sympathy with the people in the community.

I examine below three questions often raised about native or insider anthropology. (Since actual usage does not always allow us to distinguish clearly between *native* and *inside* and between *non-native* and *outside*, these words are occasionally used interchangeably. It is, however, important to note the conceptual distinction made earlier). The first question is whether or not natives know themselves best. The answer is both in the affirmative and in the negative. On the one hand, there are things that only those people brought up in the native community can feel and understand. To use the famous phrase of Malinowski (1922) and, more recently, of Clifford Geertz (1983), it is very difficult for outsiders to appreciate the 'native's point of view.' It requires a complete familiarity with the local language, as well as the willingness to engage in emotional sharing (if not identification) with the natives, to explore the native mind. On the other hand, natives are not always the best source of information. There are three major reasons for this. To begin with the obvious, some things escape natives' attention because they are taken for granted. Research by outsiders sometimes upsets natives because it lays bare the cultural unconscious, which has been buried in the mind in the process of socialization, thus provoking collective anxiety and discomfort. Second, natives' knowledge of their culture is partial and limited because they are usually indifferent to things not directly related to their everyday life. And, third, being knowledgeable about something is not the same as being able to explain it. As Ikuya Sato (1992:150) contended, practical knowledge (i.e., knowledge necessary for practicing something) is different from critical knowledge (i.e., knowledge necessary for critically analyzing it).

The second question has to do with so-called 'scientific objectivity.' A major criticism directed toward research conducted by natives or insiders is that it is 'biased' and does not meet the scientific standard of 'objectivity' (Aguilar 1981:22). In the United States, this criticism has typically been leveled against researchers from ethnic minority groups; they are regarded as representing the political interests of their group. Similarly, in the colonial non-West, many native intellectuals have been criticized for their (alleged) attempt, out of nationalistic sentiments, to advocate a re-writing of their history. Such allegations are not completely misdirected. Given, however, the wide recognition today of the subjectivity of all cultural representation, we may ask why natives of the West are so often exempted from this same criticism. For example, it is well known that David Schneider used himself as an informant when he wrote *American Kinship* (1968), and the same may be said of Marshall Sahlins' *Culture and Practical Reason* (1976). Yet neither of these works has been received with as much skepticism as is normally accorded those written by minority scholars (Bakalaki 1997:520). This difference suggests that 'scientific objectivity' is not simply about the quality of research, but is also influenced by the degree of sympathy between the researcher and the academic community to which he belongs. Put another way, research by scholars in the mainstream of society tends to be considered 'objective' and 'neutral' because it arouses sympathy among the audience, whereas research by minority scholars tends to be labeled as 'subjective' and 'biased' for the opposite reason. We may say, then, that 'objectivity' is another name for domination of the weaker by the stronger.[3]

Finally, we should discuss the social and historical implications of the word *native*. As mentioned in Chapter 1, *native* is a colonial term that reflects the power inequality between the colonizer and the colonized. Since the word *native* refers to a person born in a certain place or country, we may say that everyone is a native of somewhere. In the early stages of colonialism, however, anthropologists used *native* as a synonym for *primitive*. As Arjun Appadurai (1992:35) stated, 'We have tended to use the word *native* for persons and groups who belong to those parts of the world that were, and are, distant from the metropolitan West.' Thus, when American anthropologists study American culture, they ordinarily call it '*insider* research,' whereas either *native* or *indigenous* is used for the same type of research by non-Western scholars (Messerschmidt 1981:13). The word *native* therefore makes other people not only different, but also distant in time and space. In this context, we must remember that fieldwork conducted among 'exotic' natives in faraway lands has been, and still is, considered more authentic than fieldwork at home. This not only shows the 'colonial roots' of anthropology, but also suggests how the notion of 'the field' has developed in anthropology (Gupta and Ferguson 1997).

The US-Japan relationship in the anthropology of Japan

The complex relationship between Western and native anthropologists is clearly seen in the study of Japan. Given that William Kelly (1991) has written an extensive review on the anthropology of Japan in the United States, it will suffice to say here that the early efforts of John Embree (1939) and Ruth Benedict (1946) have spawned a vast literature in the field. We should also note that Japanese scholars trained in the United States, most notably Emiko

Ohnuki-Tierney and Takie Sugiyama Lebra, and Japanese Americans, such as Harumi Befu, have also made significant contributions. Unfortunately, there has only been limited dialogue between anthropologists in the two countries. A look at the directory of the Japanese Society of Ethnology (JSE) shows that only a handful of Americans, or for that matter other non-Japanese, are members. Furthermore, presentations by non-Japanese are very rare at JSE meetings, both national and regional. Considering the fact that JSE is one of the largest anthropological organizations in the world, with a membership of approximately 2,000 people, this situation is deplorable. Also deplorable is the paucity of Japanese anthropologists familiar with American research on Japan. The Japanese tend to assume that only they can fully understand Japan. With some notable exceptions, contributions by non-Japanese scholars have seldom been taken seriously by native Japanese anthropologists. Thus, mutual indifference and ignorance characterize the US-Japan relationship with regard to the anthropology of Japan.

Two senior scholars made illuminating comments about this situation. In 1989, JSE published a special issue of the *Japanese Journal of Ethnology*, entitled 'Japan as Seen from the Outside.' One of the contributors was Robert J. Smith, a highly respected Japanologist in the United States. He remarked that he had been surprised when a JSE editor approached him, asking him to write a review essay for his Japanese colleagues, most of whom knew very little, according to the editor, about American research. As Smith wrote, 'For a long time, I have innocently assumed that our Japanese colleagues are far more familiar with American research than Americans are with Japanese research' (Smith 1989:360). Similarly, Takao Sofue, one of the first Japanese to study anthropology in the United States after World War II, commented that the lack of communication between the two countries has been a persistent problem since he was a student (Sofue et al. 1989:411).

The situation does not seem to have improved since then. If anything, it has gone from bad to worse. In the immediate postwar days, many American academics visited Japan with the financial support of institutions such as the Asia Foundation. They were eager to develop partnerships with local scholars, and indeed made friends with them, as the Michigan project in the village of Niiike, Okayama, showed (Beardsley, Hall, and Ward 1959). Today, with research funding having greatly diminished, it has become increasingly difficult for Americans to conduct long-term research abroad. Moreover, the younger generation shows little interest in collaborating with the Japanese; many of them carry out fieldwork in Japan without consulting Japanese specialists, and 'disappear' quickly once fieldwork is completed.

A major factor behind this change is the development of a self-contained community of Japan specialists in America, which has been fostered by the maturity of Japanese studies there. When the study of Japan was a developing field, they needed the assistance of Japanese scholars, but once established, they have become more independent.[4] Unfortunately, this independence has generated indifference toward, even disrespect for, Japanese scholarship. The harsh remarks I privately heard made by a major American Japanologist about the work of Japan's leading anthropologist, ranging from 'superficial' to 'nonsense,' amply demonstrate this point. The literary critic Masao Miyoshi, a naturalized citizen of America, went further when he described Takeshi Umehara, the first director general at the International Research Center for Japanese Studies, Kyoto, as 'a confused philosophy professor.' Miyoshi even called the entire institute 'a notorious think tank so far mainly staffed by mediocre neo-nationalist writers or worse' (Miyoshi 1991:81). While Miyoshi's assessment is not totally without support in Japan, it still reveals more about his attitude than it does about the reality of the Research Center and its inaugural director. By and large, the Americans' under-estimation of Japanese scholarship is due to their inability to fully appreciate it, which stems from their imperfect command of Japanese. Compared with European scholars, who typically have a strong philological background, American Japanologists generally have an insufficient understanding of the language. The anthropologists' record is far from commendable in this respect. The national pride of Americans in being the world's sole superpower may also be related to this. Harumi Befu's comments do not seem completely misdirected:

> The ethnocentrism of Americans is worsened by their megalomania complex, in other words, their conviction of being Number One in the world. This complex spills over from military and economic spheres to scholarship. Many believe – covertly if not consciously – their scholarship is Number One and consequently lack desire to learn from scholarship in other countries (Befu 1994:39).

Despite being well versed in the problems and pitfalls of cultural relativism, anthropologists generally maintain a relativistic outlook on the world. When doing fieldwork, at least, they respect the worldview of the people they are studying, listen carefully to the stories native informants tell, and take field notes meticulously, so as to understand their 'peculiar' customs. Why, then, can they not approach native scholarship with the same sympathetic attitude? *Nihonjinron* (theories of Japan) have certainly ideological elements associated with Japan's nationalism, but this feature is not found exclusively among the Japanese. As Ernest Gellner (1983) and Nagao Nishikawa (1992), among others, have pointed out, the notion of culture is inseparably related with the political framework of a modern nation-state. It would be unfair to accuse *nihonjinron*, as Peter Dale (1986:17; 140) did, of 'conceptual counterfeiting,' labeling it as a series of 'ideological mendacities.' As Kelly (1988:368) warned, such a statement reveals 'the Orientalist conceit that only the Western observer is capable of careful thinking and accurate understanding.'

On the other hand, we must remember that there is a persistent complaint in the United States that the Japanese treat foreign Japanologists as 'children,' paying little attention to their research. To illustrate this point, I proffer one example from my own experience. For an annual meeting of the American Anthropological Association held in the early 1990s, I organized a session on 'Japanese individuality.' My purpose was to reconsider the stereotypical image of the Japanese as a group-oriented people (Kuwayama 1991). Most of the presenters were junior Japanese researchers residing in the United States. To strike a balance in terms of age, I invited an established, visiting Japanese scholar, as well as a senior American professor to be discussants. Throughout the session, the American professor seemed unhappy because the papers were, in one way or another, critical of the American approach to the study of Japan. Then, when the Japanese professor criticized the research method of his American colleague, the American lost his temper, and retaliated with acrimonious comments when he took the floor. In short, he said that our session was a quintessential example of how the Japanese criticize foreigners without reading their works. 'Do your homework!' he exclaimed. Although there was a grain of truth in his statement, the way he presented himself as an admonishing schoolmaster was totally inappropriate to the occasion. His outburst destroyed the entire session. After the session was closed, he came to me and apologized for having been too harsh. What he said was symptomatic of the difficult relationship between American and Japanese anthropologists: 'I said it' he claimed, 'because the Japanese don't read us.' It was, however, unclear just how much he had read in Japanese.

Through this incident, I keenly became aware of the difficulties of engaging in scholarly dialogue across national and cultural boundaries. It also directed my attention to the structure of anthropological knowledge that has produced similar conflict between natives and non-natives in other parts of the world, as discussed in Chapter 1.

The 'world system' of anthropology

The American, and more generally Western, lack of interest in collaboration has led native anthropologists to complain that they are treated as knowledgeable informants or even local travel guides, rather than respected, equal research partners. This problem has occasionally been cited as an example of 'internal colonialism' within anthropology. I would submit that the low status of native anthropologists in the non-Western world derives from the imbalance of 'power' between the West and the rest. 'Power' means here the totality of forces that has enabled major Western countries to occupy a dominant position in modern history. More specifically, it refers to the academic hegemony of the United States, Great Britain, and to a lesser extent France, which together constitute the center of what I call the 'world system' of anthropology.

Robert J. Smith's earlier mentioned remarks in the *Japanese Journal of Ethnology* illustrate how the world system works. Smith gave two major reasons for the inadequate attention paid to Japanese anthropology in the United States. First, as the blurring of genres has occurred, more and more American anthropologists have come to study topics that were formerly investigated by sociologists, social psychologists, educationalists, historians, political scientists, literary critics, etc. As a result, they have more to learn from Japanese specialists in these fields than from anthropologists. Second, because the geographic focus of Japanese anthropologists has shifted since the mid-1960s from Japan to other cultures (see Footnote 4), very few of them possess the expertise sought by the Americans. Therefore, Smith argued, it is only natural that anthropologists in the two countries have ignored each other (Smith 1989:363).

Despite my admiration for Smith's distinguished career, I find it difficult to accept his view uncritically because it conceals the power imbalance in the world system. First of all, we should ask if communication across different disciplines with different theories, methods, and terminologies is as easy as he claimed. In my experience, even such basic terms as 'culture' are conceptualized differently in different disciplines, which works as a barrier to interdisciplinary dialogue. I suspect that foreign specialists in disciplines other than one's own look attractive when one regards them as data providers or knowledgeable informants. The second reason given by Smith is also questionable, for the paucity of research on Japan by Japanese anthropologists is no excuse for neglecting their works. To appreciate this, ask yourself if you read Lévi-Strauss or Geertz because they are specialists about a particular region. I think not. Most of us read them because they are intellectually stimulating, not because of their expertise as regional specialists. To say, then, that Americans are indifferent to Japanese research because the Japanese do not study Japan, is tantamount to saying that Americans see little intellectual value in what the Japanese have produced. At least, Japanese scholars are regarded as producers of 'local knowledge' as opposed to general theories applicable to all regions. We must also note that Smith avoided the question of the linguistic competence required to read Japanese-language literature.

Given the relatively short history of anthropology in Japan, and considering the small number of Japanese anthropologists with an international profile, it is understandable that Japan and the United States have yet to develop a research partnership on an equal basis. My point, however, is not about the two countries' relationship per se, but about the overall power structure of anthropological knowledge. As I pointed out, the United States, Great Britain, and France are positioned at the center of the world system of our discipline. Their power is such that other countries, including small European countries, have been relegated to the periphery of the system. As Tomas Gerholm and Ulf Hannerz (1982) observed, the relationship between the center and the periphery may be likened to that between the mainland and a remote island: people living on the former can go through life unaffected by what happens to those living on the latter, whereas the island-dwellers are dependant on those on the mainland for their basic needs. Similarly, central anthropologists do not need to learn from research conducted on the periphery, whereas peripheral anthropologists must always be attentive to research trends at the center.

> It seems that the map of the discipline shows a prosperous mainland of British, American and French anthropologies, and outside it an archipelago of large and small islands – some of them connected to the mainland by sturdy bridges or frequent ferry traffic, others rather isolated. On the mainland, people can go through their professional lives more or less unaware of what happens on the islands. The reverse seems not so often to be the case. If international anthropology to a great extent equals American + British + French anthropology, in other words, then these national anthropologies need hardly take external influences into account to more than a very limited degree (Gerholm and Hannerz 1982:6, quoted in Gerholm 1995:159–160).

Furthermore, scholars in different countries located on the periphery must communicate with each other through the center because locally produced knowledge is difficult to appreciate outside the local context. This applies, of course, to the core Western countries, but their power transforms the local into the global. (For more details, see the next chapter). It should be clear from this that Smith's view boils down to the contention – covert as it may be – that American anthropologists derive such overwhelming power from their leading position in the world system that they can safely ignore indigenous scholarship without risk to their careers.

We should recall here the debate on 'scientific colonialism' during the social turmoil of the 1960s. Johan Galtung amplified this concept when he vehemently objected to the research called 'Project Camelot,' which was conducted in Latin America with the support of the American Department of Defense. According to Galtung, scientific colonialism means 'a process whereby the center of gravity for acquisition of knowledge about a people is located elsewhere.' As he explained, 'There are many ways in which this can happen. One is to claim the right of unlimited access to data from other countries. Another is to export data about the country to one's own home country for processing into "manufactured goods," such as books and articles' (quoted in

Hymes 1972:49). Based on a classic definition of colonialism in the neo-colonial context, Galtung's view reflected the radical intellectual climate of the 1960s. In a similar vein, Jacques Maquet criticized the one-way movement of discourse in scientific colonialism. He maintained that anthropological research on Africa was evaluated not by Africans, but by professional standards alien to them. As he remarked, '[Anthropologists] were integrated into the colonial system, whose frame of reference was external to the dominated country and in which rewards were measured in terms meaningful only in the outside society' (Maquet 1964:48).

In the 1960s, the concept of scientific colonialism examined the 'predatory' relationship between Western anthropologists and native informants in the Third World. Today, the concept may usefully be applied in the analysis of the center-periphery relationship in the academic world system. Indeed, exploitation of the weaker by the stronger has occurred in academic relations between Japan and the United States. From the postwar days down to the present, we have often heard stories of data being stolen from joint research projects and reported without permission from the collaborating Japanese scholars; of papers co-authored by Americans and Japanese that were published only under the American names; of Japanese-language literature being exploited without credit being given to its authors, and so on.[5] When discussing the ethics of fieldwork, anthropologists tend to limit the issue to the infringement on the rights of indigenous people living in the hinterland. Considering the above, we should expand the scope of inquiry and examine the exploitation of peripheral anthropologists by those at the center.

In his 1994 article, J. S. Eades, who has long been teaching in Japan, asked why Japanese anthropology makes little impact outside Japan. He answered the question in terms of the institutional structure and practice of Japanese higher education. I find his approach useful, but not sufficient, because a country's external influence is correlated with its position in the world system. When science is understood as a socially constructed discourse, rather than a value-free system of knowledge, we realize that different national traditions of the same science have different degrees of influence. Japanese anthropology lacks international influence, not because the Japanese have little to offer, but because their frames of thought and expression do not neatly match those of the central scholars.

Many people have maintained that Japanese scholarship is not easily accepted in the West because of the language barrier. It has been overlooked, however, that the language problem does not simply relate to language fluency or lack thereof; rather, it relates to the social construction of language, and more importantly, to inequalities in the power of different languages in relation to the dominant forms of discourse (Asad 1986:156–160). Since the core Western countries dominate anthropological discourse, desirable knowledge is naturally obtained and produced more easily in their languages than in others. Conversely, knowledge more suited to peripheral (especially non-Western) languages tends to be devalued. It would, therefore, be simplistic to assume that translation will solve all the problems.[6] Furthermore, even if written in a language from the center of the world system, works arranged in unfamiliar, foreign styles are often dismissed as incomprehensible or as inferior products (Miyoshi 1991:9–10). Hence, studying in one of the core Western countries is essential if a scholar from the periphery is to enjoy a successful international career.

The imbalance of power in the academic world system is best illustrated by the peer review system that determines what is published in the core countries' leading journals. Submissions from peripheral scholars tend to be ranked low because they do not engage directly enough with the central discourse or do so in an unfamiliar way. Even when their papers are accepted for publication, they are often required to make changes to the content (e.g., making major revisions by consulting the most recent theories available in the reviewers' country) or to the writing style or both. This is a humiliating experience that both injures the authors' pride and tests their patience. The editing process thus works to maintain and strengthen the hegemony of central scholars. Certainly, many of the submissions from peripheral scholars look unsophisticated by the standards of the center. It should not be forgotten, however, that people positioned at the center have enough power to silence foreign discourses derived from assumptions different from their own. Narayan aptly described this situation when she stated:

> While it is hoped that we will contribute to the existing anthropological pool of knowledge, we are not really expected to diverge from prevailing forms of discourse to frame what [the African American anthropologist] Delmos Jones called a genuinely 'native' anthropology

as 'a set of theories based on non-Western precepts and assumptions' (Narayan 1993a:677).[7]

Pamela Asquith made insightful observations about the unfavorable treatment of Japan in the West by taking the example of Japanese primatology (Asquith 1996). She contended that Japanese research has been neglected, sometimes intentionally, because the Japanese view of the non-human world is radically different from that of mainstream scholars in the West. This difference probably results from the different religious backgrounds. Of particular interest is Asquith's contention that although many of the Japanese findings have been reported in English, they tend to remain unknown in the West because a 'stigma' is attached to Japanese primatology, which discourages scholars, especially those not yet established, from reading Japanese journals. Consequently, it has sometimes happened that 'new' discoveries by Western primatologists have long been known in Japan. Asquith (1998; 1999) also contended that the review system for major Western journals is instrumental in maintaining the academic hegemony of the core countries, suppressing voices from the margin.

Natives as outsiders in anthropological discourse

We should now ask why anthropologists reject natives as participants in discourse when they are heavily dependent on them as sources of information. In my view, the answer lies in the structure of anthropological knowledge, particularly in that of ethnography. Ethnography fascinates readers because through reading it they can experience a romantic encounter with unseen people in unknown places. This encounter provides them with opportunities to recognize the plasticity of human culture, thereby seeing their world in a new light. For the author, ethnography is a product of cultural translation, in which the 'peculiar' customs of natives are rendered intelligible to an audience with a different cultural and linguistic background. Whether academic or general, this audience is ordinarily a community of people to which the author belongs. I contend that this structure of ethnographic reading and writing excludes natives from anthropological discourse because they are posited as objects of observation and representation, rather than as interlocutors. Natives, therefore, acquire legitimacy only as objects of thought.

To demonstrate this point, I will critically examine Dorinne Kondo's representations of the Japanese family called '*ie*,' which appeared in *Crafting Selves* (1990). The second part of this widely acclaimed book is entitled 'Family as Company, Company as Family,' in which Kondo vividly described the lives of merchant families in a lower-class district in Tokyo. Kondo's narratives began as follows:

> Masao, a young high school student, walked in my door with a troubled expression on his face. It was time for our weekly lesson in English conversation, my way of doing a favor for his family. Masao was usually enthusiastic and engaging, but this time he seemed preoccupied. After the hour ended, I casually asked him how things were going. 'Would you mind if I spoke with you for a few minutes?' he said, his voice worried and urgent. I nodded assent, wondering what the problem could be.
>
> The following week, he said, he would have to choose the division of the university to which he would apply. His real love was art, and he desperately wanted to be an art teacher. Should he pursue his own career interests, or apply to the business division and prepare to take over his family's shoe store? In other circumstances, he would have had no hesitation in applying to the liberal arts division. But matters were not so simple. His father wanted him to take over the business, and although his mother told him to do whatever he wanted, he could tell that she secretly hoped he would follow in his father's footsteps (Kondo 1990:119).

According to Kondo, Masao's grandfather had come to Tokyo from the northern region of Japan known for its poverty. He apprenticed himself to a cobbler near Ueno, a town where there used to be a railroad terminal for people coming to the capital city for seasonal work. After years of hard work, he opened a shop of his own and later became the first president of a local merchant association. Masao's father was his eldest son, and following the *ie* custom of primogenitural succession, he had taken over the family business. Masao, the only son of the present owner, was expected to do the same, but was not enthusiastic. He knew there was little economic reward for running a small shop against the pressure from big stores.

> 'I envy the children of *sarariman* [salaried man],' he said. They can take their vacations. Home and work are clearly separated. Life is more

predictable. Even the most average (*hei hei bon bon na*, an absolutely average) *sarariman* can count on that much. Still, he said, his father wanted him to take over the business, carry on the family name and occupation, keep their ties with the merchants' association, and bring them back to real prosperity. In a voice choked with emotion, he said that it would be a shame for his grandfather's hardships and his father's hard work to go to waste. It would be a shame for the enterprise to die, after a mere two generations (*ni dai kagiri*).

'I am sorry to bother you with this,' he said. 'But I go to a boys' high school, and my classmates aren't very sympathetic (*omiyari ga nai*). And teachers like Kinpachi-*sensei* [the hero in a popular television drama] just don't exist – that's a fantasy.' I murmured what I hoped were consoling words, but I frankly felt completely inadequate to advise the young man, so torn by this agonizing existential dilemma. Although nothing was resolved by our conversation, he went home saying he felt better for having talked with someone. I was left feeling stunned, for the fact that he would approach me, a foreigner to whom he was not particularly close, attested to the magnitude of his problems.

How could one so young anguish so over this decision? What gives families and family firms such power to shape people's lives? To further understand the source of Masao's dilemma and the power of the family firm it is necessary to appreciate the importance of *ie*, the family as the weight of history and obligation, and of *uchi*, the family as a center of emotional attachment (Kondo 1990:120).

Kondo then explained the structural features of the Japanese *ie*, which has been characterized as a 4-P institution: patriarchal, primogenitural, patrilineal, and patrilocal. The origin of the *ie* dates from the medieval age when the warrior class had taken control of the nation's politics. In the late nineteenth century, the *ie* system was legally instituted as the foundation of the Japanese 'family state,' but was abolished after World War II when the revision of the Civil Code took place. Although defunct as a legal institution, the *ie* has survived as a custom. As such, it has commanded the attention of many anthropologists. Kondo, after describing a few more families in Masao's town, came to this conclusion:

> The *ie* is not simply a kinship unit based on blood relationship, but a corporate group based on social and economic ties. Thus, the *ie*, the household line, and the *kagyō*, the family enterprise, are of critical moral,

social, and emotional importance. They should ideally be carried on in perpetuity, so much so that many alternatives exist to ensure that the household will not die out. The responsibility facing young Masao was thus a daunting one. As the only son and the only child, he carried the weight of history on his shoulders...For the parents with a *kagyō* to pass on, subordinating one's individual desires to that of the household enterprise takes on the character of moral virtue. Pursuing one's own plans and disregarding the duties toward the household smacks of selfish immaturity (Kondo 1990:131).

Before examining Kondo's view, I should point out a salient feature of her writing style – the abundance of indigenous words inserted here and there into the text. They not only have the effect of recreating the local atmosphere, but also register the writer's authority, just as photographs of local people and scenery authenticate fieldwork.[8]

Crafting Selves has widely been acclaimed in the United States as it conveys an immediate sense of what it is like to live in Japan, especially for young Americans. Kondo's superior ability to stimulate her readers' imagination of a foreign culture is something found in all good ethnography. But the question we must ask here is the meaning her book has for the people she described. Many Japanese would find her representations lopsided, for the significance of *ie* in a person's life differs considerably depending on his or her social position. Certainly, the *ie* is an archetype of the Japanese group, as Chie Nakane (1970), among others, has emphasized. There is no denying its pervasive influence on all aspects of life in modern Japan. Indeed, there are countless Japanese like Kondo's Masao who have suffered the constraints of *ie*. However, there is general agreement among Japanese social scientists that Japan's contemporary family cannot be explained solely in terms of the *ie*. Furthermore, even if there had been no legal change in family law, the *ie* would still have had different meanings for people in different social positions. For example, whether one is an inheriting child in a merchant family with a *kagyō* (family enterprise) to pass on, or a junior son in a poor farming family with a tiny land holding, or an urban worker's daughter who is expected to marry out, is of critical importance. Kondo was in fact well aware of such internal diversity, and discussed the multiplicity of cultural experience.[9] However, despite her opposition to totalizing discourse, her narratives ended up highlighting the *ie* as 'the weight of history and obligation,' which had been repeatedly stressed in past literature.[10]

What made Kondo echo the prosaic view that the Japanese are a self-effacing people willing to sacrifice themselves for the sake of the group? And why did she decide to study the *ie* in the first place? The answer to these questions lies, I believe, in her American background. There are some fundamental differences between Japan and the United States with regard to the conceptualization of the individual and society. In the United States, where there is a long tradition of rugged individualism, the idea of freedom is related to escape from social constraints and rules. Since human existence is social, there is no strict opposition between individual and society. Yet Americans have tended to conceive of this relationship in dialectic terms. As Robert Edgerton (1985:258) put it, 'The imagined antinomy between individual freedom and social constraint is a master metaphor of Western thought.'

To see how deeply Kondo has been influenced by this metaphor, consider her remarks about Mrs. Yokoyama, an attractive middle-aged woman who one can imagine had her pick of handsome boyfriends, but who married a dull man to carry on her family business of hairdressing. Kondo (1990:137) asked, 'Why was the household enterprise so important? How could she so calculatingly sacrifice personal happiness, even for the sake of the *ie* and the business?' Yet these questions are meaningful only when the individual is idealized, as in the United States, as an autonomous being with a separate existence from the group. In a society like Japan's where there is no strong tradition of individualism, such questions may not even be asked. Following the argument of reflexive anthropology, of which Kondo is a representative, we may say that her questions reveal more about herself as an American than about the Japanese (Kuwayama 1996a:161).

Thus, whether or not the Japanese are group-oriented is not the question here. The point is that, compared with individualistic Americans, the Japanese identify with groups to which they belong, and this characteristic is best expressed in the symbolism of *ie*. In other words, the *ie* provided Kondo with a prism through which she could see the differences between the two nations most clearly. As long as the *ie* is useful for Kondo and her American readers' understanding of Japan, the meaning of *ie* for the Japanese becomes a secondary issue.

We could further clarify this point if we translated Kondo's book into Japanese. Her writing strategy of using narratives is innovative, but many of the stories she told are, when read in the local context, merely *sekenbanashi* (gossip). Indeed, *Crafting Selves* would make an ideal target for the persistent Japanese criticism that foreigners' writings on Japan are boring because they are merely common sense. As I will argue later, this criticism does not consider the question of audience (readers) in ethnographic writing. Since Kondo wrote for Americans, it would be unfair to judge her work without examining the value it has for them. Kondo's elegant narratives stimulated her American readers' imaginations regarding Japanese culture. An understanding of the Japanese based on these imaginations was meaningful for Americans as it helped them become aware of their individualism through the contrasted collectivism of the Japanese. Kondo thus demonstrated the reflexive nature of anthropological knowledge. In this regard, she followed Clifford Geertz, who remarked, 'All ethnographical descriptions are homemade [and] they are the describer's descriptions, not those of the described' (Geertz 1988:144–145).[11] Michio Suenari, a senior Japanese anthropologist, presented a similar view:

> When I read some American ethnographies of Japan, I noticed that there were descriptions that might be very interesting to American readers, but banal to the Japanese. However, things that are commonsense to natives are essential elements of ethnography. If anything, monographs that eliminate everything taken for granted by local people would be extremely difficult to read. It would be unproductive to take up only what is commonplace for the Japanese and criticize foreign anthropologists as being trite or incompetent (Sofue et al. 1989:416).

An important question overlooked in this shrewd observation is, 'For whom does ethnography exist?' Geertz's view of ethnographic descriptions as 'homemade' is felicitous. But if it were intended to justify the describer's exclusion of the described, it would be a questionable position. In this context, it is worth noting that a major problem with postmodern ethnography is its extravagant concern with the self. Kondo and others of her persuasion are interested in ethnographic *writing* and *reading*, but have passed over the question of what it means to *be written*. As a result, they have eliminated natives – the people described – from the circle of dialogue. This problem is immanent in all anthropological writing, but particularly conspicuous in postmodern/reflexive ethnography. In the words of Johannes Fabian (1983:85), the 'dialogic Other' of an anthropologist is the 'other anthropologist, the scientific community.' Natives are 'posited (predicated),' but are 'not spoken to.' It is understandable, then, that the experience of Kondo's Japanese has been interpreted by using prestigious Western theories, such as the post-structuralism of Michel Foucault, instead of local, Japanese theories. To the extent that the local carries weight in relation to the global as defined by the center of the academic world system, Kondo provides a classic example of what may be called 'token localism.'

Edward Said's critique of Orientalism illuminates this point. He argued that the Orientalist's main task is to render the Orient intelligible to fellow Westerners. Their portrait of the Orient continues to be appreciated in the West, even if it is different from the Orientals' Orient, as long as it is useful for the Westerners' understanding of the Orient. Thus, whether or not 'Orientalism makes sense at all depends more on the West than on the Orient' (Said 1978:22). In this structure of knowledge, the value of an Orientalist's work is determined not by Orientals themselves, but by other Orientalists in the West. The former is placed outside the latter's discourse – a situation parallel to that in scientific colonialism.

Also important is Said's argument that Westerners have defined themselves in contrast with Orientals. As I have argued elsewhere (Kuwayama 1999:213), 'contrast' is different from 'comparison.' In 'contrast,' the self is understood as the opposite of the Other, whereas in 'comparison' both differences and similarities are examined. Kondo approached the *ie* as a prism through which to see Japanese collectivism as opposed to American individualism. This explains why she lacked the comparative perspective of Eitaro Suzuki (1940), for example, who had defined the *ie* as a Japanese form of 'familism' commonly observed in rural communities throughout the world (Sorokin et al. 1965). Since Kondo's approach was contrastive, the Japanese were inevitably portrayed as a people radically different from Americans. Indeed, her Japanese were more Japanese than the Japanese thought they were. Said's warning that the Orientalist propensity to polarize the world into 'us' and 'them' has made the Orient more Oriental and the

West more Western (Said 1978:46) is perfectly applicable here. That the postmodern Kondo chose to discuss the premodern *ie*, from which emerged a very traditional image of the Japanese, is not an irony, but a natural outcome of the logic of Orientalist ethnography.

Changing relationships between the describer and the described

Native anthropology, the anthropology of natives by natives, is a major issue today because the relationship between the describer and the described has undergone a fundamental change as the result of changes in international post-World War II politics. The 'primitive' world, where much of the anthropological fieldwork was carried out, has been integrated by and large into the Third World, and is no longer an isolated, self-contained community.[12] Furthermore, globalization has affected all parts of the world, and non-Western civilizations have been brought into closer contact with the West than ever before. Under these circumstances, anthropologists have encountered a different kind of the Other to which they have traditionally paid only scant attention – natives who read ethnography written about their culture. In the past, natives were merely objects of representation. Today, they not only read outsiders' ethnography, but also protest against it, if objectionable, by taking advantage of what little political influence they have gained. So far, not many anthropologists have been forced to confront militant natives squarely, but sooner or later they will have to postulate them as 'dialogic partners.' As Renato Rosaldo wrote:

> We should take the criticisms of our subjects in much the same way that we take those of our colleagues. Not unlike other ethnographers, so-called natives can be insightful, sociologically correct, axe-grinding, self-interested, or mistaken. They do know their own cultures, and rather than being ruled out of court, their criticisms should be listened to and taken into account, to be accepted, rejected, or modified, as we reformulate our analyses (Rosaldo 1989:50).

The describer, too, has changed. Historically, anthropology developed as a science that aimed to explain the 'exotic' people Westerners had encountered as they expanded their influence throughout the world, hence the 'colonial roots' of anthropology. (Japan has a colonial past of its own, but its power was limited to the Asia Pacific region. Japan's 'betwixt and between' status in the modern world will be discussed in Chapter 4). Today anthropology does not belong exclusively to Westerners. In the Third World, there are many talented scholars trained in the West. In Japan and other non-Western industrialized countries, we find home trained anthropologists, who run professional societies according to their own tradition. The anthropological self, that which observes and describes culture, has diversified and spread to all parts of the world, including former colonies. Thus, in many parts of Asia and Africa, it has become common for indigenous scholars to study and write about their society in their language for readers in their country. As the influence of native anthropologists spreads, researchers from the former colonial powers will increasingly have to negotiate with them as 'professional others.'

A major problem in the encounter between native and non-native anthropologists concerns the subjectivity of cultural representation. The described may not see their culture in the same way as the describer has seen it. Furthermore, when the same culture is observed by more than one researcher, conflicting pictures are often presented, as the debate between Robert Redfield (1930) and Oscar Lewis (1951) shows, and more recently, between Margaret Mead (1928) and Derek Freeman (1983). Since the publication of *Writing Culture* (Clifford and Marcus 1986), subjectivity has been widely debated. In his influential introduction, James Clifford maintained that it is impossible to attain objectivity in the study of culture, defining anthropological knowledge as 'partial.' He declared, 'In cultural studies at least, we can no longer know the whole truth, or even claim to approach it' (Clifford 1986:25). Although insightful, this view is not entirely original. As early as the late 1960s, Maquet (1967) pointed out that all forms of social knowledge are subjective and partial because they have been gained from a particular perspective. The novelty of Clifford's view lies in his challenge to the hitherto unquestioned claim of anthropology as an objective science. (But who would think of anthropology as a 'science' after reading Benedict?) Clifford's argument is worth careful attention, but too much emphasis on subjective partiality would infuse anthropology with a nihilism that produces fragmentary pictures of a people in the manner of 'the five blind men and the elephant.'

Harumi Befu was among the first to note the subjectivity of cultural representation in Japanese studies. His book review of *Heath, Illness, and Medical Care in Japan* (1987), edited by Edward Norbeck and Margaret Lock, resonated with Clifford's view.

> This book, like most other books in English on Japan, is designed to make Japan more understandable to North Americans. Whether that understanding helps Koreans or Pakistanis to understand Japan is totally a different question. In short, anthropology is a culture-bound discipline: there is no single discipline of Anthropology with a capital 'A.' Instead there are multiple anthropologies seemingly doing the same thing but in fact engaged in different endeavors: North American anthropology dedicated to making foreign cultures understandable to North Americans, French anthropology designed to make foreign cultures comprehensible to the French, etc. I wonder how French anthropology's understanding of Japanese health, illness, and medical care in Japan is different from North American anthropology's (Befu 1989:266).

Befu later examined how Japan had been portrayed by scholars in ten different countries (Befu and Kreiner 1992).

A question remains, however, as to whether it is sufficient to attribute such differences in representation to the different cultural backgrounds of the authors. I would submit that subjectivity is meaningful in the public sphere only when it is oriented toward some sort of objectivity. The study of Srinivas (1966) sheds light on this issue. Like Befu, Srinivas acknowledged the importance of examining one's ideas in terms of one's social background and intellectual history. He maintained, however, that the awareness of subjectivity is only 'a first step toward achieving greater objectivity,' which in his opinion required cooperation among professionals of diverse backgrounds. 'International cooperation is indispensable for achieving greater objectivity in sociology' (Srinivas 1966:154). Following Srinivas, I contend that a certain measure of objectivity is possible and desirable in the study of culture and that it can be achieved by cross-examining different subjective realities. I further contend that the postmodern emphasis on subjectivity in cultural representation has only located the problem, and has failed to advocate a strategy to overcome it. The fact that so much has been said about writing, while neglecting the question of what to do in the field, attests to this point. In my mind, the important thing is that we can build on this awareness of subjectivity.

Paul Roscoe (1995) argued that anthropologists have been enthralled by the postmodern critique because in anthropology one scholar has usually monopolized a research site, which makes verification by other scholars difficult. This practice contrasts with that of the natural sciences, in which the same phenomenon is observed by more than one researcher, attempting to test one theory against another. To restate Roscoe, anthropologists have been captured by the idea of 'partial truths' (Clifford 1986) because they are not trained to compare different subjective realities in order to establish what may be called an 'inter-subjective reality.' Postmodern thinkers have contributed greatly to the clarification of hidden problems in anthropology, but the following warning is worth heeding:

> Anthropology would be better served by contemplating a path that leads less to postmodernism than to pragmatic ways of breaking down [the lone ethnographer's] observational and representational authority... Multiple ethnographers might be pitted one against another in the same field, or anthropological journals and book editors might invite literate members of a [native] society to critique ethnographies of their culture (Roscoe 1995:498).

It should be noted in this context that a major pitfall in the discussion of cultural representation is that little attention has been paid to the sentiments of the people who have been described. Following Befu, we may say that Americans have represented the Japanese in one way, the French in another, and that their attempts are both legitimate. Although this argument makes sense from the standpoint of the describer, it shows little or no consideration for the described. It does support the psychoanalytic thesis that the describer's self will be projected onto that of the person being described, but hardly says anything about that person's self-image. Indeed, how would we feel if we were portrayed by more than one artist and found that their works were very different from each other and from our self-image as well? And what should we do if the artists adamantly asserted that their works were authentic? Nothing would be more humiliating than being forced to accept such a representation merely because one did not possess enough power to resist the artists' claim. Postmodernists would argue that visual art is not obliged to replicate an 'objective' reality, but this argument, when applied to the study of other cultures, effectively ignores the reactions of the people portrayed. (See the next section for some American anthropologists' reactions to what they perceived as 'inhumane' analyses of their friend's anguish). As Said's critique of Orientalism has demonstrated, representation is a political act. It is especially problematic when there is power asymmetry between the describer and the described.

How, then, can describers achieve objectivity by transcending each other's subjectivity in ways that satisfy the described at the same time? In my view, the key to this question lies in the notion of 'open text.' By 'open,' I mean the kind of representation that posits a diverse audience, both native and non-native, which contrasts with the 'closed' representation that assumes, as reflexive ethnography such as Kondo's does, a homogeneous audience from within one's own cultural and linguistic community. Open texts are not complete in themselves. On the contrary, they invite diverse people to contribute to the author's text. Thus, open texts permit 'co-authorship' by the observer and the observed, as has already been experimented with in the construction of life histories. They even allow 'plural authorship,' in which ethnographic texts are written by more than one person, with the authors taking turns writing and reading to produce an open-ended forum for dialogue. Until quite recently, this idea existed only in the realm of imagination, but the advent of the Internet has provided the technological basis for such dialogue on a global scale.[13]

Yoshinobu Ota's concept of 'open discourse' is relevant here. Ota (1993) contended that anthropologists should discard their attachment to ethnography and establish instead a broader category of cultural descriptions that would provide an open forum for discussion among diverse people, such as literary critics, historians, local ethnographers, and natives. Ota suggested that, instead of confining cultural discourse to the academically authorized style of ethnography, we should conceive of it as 'a sequence of renewable texts,' in which different voices from different people are linked continuously without being ranked by the established standard of excellence. In open discourse, 'anonymity' will substitute for 'authorship' (Ota 1993:487).

Ota derived his idea from the computer conferencing. Interestingly, there is a classic style of Japanese poetry that realized Ota's open discourse in premodern times. Called *'renga'* (linked verse), this particular style of writing is associated with the notion of *za*, which the Korean literary critic O-Young Lee (1984) interpreted as a 'communal theater.' In the *za*, the distinction between actor and audience, host and guest, subject and object, etc., disappears as the two parties gather and perform together to become one. The sense of unity created in the *za* is to be observed in many places throughout Japan. A most famous example is that of the Kabuki theater, which has a runway protruding from the center stage into the audience's seats, which has the effect of enhancing a sense of participation among the viewers. Other examples include the tea ceremony, in which the host makes tea in front of his guests, not behind a wall, and shares the moment of drinking, and *sushi* bars in which the chef cooks on the opposite side of a long dining table where customers are seated. Pointing out the historical affinity between *renga* and the tea ceremony, Lee wrote:

> Like the tea ceremony, linked verse is written, or performed, in a Japanese-style room with a flower arrangement on the ceremonial shelf and a scroll on the wall. And while tea has a host and guests, in a linked verse meeting one member acts as a kind of leader. He begins the poetry sequence by offering the opening verse, just as the host at a tea ceremony offers a cup of tea. Tea ceremony guests drink in turn, and, likewise, the poets at a linked verse meeting compose their verses in turn. When a hundred verses have been written, a title is affixed to the sequence and the meeting is over. Furthermore, the composition of verses is as strictly regulated as are the actions in the tea ceremony...Individuality is detrimental to linked verse. Since everyone is working together, the first verse is of the utmost importance for it must be one that the other poets can build from. And although each verse thereafter is composed individually, the rules of linking mean that by definition any single verse will be influenced by the one before it and will in turn influence the one following (Lee 1984:142–143).

Clifford, too, suggested the possibility of such plural authorship. He called it a 'utopia,' however, because 'the very idea of plural authorship challenges a deep Western identification of any text's order with the intention of a single author' (Clifford 1988:51). I find his argument unconvincing, for just because something is a tradition is no excuse for continuing it forever. If an alternative approach to ethnographic writing is not to be found in the

Occident, why not look elsewhere and borrow one from the Orient? Clifford should have taken himself more seriously when he said, 'Anthropologists will increasingly have to share their texts, and sometimes their title pages, with those indigenous collaborators for whom the term informant is no longer adequate, if it ever was' (Clifford 1988:51).

As things stand today, neither 'plural authorship' nor 'anonymity' is feasible because the question of how to assign and protect academic credit for such new forms of publication has been unresolved. Consider, for example, the current low status accorded to electronic publishing, which is most suited to 'linked' writing (cf. Schwimmer 1996). Thus, as an interim alternative, I propose to publish a new type of journal, in which native scholars comment on articles by outside scholars, who in turn reply to the comments they have received, thereby re-conceptualizing their ethnographic observations in both native and non-native contexts. Publication both in print and on the Internet would be useful. A similar sort of exchange has been going on in *Current Anthropology*, but it seems limited mostly to professional circles with similar cultural and linguistic backgrounds. Although far from ideal, my proposal at least has the effect of opening up the hitherto closed anthropological discourse, promoting dialogue between the describer and the described, between natives and non-natives.

When Western anthropologists are excluded from discourse

Finally, the following anecdote describes how Western anthropologists responded when they were placed in the position of the described. At an annual meeting of the American Ethnological Society (AES) held in the mid-1990s, there was a panel on the subject of the boundaries of anthropological discourse. Of the four panelists, two were literary critics. Both of them took up the introductory chapter of Renato Rosaldo's *Culture and Truth* (1989), in which the author, then president of AES, recounted his anguish over the tragic death of his wife Michelle Rosaldo, who had been killed in an accident while doing fieldwork in the Philippines. The critics treated Michelle's body as an 'object' and analyzed Renato's descriptions as a text.

Their analyses were skillful, but after the presentations, questions were raised from both the discussant and the floor about whether it was morally correct to speak of the human body as an object. Most of the people who commented agreed that the critics' attitudes were cold, inhumane, and immoral. One anthropologist challenged them, saying they 'must' change their attitudes and pay more respect to the person they are describing. Another anthropologist, who was a close friend of the late Michelle, protested against the ways Renato's grief was represented. She reproached the critics for having made no genuine attempt to understand his suffering. Unable to suppress her emotion, she shed tears as she spoke. Moved by her tears, many of the people who were present turned their eyes critically to the 'inhumane' literary critics. Exposed to the condemnation from the floor, one of them fought back, saying, 'I don't understand. What's the problem? Are you saying I'm just an unsympathetic reader?' After a few more exchanges with the participants, the critics left the conference room, openly displaying their exasperation over what they thought was the anthropologists' unprofessional response.

Never before or since have I seen such an emotional exchange at an academic conference in the United States. Putting that aside, this incident clearly showed what it means to be described. Being described or represented by other people means having oneself portrayed by people who have the power to determine one's identity for oneself, which, despite one's will, may take on a life of its own and speak against oneself. When the describer and the described (or people who identify with them) meet on an equal basis, as was the case with the AES meeting, the latter is able to object. When, however, there is a great difference of power in their relationship, as between the West and the colonized non-West, people who have been described are put at the mercy of the describer.

Concluding remarks

The literature on native anthropology is growing, but it remains small. Generally, research on this issue has been conducted by non-Western or ethnically minority scholars outside the mainstream of the academic community. Since most of their works have appeared in minor journals, the voices from the margin have seldom reached the center. Even if they have been heard, they have tended to be labeled as 'subjective,' 'biased,' and 'distorted' or simply ignored as 'noise.'

In this chapter, I have examined the epistemological and political basis of this situation. By way of summary, I enumerate below my major points: (1) natives are structurally excluded from anthropological discourse, especially from ethnographic representation; (2) this exclusion has been made possible by Western hegemony in the modern colonial system; (3) native anthropologists have been forced to play a minor role because they are placed on the periphery of the academic world system; (4) the United States, Great Britain, and to a lesser extent France occupy the center of the academic world system, in which they set the standards of excellence by which to evaluate different kinds of knowledge; (5) the concept of 'open text' is useful for attaining an objectivity that transcends the subjectivity of individual researchers; (6) anthropologists need to establish a forum for dialogue or 'dialogic space' that would allow diverse people, including natives (especially those professionally trained), to participate on an equal basis.

Regarding the last point, Befu (1994) proposed that 'a World Association of Japanese Studies' should be established in order to promote communication among Japan specialists throughout the world. He contended, however, that Japanese scholars should only participate as 'observers' because, in his view, the Japanese influence is already so strong that foreigners find it difficult to do research independently. As Befu (1994:44) remarked, 'In deliberating on the significance of the study of Japan from abroad I believe there should be space where they can think and debate without Japanese scholars.' Putting aside the intricate question of which language to use in the proposed world association, I think Befu's proposal is dangerous because denying an active participation to the people being studied will deepen the gap that already exists between the describer and the described.

Behind Befu's proposal is the discomfort, even a sense of threat, among many non-Japanese scholars about the growing influence of the Japanese government that is exerted through Japan's national research institutions and funding agencies. For example, when international symposia are held with financial support from Japan, the Japanese staff ordinarily makes decisions regarding the topics for discussion and participants (Befu 1994:43). Befu claims this practice imposes many restrictions on academic freedom. His criticism is legitimate, but in my view a more pressing and important problem relates to the complaints of non-Japanese scholars that the Japanese treat them as 'children' or apprentices at best.

I have already touched on this, but as someone who did postgraduate study in the United States, I have myself been called 'immature,' so it is on that basis that I dare to offer this criticism to my Japanese colleagues. Often I am compelled to cover my eyes when I see some Japanese anthropologists, who, in the deepest recesses of their mind, feel ashamed that their profession is a Western import, compensate for this feeling by assuming an overbearing posture when it comes to the study of Japan. For example, when Benedict's *The Chrysanthemum and the Sword* was published, gossip was heard, along with praise, which in essence said, 'After all, Americans cannot do any better.' Also, there are more than a few anthropologists in Japan who reject outright introductory books on Japan written in English, labeling them as 'scholarly common sense.' Such remarks and attitudes reflect a complete failure on their part to understand that lecturing about Japan in a foreign language to a foreign audience whose cultural background is completely different from that of the Japanese, is fundamentally different from speaking about Japan with the Japanese in Japanese.

It is neither the arrogance of central scholars in the core Western countries nor the ignorance of peripheral scholars in Japan that I am criticizing here. My point is, rather, that both sides are so stubborn that they have produced a 'closed' discourse on Japan. We have already seen that in the United States there is a vast literature on the anthropology of Japan. This field has developed to a point where a self-contained community of specialists has been formed. In Europe, too, Japanese studies is thriving owing to the efforts of leading members of academic societies, such as JAWS (Japan Anthropology Workshop). Japanese studies abroad has come of age, and there is good reason for celebration. We must remember, however, that the opposite side of this development is the accelerated tendency to rule out the Japanese as interlocutors. I do not think I am alone in feeling a sense of crisis in this state of affairs. To overcome this crisis, Japanese scholars should stop finding fault with foreigners' research and contemplate instead how to create space for fruitful dialogue.

A good deal of the plight of native anthropologists derives from the power inequality between the center and the periphery in the academic world system. As the above account of Japanese studies suggests, however, the problems surrounding native versus non-native anthropologists are often mutual. At the risk of sounding moralistic, I submit that the only solution to these problems lies in learning to respect each other as equal partners, to develop sympathy for what the others are doing, and to engage in dialogue with a sense of humor and patience.

3 The 'World System' of Anthropology: Japan and Asia in the Global Community of Anthropologists

As offspring of a Western science with 'colonial roots,' anthropologists used to observe and write about people in distant lands without considering seriously how the people who had been described would respond to their representation. The distant, 'exotic' others were objects of research whose frame of reference was largely alien to them. Except as informants, they seldom had opportunities to make themselves heard in the civilized world, where knowledge about them was produced. In the second half of the twentieth century, however, many former colonies gained political independence, and anthropologists were no longer able to keep a comfortable distance from the people they studied. Indeed, today's anthropologists are in a position of being observed by the 'exotic' others, who, in some instances, possess enough power and resources to contest their authority. Recent worldwide support for indigenous people's rights has worked to uphold native claims. The anthropologists' gaze has been returned. At the center of the current debate on native anthropology is the question of whether or not reciprocity is possible between the describer and the described as research partners.

The relationship between the two is particularly difficult and complex when the described are literate and have a native tradition of scholarship that may be used to challenge the describer's authority. In the previous chapters, I have examined this problem, noting the power difference between the describer and the described. In this chapter, I expand on the arguments I have presented and discuss the 'politics' regarding the production, dissemination, and consumption of knowledge about other cultures on a global scale. In the first section, I clarify the concept of 'academic world system' by responding to various critiques of my

1997 Japanese article (Kuwayama 1997a; see Kuwayama 1997b for a detailed English summary), on which Chapter 2 was based. One such critique, made by the Dutch anthropologist, Jan van Bremen (1997), raised some important questions that helped refine some of my key ideas. As explained in the Preface, these critiques were also instrumental in making my thesis known outside of Japan. In the second section of this chapter, the focus shifts from the relationship between the center and the periphery in the world system to relationships between peripheries in Asia. The main purpose of this chapter is to raise awareness of the imbalance of power in anthropological practice and of various problems that result from it, rather than offering concrete solutions.

The center and the periphery in the 'world system' of anthropology

Before getting down to specifics, I must acknowledge my debt to the late Swedish anthropologist, Tomas Gerholm, whose work inspired me greatly. In his article entitled 'Sweden: Central Ethnology, Peripheral Anthropology,' Gerholm (1995:159) wrote, 'Both ethnology and anthropology have enough practitioners internationally for us to be able to speak of a world-system of ethnology and a world-system of anthropology. These world-systems of academic disciplines, just like any world-system, have their centers and their peripheries.'

Van Bremen's main criticism of my conceptualization of the world system of anthropology is that it is both monolithic and static. 'The problem,' he wrote, 'in Kuwayama's analysis is the excessive weight given to center-periphery relations and positions and the static view taken of them.' He also stated, 'More disturbing is Kuwayama's suggestion that there is an inherent discord between peripheral native and dominant center anthropologists' (van Bremen 1997:62). Gordon Mathews, an American anthropologist teaching in Hong Kong, made a similar point. He commented that, instead of a single center and a single periphery, there are a few centers and multiple peripheries, and that most anthropologists, regardless of their nationality, feel more or less marginalized relative to a small number of heroes at the dominant centers (personal communication). Van Bremen and Mathews were probably not alone in pointing out the need to rethink the binarism postulated in the idea of academic world system. Obviously, this binarism parallels oppositions like the West/the rest, colonizer/colonized, us/them, etc.

To clarify my position, I will focus on three issues. First, regarding the plurality of the center and the periphery, this was implied in my original thesis, though was not made explicit. To begin with the former, following Gerholm and Hannerz (1982), I maintained that the center of the world system of anthropology is located in *three* countries – the United States, Great Britain, and France. Besides the fact that these constitute three centers rather than one, it is important to note the differences between them. Since it is obvious that France belongs to a tradition different from that of the United States and Great Britain, I will compare America and Great Britain. In Japanese studies, the British are generally more interested in collaborating with Japanese and other European scholars than are Americans. For example, Joy Hendry (1998:2) noted that a major strength of her edited volume *Interpreting Japanese Society* (2nd edition) is the collaboration between Japanese and European scholars. She compared this feature with 'the rather closed American literature' on Japan. Also, Harumi Befu (1992:28) remarked that scholarly communication is naturally more intensive within the same linguistic community than between different communities, but that the Europeans 'tend to be much more aware of scholarship in the United States than American scholars are aware of European scholarship on Japan.' These comments in no way blame Americans for being parochial. They do suggest, however, that with the largest anthropological organization in the world, the United States is by far the most powerful of the three core countries.

Second, regarding the plurality of the periphery in the world system, it should be noted that Japan is not the only marginalized country. On the contrary, many small European countries, to speak nothing of the majority of non-Western countries, are in a similar situation to Japan. Unfortunately, the internal diversity of Europe has too often been overlooked because of the all-inclusive word 'the West.' It is important to remember that 'the West' is a relational concept that has meaning only in comparison with, or in opposition to, other such categories as 'the East.' In a way similar to the relativist conception of culture, it dramatizes the differences between the West and the non-West, while minimizing the differences within the West. In other words, the notion of 'the West' homogenizes the Euro-American self as it constructs the heterogeneous Other called 'the East' or 'the Orient.' The homogenized 'West' has made it difficult to see the different, sometimes competing, traditions of anthropology in Europe and the United States. Significantly, the critique by Gerholm and Hannerz of the academic world system came from the periphery within the dominant West.

Finally, marginalization within the center is different from marginalization on the periphery. This point is critical to an understanding of the world system. In American anthropology, the study of Japan has been pushed toward the periphery for a variety of reasons, and Japan specialists have long been suffering a sense of alienation. (For that matter, we might even complain about the marginal status of anthropology as a discipline throughout the world!). Yet their marginalization has taken place within the most powerful center of the world's anthropologies. And their objection, as well as their demand for more respect, occurs in the context of a competition for access to a kind of power barely imaginable to those living in the periphery. Thus, even if successful, their contestation will merely replicate the existing power structure of the world system and may even strengthen the dominance of the center over the periphery. Indeed, it may end up in an increase in the power, small as it is at the center, but not negligible vis-à-vis the periphery, which American specialists of Japan already have over their native counterparts in the international community. By contrast, the objection to marginalization voiced by peripheral scholars has seldom reached the center, but it does have the potential to change the power structure itself. In this regard, resistance on the periphery is 'transformative' and 'counterhegemonic' (Dirks, Eley, and Ortner 1994:18–19).[1]

Another criticism of my notion of the academic world system relates to my view of Japan as peripheral. Van Bremen argued strongly that Japanese anthropology is not as marginal as is commonly thought. To support his view, he cited three Japanese anthropologists who (in his opinion) had influenced their Western colleagues, especially in the study of Southeast Asia: Toichi Mabuchi (1910–1988), Chie Nakane (b. 1926), and Shigeharu Tanabe (b. 1943). According to van Bremen, when Rodney Needham formulated his theory of 'dual sovereignty,' he drew on Mabuchi's 1964 work, 'Spiritual Predominance of the Sister.' Van Bremen also contended that this article, along with another paper by Mabuchi, inspired Claude Lévi-Strauss when he wrote Chapter 11 of *The View from Afar* (in which Mabuchi is mentioned once in passing). In addition, van Bremen remarked that Tanabe's book, *Ecology and Practical Technology* (1994), has been internationally acclaimed as a major achievement in the study of Thai society. As for Nakane, she is a leading figure in structural functionalism, and is widely known as the author of *Garo and Khasi* (1967) and of *Japanese Society* (1970), one of the most influential books in the anthropology of Japan. Therefore, van Bremen maintained, 'Japanese anthropology is not so marginal, certainly in Asia, where over the past century it has been a veritable presence.' He then pointed to 'the need to be more precise and inclusive in one's statements about the place of Japanese anthropology in the world' (van Bremen 1997:60)

This criticism is pertinent, and Japan may better be called 'semi-peripheral' rather than peripheral. In purely numerical terms, Japanese anthropology is neither negligible nor powerless, given that the Japanese Society of Ethnology has a membership of approximately 2,000 academics. Also, in terms of research and teaching, Japan has had a degree of influence over its Asian neighbors, especially China and Korea, from which many students have come to study ethnology/anthropology since the days of Japan's colonial rule. These facts show that while Japan is peripheral to the center, it is central within the periphery, so that it should be defined as 'semi-peripheral.' While this definition has the advantage of reflecting the Asian reality more accurately, it is somewhat akin to the apartheid system which designated the Japanese as 'honorary whites' due to their economic power. It has the disadvantage of overlooking the inequalities that do exist between Japan and the core Western countries, concealing the power dimension of the world system of anthropology.

Perhaps the most difficult problem with which peripheral anthropologists are faced is the use of a non-native language, especially one that is completely different from their own, such as English for the Japanese. As mentioned earlier, this difficulty does not simply relate to language fluency or lack thereof; rather, it relates to the social construction of language, and more importantly, to inequalities in the power of different languages in relation to the dominant forms of discourse (Asad 1986:156–160). As long as the dominant anthropological discourse is constructed using the languages of the core countries (i.e.,

English, and to a lesser extent French), knowledge that is considered 'authentic' and 'legitimate' is more easily obtained and produced in those languages than in others. Conversely, knowledge more easily conveyed in peripheral languages, including Japanese, tends to be devalued *unless* it is successfully related to the dominant discourse. Thus, 'local knowledge,' to use the celebrated phrase of Clifford Geertz, may only be appreciated when it is rendered intelligible to the center.

Herein lies a major source of discontent among peripheral/native scholars who are forced to conform to the dominant discourse at the center in order to be recognized. The center inevitably influences, if not determines, the choice of the language and style in which they can present their arguments, as well as the theories and methods they must use. The power imbalance between the center and the periphery is such that only those who are familiar with the major academic traditions at the center (usually those people who have studied there) can manage to meet these demands. This structure produces a result not desired on either side of the system – the Anglo-Americanization of peripheral/native anthropologists, with a hint of French flavor. It explains why these scholars seem to lack originality. Compelled to develop and express their ideas according to the Anglo-American (and less often French) pattern in order to reach the international community beyond their own, whatever originality they may have possessed tends to be filtered out in the process. Thus, anthropologists outside the core countries are caught in a 'Catch 22' of cross-cultural conformity.

Discourses constructed in different languages and drawing on different intellectual traditions have merits of their own. It is unlikely that anthropologists who practice cultural relativism in 'the field' when doing fieldwork miss this point. However, their respect for difference is frequently lost on the return trip home. What we see instead is a judgment of foreign discourses, and even the act of ranking them, according to home-based standards. A case in point is the review process for leading journals in the core countries, which was explained in Chapter 2. This process poses a great dilemma for peripheral/native scholars because conformity to the center may be derided as imitative, whereas non-conformity will likely result in dismissals of their work for being incomprehensible.[2] The late Edwin Reischauer (1995:200) captured this dilemma when he wrote, 'The Japanese are often accused of being intellectually not very creative...When thinkers have drawn more heavily from native Japanese inspiration, as in the case of the philosopher Nishida Kitaro [written with the family name first] in the first half of the twentieth century, who was strongly influenced by Zen concepts, the rest of the world has not been much impressed.'

This dilemma bears a close parallel to Third World novels. In his book *Off Center* (1991), the literary critic Masao Miyoshi observed that texts written by Third World writers produce an acute sense of difference and even discomfort in First World readers. To 'domesticate' or neutralize the exoticism of the texts, the First World will try to tame them according to its own patterns. If a text turns out to be intransigent, however, it will be dismissed as an inferior product. As Miyoshi wrote:

> Every experience of reading a marginal text is at least potentially upsetting. When a Third World text is read in the First World, the sense of unfamiliarity is often marked, and the reader's discomfort is proportionately acute. To restore the accustomed equilibrium, the reader either domesticates or neutralizes the exoticism of the text. The strategy of domestication is to exaggerate the familiar aspects of the text and thereby disperse its discreteness in the hegemonic sphere of First World literature...Third World texts will be tamed, with the hegemony of the First World conferring the needed authority. Should a particular sample happen to be intransigent, it can always be rejected as an inferior product. The principle of canonicity never fails. The experience of reading a foreign text is nearly always transformed into an act of self-reaffirmation (Miyoshi 1991:9).

Van Bremen's view that Japanese anthropology is not marginal should be examined in this context. The three scholars he cited as examples of Japan's international influence – Mabuchi, Nakane, and Tanabe – have been acclaimed, not simply because they are excellent, but because they wrote in English. A more crucial factor, though, is their familiarity with European and American anthropologies, which has enabled them to think and write in terms familiar to the people who have the power to determine their value in the international market (Kuwayama 1997c). Many other brilliant anthropologists in Japan have remained unknown abroad because they lack the qualities that have brought international recognition to their more fortunate colleagues.

This is, of course, not to say that all scholarly work is of equal value. On the contrary, there are both good and bad writings in any academic community, whether central or peripheral. Poor-quality scholarship that does not even deserve domestic attention is not an issue. The problem arises, however, when there is *a consistent pattern of neglect* regardless of the quality of research. When this neglect is justified by the assumption that only the West is able to produce knowledge worth dissemination – and here I am putting aside the differences within the West that have been discussed – we may say that it is ideologically motivated. By 'ideology' I mean a discourse that serves to 'establish and sustain relations of domination' (Thompson 1990:56). As such, ideology legitimizes the power of a dominant group or groups, which in our context refer to those situated at the center of the academic world system.[3]

In a different context, Henrietta Moore (1996) asked, 'Who are the producers of knowledge?' She maintained that anthropologists acknowledge non-Western people as producers of knowledge about cosmological theories and medical cures, for example, but that they have seldom considered non-Western knowledge useful outside the local context. As she argued, this failure to recognize the different 'others' as producers of knowledge that may provide alternatives to existing Western theories, is, ironically, also to be observed among deconstructive/post-modernists who insist on the partial and local nature of all theories. Moore could have been speaking for myself when she remarked:

> Anthropologists from the developing world, for example, may produce theoretically innovative work, but if they claim that it draws on theoretical traditions outside mainstream western social science, they are likely to find that it will be denigrated as partial and/or localized. If they are critical of western social science, they may find that they are sidelined. Western social science consistently repositions itself as the originary point of comparative and generalizing theory (Moore 1996:3).

Akhil Gupta and James Ferguson made a strikingly similar observation:

> In most standard accounts of the history of anthropological theory, the canonical narrative examines the relationship between national traditions of anthropology only in the United States, Britain, and France. Other

national traditions are marginalized by the workings of geopolitical hegemony, experienced as a naturalized common sense of academic 'center' and 'periphery.' Anthropologists working at the 'center' learn quickly that they can ignore what is done in peripheral sites at little or no professional cost, while any peripheral anthropologist who similarly ignores the 'center' puts his or her professional competence at issue (Gupta and Ferguson 1997:27).

I must hasten to add that the works of Moore and of Gupta and Ferguson came to my attention after my Japanese article on native anthropology (Kuwayama 1997a) was published. I make this seemingly trifle note lest I be accused of plagiarism. That I am forced to make such a statement, while the reverse would hardly apply, demonstrates the power difference between the center (Great Britain and the United States) and the periphery (Japan) that Moore and Gupta and Ferguson have criticized.

There are certainly weaknesses in dividing the world into the center and the periphery, conceptualizing their relationship as one of binary opposition, because there is always interaction between them, whether academic or personal; no country or individual, however powerful, is completely free from an external influence. Dualistic models have the weakness of neglecting this complex, fluid reality. Also, we should note that the relationship between central elites and peripheral elites is often stronger than that between elites and non-elites within each region. As Immanuel Wallerstein (1979:102) pointed out, elites in central and peripheral countries tend to form a symbiotic relationship.[4] In the academic world system, however, such relationships are controlled by central scholars, who set the standards of excellence by which peripheral scholars are judged. Thus, it is important to not lose sight of the power inequality and of the concomitant relations of domination in the world's intellectual community.[5]

Relations on the periphery in the 'world system': The Asian case

I now turn from the center-periphery relations in the world system to the relations between peripheries in Asia. The first point we must make about Asia is one I often made while teaching in the United States from 1989 to 1993, namely, that 'there is no Asian in Asia' (Kuwayama 1994). In the Old World, 'Asia' or 'the Orient' is a concept that only has meaning in relation to 'Euro-America' or 'the Occident.' Its internal diversity makes it difficult to lump together all the countries located in the region and to label them as 'Asian' as if there were some sort of unity among them. The same is true, as we have already discussed, with 'the West' and also with such categories as 'Hispanic' (Oboler 1995). However, the complexity of Asia far surpasses that in any other region of the world, especially in terms of language and religion. If we take the example of East Asia, the meaningful distinction is whether one is Chinese or Korean or Japanese. Any sense of solidarity that Asians may have as a group will emerge only when they are pitted against or compared with Americans, for example. It is important to remember the complex multiplicity of Asia because in the United States, and to a lesser extent in Europe, there is a 'generalized Asian stereotype' (Johnson 1988:8) that erases the vast differences among Asian countries.[6]

To illustrate this point, I will briefly compare Japan with a few of its Asian neighbors. Japan is one of the few non-Western countries in the world in which almost all academic instruction is given in the national language from elementary to graduate schools. Obviously, this fact derives from Japan's modern history as an independent nation that has escaped colonization by Western Europe and the United States. There is no denying the Western influence on Japan in every aspect of life, but it remains that, with so many translations of Western scholarship available in Japanese, intellectual activities can be conducted without the use of a dominant European language such as English. Thus, Japanese anthropologists, or for that matter scholars in any other field, can think and write in Japanese and continue to pursue their careers. Moreover, anthropology, which specializes in the study of other cultures, is a thriving field in Japan, where the slogans of 'internationalization,' or more recently, 'globalization' are on the lips of the country's leaders. The large domestic market for anthropological books, both at the professional and non-professional levels, has even made some anthropologists (e.g., Tadao Umesao, Chie Nakane, and Masao Yamaguchi) nationally recognized figures.

All this points to the fortunate situation in which Japanese anthropologists find themselves. There is, however, an opposite side to the picture: what is fortunate inside Japan is a misfortune outside it. Because the Japanese can easily find an outlet for their writings domestically, they do not feel the need to write and publish in the dominant languages of the world, even though Japanese academics know very well that, as long as their publications remain in Japanese, the rest of the world will not comment on them. The only exception may be books on Korea, which, according to Abito Ito (1996:8–9), are often subjected to the scrutiny of Koreans who suspect an Orientalist bias on the part of their former colonizers. It is only natural, then, that Japanese discussion tends to be self-contained and for 'domestic consumption' only. The same may be said of Americans, but as already mentioned, their dominant position in the world system means that what is domestic is also international.

The Japanese situation contrasts with that in Southeast Asia, where, despite its ethnic diversity, elites constitute a unified world through the use of a common language – English (Nakane 1987:159). This linguistic unity, as well as a limited degree of intellectual unity that arises from it, has its roots in the unfortunate experience of colonization by the Western powers. (Much of Southeast Asia was occupied by Japan during World War II, but its influence was limited). Its positive side should not be overlooked, however. At international conferences, for example, Southeast Asian intellectuals are far more confident and eloquent than the Japanese, not simply because they speak better English, but because their Western-style intellectual training has made it possible for them to argue in ways that appeal to the Western-dominated, international academic community. Perhaps one of the positive legacies of Western colonialism is that it has educated a class of local elites who know how to 'talk back' to their colonizers using the colonizers' own languages.

I suspect that the 'peculiar intimacy' between the colonizer and the colonized to which I have just alluded has contributed to the prominence of India and its adjacent countries in the world of anthropology. Although India was colonized by the British, the British were, unlike the Japanese, victors in World War II, and many of the leading figures in postwar India were educated at prestigious universities in Great Britain. The ability to speak English with British accents is in fact a distinct marker of social prestige. From this background have emerged personal networks of intellectuals between the two regions, which go beyond the simple binarism of the colonizer/ruler and the colonized/ruled. In particular, the familiarity of Indians with the discourse at the center of the world system on the one hand and their colonial experience on the other has enabled them to theorize their 'otherness' – the Indian self as the Other to Westerners – by using the language of the colonizers. 'Language' should be understood here not merely as a medium of communication, but rather as a totality that expresses the 'world view' of the people who speak it. Referring to Homi Bhabha's exposition of 'hybridity,' Kuan-Hsing Chen (1998:23) wrote, 'Although the colonizer looks down on [the colonized], the latter can still use the colonizer's language to insert denied knowledges and traditions into the dominant discursive space, and in turn, the colonizer's unfamiliarity with this whole set of cultural codes puts the colonizer in crisis, and hence undoes his authority.' It would not be wide of the mark to say that although colonization by the Western powers has been an unfortunate experience, it has nevertheless worked in some positive ways, as is shown in the prominence of Indian scholars in postcolonial studies. Japanese intellectuals, too, have had a similar colonial experience since the mid-nineteenth century, but Japan's fortunate past as a politically independent nation (except for a short period after World War II) has ironically worked against them in making themselves understood by the outside world.

Not only was Japan independent, but it also had its own colonies in Asia. Indeed Japan's colonial past, which has no parallel outside Western Europe and the Untied States, has left deep scars in East and Southeast Asia. Like European anthropology, Japanese ethnology/anthropology was a product of colonialism, but its reputation was damaged more severely than its Western counterparts because of the harshness of Japan's colonial rule. Even today, the word *minzokugaku* (ethnology) is associated with colonialism and arouses suspicion both inside and outside Japan. In 1995, it was proposed to change the name of Japanese Society of Ethnology as a possible solution to this problem, but the proposal was rejected for complex reasons (JSE 1995a; 1995b; 1996; 1997). It took eight more years of deliberation before an agreement was made to change the name to Japanese Society of Cultural Anthropology (to be effective April, 2004).

This cursory review makes it clear that not only is the Asian intellectual community diverse, but that there is also not much substance in the notion of a unified 'Asian anthropology.' (Note that this term is used here in the singular as distinguished from 'Asian anthropologies' in the plural). At least, it is something in the making, not a reality yet, which reflects the growing awareness among Asian scholars that it is time to make a social science of their own, one free from Eurocentrism.[7] This, then, is the one thing that unites Asian anthropologists – the fact that all of them belong to the periphery in the academic world system. The complex relations between anthropologies in Asia may only be understood by considering their peripheral status vis-à-vis the center.

Using the mainland/island metaphor again, we may say that the island people's eagerness to form ties with the dominant mainland has resulted in the neglect of the relationships *among* themselves. Thus, while there is frequent 'ferry traffic' between the mainland and the islands, the traffic is sporadic between the islands, which have remained isolated from each other.

The mutual ignorance and indifference among Asian anthropologists may be explained from this point of view. Not only do they not know each other's work well, only few of them have made serious efforts to rectify that situation. Unfortunately, the intellectual distance between Asian countries is far greater than that between Asia and Europe or America. Geographic proximity does not always bring about intellectual exchange. To give an example, very few Japanese anthropologists are familiar with scholarship in Korea, Japan's closest neighbor. Since 1968, the Korean Society for Cultural Anthropology (KSCA) has been publishing a journal called *Korean Cultural Anthropology* (in Korean). In the spring of 2003, the KSCA's Committee for Developing Educational Materials, headed by Kyung-Koo Han, released a new introductory textbook entitled *The First Encounter with Cultural Anthropology* (in Korean). Designed specifically for young students, it emphasizes the discipline's contemporary significance. Yet such accomplishments are little known in Japan or anywhere else in Asia. As this example shows, peripheral scholars must overcome the double barrier between mainland and islands on the one hand, and between islands on the other.

Carol Gluck's (1995:36) observation of Japanese historiography neatly applies to anthropologies in Asia. She pointed out that Japanese historians have long been engaged in a conceptual exchange with Western historians. Although the 'balance of trade' has been in favor of the West due to the one-way traffic of translations, there has still been a sustained and active intellectual exchange between the two regions. According to Gluck, this has brought about surprising similarities between Western and Japanese historiographies. By contrast, the trade between Japan and the rest of Asia has been virtually non-existent. The need to establish or re-establish commonality in Asia has been recognized, but much of the task still remains to be done.[8]

Regarding the relations of domination involved in the academic world system, Asian anthropologists, and for that matter those in any other peripheral region, should be cautious of the danger of cultural nationalism. As the political scientist Hans Kohn (1944 [1994]) pointed out during World War II, developing countries in modern times have often been trapped in a cultural nationalism that stresses their distinctiveness and even spiritual superiority over rivals that are materially more powerful. A look at prewar Germany and Japan shows how destructive the consequences of cultural nationalism can be. In particular, Japan's search for spiritual autonomy and political independence from the West (e.g., the idea of the 'family state' centered on Emperor worship) brought about what may be called an 'anachronistic fantasy.' This point is very important to remember because culture and politics are inseparably related in modern nation-states. The quest for cultural (including academic) autonomy may easily be politicized. If the problems of European and American anthropologies come from their colonial past, the problems of Asian anthropologies stem from nationalism or the nationalization of culture.

The aforementioned attempt to create an 'Asian social science' free from Eurocentrism is understandable, given the subordinate role Asia has been forced to play in modern history. However, if this attempt, out of national or regional pride, refuses to see the power inequalities that undoubtedly exist between Asia and Euro-America, it will merely result in a Utopian struggle. And if the refusal to see the reality of power leads to the wishful thinking that an Asian science can be created without drawing on the intellectual legacy of the West, it will be self-defeating. As earlier mentioned when discussing the Japanese folklorist, Kunio Yanagita, there is hardly any modern indigenous system of thought that has not been influenced in one way or another by Western science.[9] In the academic world system, the periphery is enmeshed with and dependent upon the center in much the same way as the countryside is connected with urban centers in a modern state. Dogmatically denying this relationship or attempting to subvert it without a sufficient basis of power might have the effect of temporarily satisfying a heightened sense of national or regional pride, but in the long run it will merely damage one's intellectual potential.

A more practical and fruitful approach is, in my mind, to accept the core countries' achievements as the common heritage of all anthropologists throughout the world. Just because E. E. Evans-Pritchard, for example, was British and his bust is displayed at the Institute of Social and Cultural Anthropology, University of Oxford, does not mean that he belongs exclusively to the British; rather, he left us a legacy on which to build better theories for a better understanding of human beings. It certainly injures the pride of Asians that their intellectual ancestors have not been regarded as highly as Evans-Pritchard, even if they were of his caliber, but origin is not the most important thing. After all, great ideas transcend ethnic and national boundaries and refuse to be identified with a particular group or nation.

This is not to say, of course, that central anthropologists can be complacent about past achievements. They should, first of all, become aware of their privileged position and understand that the plight of peripheral anthropologists is not solely their responsibility, but often comes from the unwillingness of the people at the center to listen to the voices from the margins.

Conclusion

In this chapter I have delivered two different messages to two different audiences. My message to the anthropologists of the center, in the United States, Great Britain, and France, is a plea to realize, first, that their overwhelming power has created relations of domination and subordination in anthropological practice; and, second, that because of their dominant position they have, intentionally or not, suppressed the voices from the margins. To peripheral anthropologists in Asia and other regions, my message is about the danger of becoming nationalistic or even chauvinistic and of dogmatically rejecting everything Western (i.e., the central discourse) in their desire to be intellectually independent.

With the globalization of anthropology, the anthropological self – that which observes and describes other cultures – has diversified. Anthropology is no longer the monopoly of a few major countries in the West. It is practiced today in many other countries in many regions, which used to be objects of anthropological inquiry. Under these circumstances, we have no Anthropology with a capital A. Instead, we have a multiplicity of anthropologies. The attempt to create an 'Asian social science' is just one example of the fundamental changes taking place in the academic world system.

This does not mean, however, that the gravity of power is shifting from the core Western countries to the peripheries. On the contrary, we may say that they are strengthening their hold as the main generator of the forces of globalization. As I have emphasized throughout, there are *persisting* inequalities between the center and the periphery, and no analysis of anthropological practice would be complete without considering this fact. Theorizing the complex flow of knowledge caused by globalization, without losing sight of the power differences involved, is what is called for. My approach to the world system is an attempt at such a theorization.

4 'Global' and 'National' Studies of Folklore: Lessons from Kunio Yanagita, an Intellectual Giant of Modern Japan

Kunio Yanagita (1875–1962) is widely regarded as the founder of Japanese folklore studies or folkloristics.[1] Not only are his writings numerous, there is also a voluminous secondary literature on his works and career. Unfortunately, most of them have not been translated into other languages and, as such, Yanagita's contributions are little known outside Japan.[2] In this chapter, I will discuss an important aspect of his thought, which, for one reason or another, has been neglected by earlier scholars – the idea of 'global folkloristics.' Presented in his 1934 book, *Minkan Denshōron* (*The Science of Popular Tradition*), this might have developed into a major international project, but instead has, to date, remained an unfinished task, the potential significance of which has yet to be explored.

Different interpretations are possible, but I contend that Yanagita conceptualized global folkloristics as an attempt to study folk cultures throughout the world by examining them first in their country or nation and then comparing and generalizing the research results on a global scale. This idea was innovative because it regarded people in each country as the primary *subjects* (as opposed to objects) of research. In contrast to the Western approach to ethnography, which dealt with indigenous people as objects of research, they were fully recognized as knowledge producers. In my view, a major objective of global folkloristics was to create a 'dialogic space' open to all scholars from around the world, in which different kinds of knowledge produced in different parts of the world could be examined without privileging one or a few leading countries. I therefore submit that, if modified to suit today's circumstances, global folkloristics has the potential to change the academic world system into a structure that gives equal representation to both central and peripheral scholars. It is, of course, impossible to apply Yanagita's ideas as he presented them more than half a century ago, but they are still useful in rethinking anthropological practice.

Despite the merits of Yanagita's vision, it also reveals some of the limitations characteristic of modern intellectuals in developing countries. Particularly problematic is his cultural nationalism, which lurks in the assertion that only natives can understand their culture and are therefore qualified to study it. Theoretically speaking, this assertion derived from Yanagita's prioritization of the natives' 'embodied understanding' over the outsiders' 'analytical understanding,' a topic to which I will later return. Politically speaking, it stemmed from his desire to defend Japan from Western encroachment by excluding Western researchers. This desire, in turn, sprang from Yanagita's attempt to 'possess' his culture, which reflected the strong nationalism of modern Japan.

Below, I will first outline the idea of global folkloristics under eight headings, then show its significance for today's anthropology, and finally discuss its limitations. The arguments to be presented are based on my earlier work written in Japanese (Kuwayama 2000). I have drawn on the newly edited *Yanagita Kunio Zenshū* (*Complete Works of Kunio Yanagita,* 38 volumes), which started to be published in 1997. All of Yanagita's words to be quoted have been translated by the author. Readers should remember that no translation could perfectly replicate his distinctive style of writing.

Re-Viewing global folkloristics

First, an explanation of terminology is required. The expression Yanagita used for global folkloristics is *sekai minzokugaku,* 'world folklore studies,' which, as mentioned earlier, first appeared in *Minkan Denshōron*.[3] The first chapter of this book also introduced another important concept, *ikkoku minzokugaku,* which literally translates as 'one-country folklore studies.' Whether these concepts form a contrasted pair or a complementary relationship is a point of contestation, one I will discuss shortly. For now, suffice it to say that from hereon *sekai minzokugaku* and *ikkoku minzokugaku* will be translated as 'global folkloristics' and 'national folkloristics,' respectively.

What is global folkloristics?

It is widely argued that Yanagita was solely interested in the study of Japan, and refused to compare it with other countries. His concept of national folkloristics has often been cited in support of this argument. Global folkloristics, on the other hand, has been considered to involve cultural comparison. For this reason, national and global folkloristics have long been regarded as having opposite orientations, and most Japanese folklorists have reasoned that global folkloristics was merely a 'whim,' an aberration, in Yanagita's long career. The fact that he seldom mentioned it after the publication of *Minkan Denshōron*, and his own remark made in old age that it was a failure, have been taken as proof of this point.

However, a careful reading of Yanagita's writings reveals this to be a misunderstanding. Contrary to the common supposition, he conceived of national and global folkloristics as two sides or stages of the same project, regarding the former as the constituent unit of the latter. In other words, he expected each country to establish an academic tradition of its own, through which it would employ local theories and methods to investigate its own folk customs. (Whether or not it is proper to take the country or nation as the unit of scholarship will be examined later in this chapter). Once a sufficient number of countries had embarked on this process, he thought, a global community of folklorists would naturally emerge. Global folkloristics was therefore conceptualized as a sort of 'town meeting' in which folklorists gathered from different parts of the world to exchange their ideas and research findings. The following remarks by Yanagita clearly attest to this point: 'We should first establish national folkloristics in order to prepare the ground for creating global folkloristics in the future' (Yanagita 1998b:25); 'When national folkloristics is established in each country, it will become possible to make comparisons and generalizations on an international scale. And when the research results are sufficiently generalized to be applicable to all nations or ethnic groups, we may say that we have seen the dawn of global folkloristics' (Yanagita 1998b:47).

Global folkloristics and comparative folkloristics

On one of the rare occasions when Yanagita discussed cultural comparisons, he defined *hikaku minzokugaku* (comparative folkloristics) as a field that studied the folk customs of different countries by comparative methods (Yanagita 1964). Drawing on this definition, later generations of Japanese folklorists have argued that comparative folkloristics 'aims to capture Japanese-ness by comparing Japan's folk culture with that of other people' (Sano 1998:116). They have, however, paid little attention to how comparative folkloristics is different from global folkloristics. In many cases, the two fields have been considered almost identical, except in the scope of research; Japanese comparative folkloristics is practically limited to the study of East Asia, whereas global folkloristics covers all regions of the world – an ideal that is not yet a reality, but may someday be realized.

In my view, there is a fundamental difference between the two. This difference concerns the meaning of 'comparison' involved in each field. In comparative folkloristics, the objects of comparison are the different folk cultures in different parts of the world. For example, Japan is compared with Korea or China or both, and by examining the similarities and differences between these countries, scholars draw conclusions about what makes Japan distinctive. Collaboration with local researchers is encouraged throughout the process. By contrast, global folkloristics compares different *kinds of knowledge* produced by folklorists in different parts of the world. In the study of Japan, for example, research is first carried out exclusively by Japanese scholars. It is only after they have analyzed their findings according to their own academic traditions that foreigners are invited to examine the relative merits and demerits of the overall research results. This 'exclusion' of foreigners was derived from Yanagita's conviction that no outsider was capable of fully appreciating another people's culture, especially its psychological domains, which he called '*shin'i genshō*' (literally, psycho-semantic phenomena).

The objective of global folkloristics

Nowhere in *Minkan Denshōron* is the objective of global folkloristics clearly spelled out, though the following passage, taken from the opening paragraph of the second chapter, sheds some light on the issue:

> The mission of the science of folk traditions is not complete merely because the discipline of folkloristics has been established in a country,

such as Japan, where data are plentiful. Our aspirations should be aimed higher. If our methods of investigation are systematic enough to deserve the name of science, and if they prove truly useful in exploring that part of human history not accessible to conventional historiography, which relies on archival documents for verification, then our experiment should be applied to the study of our neighboring countries, and even to those unfortunate races that exist without a country. Furthermore, it is not the exclusive right of other disciplines to attempt to discover the forces and laws underlying this exceedingly complex universe that we now conceive of as constituting a single entity. We must discard our old habit of taking pleasure in making small discoveries, and instead we must be determined to contribute to the great task of discovering human unity (Yanagita 1998b:34).

Since Yanagita regarded folkloristics as a branch of historiography, his emphasis on discovering 'laws' and 'unity' appears, at least initially, to contradict such a notion. He was, however, interested in studying the general *pattern* of history, the ways in which the daily lives of ordinary people are changed, rather than unique, momentous events. Yanagita was, in fact, strongly influenced by British empiricism, as his definition of folkloristics as 'an inductive science' shows (Yanagita 1998b:191). Moreover, his admiration for the nomothetic nature of science was revealed in statements, such as, 'Our discipline came into being in order to study the laws of life that run throughout human history – laws yet to be discovered by the existing sciences' (Yanagita 1998b:113).

Community studies, national folkloristics, and global folkloristics

Yanagita strongly advocated community studies called '*kyōdo kenkyū*' (literally, the study of one's hometown). His major work in this field, *Kyōdo Seikatsu no Kenkyūhō* (*Methods in the Study of Community Life*), was published in 1935. In this book, and elsewhere, Yanagita emphasized that community studies should begin at home, namely, with the study of one's own village or town – a view compatible with his assertion that natives should be active agents in research into their culture. In the 1930s, Yanagita founded a nationwide network of amateur researchers. These researchers reported their local findings to Yanagita, who then subjected them to detailed analysis, and from this he drew more generalized, nationwide conclusions. He was convinced that the entire nation of Japan constituted a single community. Thus, a particular local community was not studied as an end in itself, but was treated as the basic unit for comparison on a national scale (Yanagita 1998b:64–66). Yanagita's objective was to explore Japanese folk culture in its entirety, both past and present, by examining different patterns of community life throughout the country (cf. Kawada 1993:127).

His notion that global folkloristics comprises a community of folklorists from around the world may be considered an extension of this approach. He conceived of global folkloristics as involving two stages of development: (1) establishing in each country a distinctive tradition of folkloristics on the basis of community studies carried out in different parts of the country; and (2) establishing a global science of folklore by integrating the different types of national folkloristics practiced in different parts of the world. In Yanagita's mind, then, community studies, national folkloristics, and global folkloristics constituted a continuum. (Again, we might question whether there is only one academic tradition in each country. This, though, was certainly Yanagita's belief). Consider, for example, the following statements:

> If a powerful institution was located at the center [of Japan], we could then collate all the locally conducted research and make the overall results available to the wider, national community…I sometimes dream of making an international network of knowledge exchange (Yanagita 1998b:75–76).

> Whatever may be said, the basic unit for folklore research is the ethnic group. It is necessary for people in each nation to conduct local research and then for the results to be generalized. It is only after we have built up a respectable library of data that it will become possible to generalize and classify the world's folk customs…Data collected and analyzed in each country should be actively translated. Taking language or ethnic groups as the basic unit, we should first create a domestic community of scholars and then engage in international collaboration (Yanagita 1998b:81).

Relationships with ethnology/anthropology

In 1925, when Yanagita was browsing in a used bookshop in Berlin, he met by chance Franz Boas, a German-born Jew who, having emigrated to the United States, was teaching anthropology there. According to Yanagita, Boas told him that in German the terms 'folkloristics' and 'ethnology' roughly corresponded to *Volkskunde* and *Völkerkunde*, respectively (Yanagita 1998a:164). Yanagita's distinction between folkloristics and ethnology (what is more commonly known today as cultural anthropology) seems to have been influenced by this German classification.[4] For example, he defined folkloristics as 'research from the inside, conducted in a small number of advanced countries in order for them to know about themselves,' and, ethnology, as 'research from the outside, conducted to teach the people of advanced and civilized countries about the various ethnic groups in the world' (Yanagita 1998b:40).

Because of his conviction that only natives can fully appreciate their culture, Yanagita regarded folkloristics as superior to ethnology, remarking, 'Foreigners' observations, however carefully made, are no equal to the compatriots' insights into their culture. Folklorists have demonstrated this to ethnologists' (Yanagita 1998b:38). At the same time, he welcomed the advance of ethnological research, which showed that some 'primitive' customs had survived in the civilized societies of Western Europe well into the twentieth century. Contending that this finding had greatly stimulated the study of one's own culture, Yanagita stated, 'The advance of ethnology will further stimulate the growth of folkloristics in each country. Eventually, it will help establish global folkloristics. This is the mission of ethnology' (Yanagita 1998b:48).

The establishment of national folkloristics by natives

Yanagita declined to compare Japan with other countries, not because he found cultural comparison worthless, but because he believed the time was not yet ripe for such study. Because of his conviction that only natives could understand their culture, Yanagita asserted that until tribal peoples possessed the ability to study themselves, a truly meaningful comparison of the world's cultures would remain an impossibility.

Yanagita repeatedly argued that the deeper layers of a culture were inaccessible to outsiders. In *Seinen to Gakumon* (*Youth and Scholarship*), published in 1928, he wrote, 'As foreigners' descriptions of Japan show, outsiders' observations and conjectures are prone to gross mistakes, no matter how elaborate their research methods are. The language barrier is mainly responsible for this. Thus, we can hardly put our complete confidence in their research' (Yanagita 1998a:27). In *Minkan Denshōron*, Yanagita developed a famous model of folklore research consisting of three parts. The first is concerned with visible phenomena, which just scratch the surface of a folk culture. This is the level of research done by 'travelers.' The second part is concerned with audible phenomena, which are more complex than the first because understanding them requires language competence, but are still not particularly deep. Research on this level is undertaken by 'temporary residents.' The third part is the most complex, being concerned with *shin'i genshō* (psycho-semantic phenomena) or 'mentalities,' in the sense of the term as used by the Annales school of French social history.[5] Yanagita contended that only *jikokumin* (compatriots) could see how mentalities work, stating, 'With only a few exceptions, foreigners are incapable of conducting research into the native mind' (Yanagita 1998b:14). In *Kyōdo Seikatsu no Kenkyūhō*, he reiterated this point when he said, 'After all, foreigners cannot probe into *shin'i genshō*. We have to wait until natives have learned to look at themselves objectively' (Yanagita 1998c:347). Perhaps the following remarks best express Yanagita's view:

> A most notable difference between folkloristics and ethnology is that the former studies its own people, while the latter studies people of different races from the viewpoint of travelers and temporary residents. Although scholars in both fields draw on data obtained by firsthand research into the actual life of a people, folklorists are able to accurately probe into deep psychological phenomena, whereas ethnologists can only make general observations about the surface of a culture. This is why I contend that, as a scholarly field, folkloristics should restrict itself to being national before becoming international (Yanagita 1998b:47).

The facts of a culture's life reveal themselves differently to different people. All that is visible to foreigners is the surface. By contrast, for compatriots, seeing the facts is tantamount to knowing and thinking about their significance. My assertion that national folkloristics should be established before anything else is premised on this fact (Yanagita 1998b:110).

Global folkloristics and Japan's mission

Yanagita vehemently maintained that it was Japan's mission to establish a strong, national tradition of folkloristics before any other non-Western country did so. (It is unclear to what extent he knew about the non-Western world other than East Asia).[6] This contention was based on his observation that although 'primitive' societies had many materials useful for folklore research, their people lacked the ability to investigate them for themselves. By contrast, 'civilized' societies in Western Europe had the intellectual resources, but were hampered in their efforts by modernization, which had buried the old cultural layers, making them difficult to find. Yanagita regarded Japan as an ideal place for folklore research because, although a modern nation, it had industrialized relatively late and had thereby retained access to the old world, while gaining the resources needed to study it provided by the new. As he remarked, 'Among the Japanese, the facts of everyday life speak for an age that is becoming a past...In many cases, thinking about them is at the same time collecting data, as well as making classifications and generalizations. Nowhere in the world is it possible to collect materials necessary for historical reconstruction as easily and as perfectly as in Japan' (Yanagita 1998b:31). Japan was, therefore, a 'treasure island' of folklore research (Yanagita 1998c:215). This in-between status of Japan stemmed from its liminal position in modern politics; Japan was dominated by the Western powers in the wider world, but in Asia it was a great regional power.

Yanagita was moved by nationalistic sentiments when he commented that whereas 'primitive' people had to be represented by Westerners, the Japanese possessed the intellectual resources to represent themselves. Criticizing outsider research as 'touching the skin, but failing to reach the heart,' he wrote, 'Herein lies the great misfortune of uncivilized people who do not possess historians of their own. Since they are incapable of studying their past, they must have it represented by foreigners with motivations. By contrast, the Japanese are fortunate enough to be able to trace the history of our culture, if only we have the will to do so' (Yanagita 1998c:234). Yanagita further commented, 'Even if foreigners flock together to make scientific observations, the results will be no more than those of 'the five blind men and the elephant.' It is truly significant that our fellow countrymen, who are familiar with the world's scholarship, are setting out to study our own culture' (Yanagita 1998a:160). The following statement summarizes Yanagita's intellectual nationalism: 'We must study ourselves. Not only should we attempt to know ourselves better, we must also lead Western folklorists who have gone astray. This is Japan's noble mission' (Yanagita 1998a:171).

Yanagita's counter-hegemonic discourse

Yanagita was counter-hegemonic in two respects. First, he challenged mainstream Japanese scholarship, especially orthodox historiography, which relied almost exclusively on written records for describing the lives of great individuals. This orientation contrasted with Yanagita's emphasis on the importance of collecting data through fieldwork, which enabled the writing of the history of what he called '*jōmin*' (literally, ordinary people or the plebeian). Also, he criticized the attitudes of many of Japan's intellectual elites who produced very little by way of indigenous discourse, but diligently studied Western ideas in translation. He repeatedly argued that it was futile to uncritically apply Western frameworks to the study of Japan.

Second, Yanagita challenged Western academic hegemony. In the opening chapter of *Seinen to Gakumon*, Yanagita praised the advance of Western ethnology on the one hand, and criticized its colonial roots on the other. He contended that 'white men's activities' had posed a challenge to young, ambitious Japanese people. He was angered when he found that no Japanese had been invited to attend an international conference on Pacific studies to be held in Brussels. He objected, saying that Japanese scholars should participate because Japan is 'a major nation in the Pacific region' (Yanagita 1998a:29). Similarly, in *Minkan Denshōron*, Yanagita denounced a world almanac of folklore, edited by a Swiss scholar, for being too Western-centered. As he remarked, 'How can they call it "international" when there is no reference to Japanese research, which has played an important role in the development of this field? No future almanac would be complete without Japanese participation. They *must* invite us' (Yanagita 1998b:81). Furthermore, in *Kyōdo Seikatsu no Kenkyūhō*, Yanagita cynically commented on H. G. Well's *Outline of History* (1921), saying that it was not a true history because it merely described 'the facts known in the West' (Yanagita 1998c:206).

Today, Yanagita is often criticized for having been indifferent to the politics of folklore, especially to the connection of Japanese folkloristics with Japan's own colonial rule. These criticisms are legitimate, but they point to one important aspect of modern Japan and overlook another. From the late nineteenth century onwards, the Japanese colonized and ruled much of the Asia Pacific region, but they were dominated by the Western powers in the wider world. This duality regarding Japan cannot be overemphasized because, now that Japan has achieved an economic status equal to that of any major European country, it is a fact too frequently overlooked. Referring to the future of folkloristics, Yanagita wrote, 'Considering the possibility that this discipline would flourish in countries like Japan, where data are plentiful, we should be prepared to re-write Western theories by reconsidering them in light of the Japanese data' (Yanagita 1998b:155). Such counter-hegemonic discourse may only be understood by considering the Western domination of Japan in almost every field, including scholarship.

The contemporary significance of global folkloristics

In the previous chapters, I have analyzed the Western neglect of Japanese scholarship in terms of the academic world system. To show how the system works in folklore research, I give here a renowned American folklorist's account of Yanagita. Alan Dundes, the 1993 winner of the Pitre Prize, one of the highest honors to be conferred on folklorists, edited a collection of classic essays entitled *International Folkloristics: Classic Contributions by the Founders of Folklore* (1999). This volume introduces the reader to twenty European (including Russian) and American scholars, people such as Jacob Grimm, Kaarle Krohn, Arnold van Gennep, and James Frazer. While Yanagita is recognized as 'the founder of folkloristics in Japan,' the following brief description is not only totally inadequate but also fundamentally inaccurate:

> His major works have been published in a set of thirty-six volumes, but except for a very occasional essay that was translated into German…, Yanagita's materials remain closed to anyone unable to read Japanese (Dundes 1999:56).

This statement is completely without foundation. Some of Yanagita's major works have long been translated into English, including *The Legends of Tōno* (orig. 1910; trans. 1975), *Japanese Manners and Customs in the Meiji Era* (orig. 1931; trans. 1957), *About Our Ancestors* (orig. 1946; trans. 1970), and *Japanese Folklore Dictionary* (orig. 1951; trans. 1958). To my knowledge, these books are available for loan at some leading university libraries in the United States. We may well wonder how Dundes could, for so long, have remained uninformed about such a simple fact.

The answer to this question is equally simple. Positioned at the center of the academic world system, Dundes did not have to worry about such 'trifle' matters. In fact, his ignorance has scarcely damaged his reputation. (Of course, the inverse would not have been true. Imagine if a prize-winning Japanese folklorist admitted to having heard about Frazer, but to not knowing much about him because his work has not been translated into Japanese. His international reputation would be in tatters). For Dundes, Yanagita is just a local hero whose contributions he can ignore at little or no professional cost. In the 1930s, Yanagita deplored the fact that Japanese research had been neglected in the 'international' almanac of folklore edited by a European scholar. Unfortunately, the situation has little changed since then – a fact that clearly demonstrates the continued inequality between central and peripheral scholars.

Herein lies the contemporary significance of global folkloristics. Conceptualized as a community of folklorists from around the world, it will provide, if modified to suit today's circumstances, the much needed forum for dialogue – what I have called 'dialogic space' – in which scholars with different national traditions exchange their views on an equal basis. The Internet has already provided the technological basis for such dialogic space. Unlike the traditional methods of communication, especially printing, in which information flows in one direction from the sender/writer/describer to the receiver/reader/described, the Internet has made it possible to connect diverse people instantaneously on a global scale. In particular, it has proved to be a valuable gift to those people living in the marginal areas that have been left out from the global network of communication. At present, because of the so-called 'digital divide,' access to computer facilities is often difficult in these areas, but this gap will hopefully close in the near future. What remains to be seen is a theory of the dialogic space or the social basis thereof. Yanagita's idea of global folkloristics is illuminating in this respect. Figuratively, it may be considered to be an attempt to create the ethnographic *za*, which has been rendered in Chapter 2 as the 'communal theatre.'

As I will examine in the next section, Yanagita's view of the country or nation, both of which are expressed in Japanese by the same word, '*kuni*,' as the unit for ethnographic analysis and for knowledge production is contestable, especially in the context of today's deconstructionist movement. His assertion that only natives can appreciate their culture is also questionable. We should, however, remember that Yanagita's project was conceived in the 1930s. Instead of rejecting it altogether, we should assess his arguments with the benefits of hindsight and see if there is anything we can learn from them.

To reiterate, Yanagita emphasized that the deep layers of a culture are inaccessible to outsiders. Foreign 'travelers' or 'temporary residents,' as he called them, might be able to analyze the surface phenomena visible to their eyes or audible to their ears, but only trained natives could grasp the deep meanings lying beneath the surface of local life. His assertion that folkloristics should be a 'national pursuit' stemmed from this belief. Yanagita often described his discipline as '*jiko shōsatsu no gaku*' (a science of introspection). He expressed his hope that a similar science would develop in other non-Western countries, but maintained a pessimistic attitude. Referring to the deprived conditions of Japan's Asian neighbors, Yanagita remarked in a rather ethnocentric manner, 'We the Japanese are fortunate enough to be competent to study our distant past by using our mother tongue. Not only should we take full advantage of it, we also have the duty to share our happiness with the neighboring countries' (Yanagita 1998a:27). This statement shows how the Japanese could be arrogant toward the people they had colonized, but considering the small number of folklorists in the rest of Asia, it was not completely off the mark. (For the situation in India, see footnote 6). Yanagita further stated:

> And what should be done about those island people who don not possess a natural aptitude for study? Should we teach them step by step how to study themselves? Or should we study them on their behalf before it is too late? It is not easy to decide which will turn out to be the better choice.

> Ideally, they should learn to research their own people, as the Japanese have done. Since, however, their culture is rapidly vanishing, there is no alternative but to have outsiders study and describe it, regardless of the inevitable inaccuracies of such descriptions (Yanagita 1998a:27–28).

Careful readers will note that these remarks are very similar to those of Malinowski quoted at the beginning of Chapter 2. A major difference is that Yanagita regarded outsiders' accounts as inherently 'inaccurate and imperfect,' whereas Malinowski did not seem to have such misgivings. If anything, he believed in the superiority of Western ethnography.

Yanagita's counter-hegemonic position led him to maintain that the advance of folklore research in Japan was 'instrumental in making Western scholars recognize a major weakness of ethnology, namely, that it is far from complete without the participation of the people being studied' (Yanagita 1998b:44). He also remarked, 'In about half a century, when people look back on the development of ethnology, they will note that the emergence of Japanese ethnography of their own people has been the single most important turning point in the history of this discipline' (Yanagita 1998b:44–45). Whether or not the Japanese really had as much to offer as Yanagita thought is not the issue here. The point is that he was aware, to a degree uncommon among his Western contemporaries, of the limitations of ethnographic research that did not involve natives as active agents. Perhaps the following best expresses his position:

> We hope and believe that one day the history of all the primitive peoples on earth, whose pasts have not been recorded in written documents, will be explored through the methods of *kyōdo kenkyū* (the study of one's hometown) and that folklorists will regard all the people in the world, whether from one's own country or not, as proper objects of research (Yanagita 1998c:233).

Junzo Kawada, one of the leading anthropologists in Japan, remarked that Yanagita's hope is becoming a reality. He gave two major reasons for this: the appearance of native anthropologists in former colonies and the globalization of information. In a recent lecture delivered at the Institute for the Study of Folklore, Seijo University, Tokyo, where Yanagita's materials are kept, he commented:

> In Europe, in the case of African studies, students come from Africa to study at major universities in large numbers. They carry out research on their own country and write doctoral dissertations, which are then submitted to French universities, for example. Furthermore, they can read and critically comment on the works of French scholars who have conducted research in Africa. The interaction between the researcher and the researched is far more frequent today than in the past. Not only has it become possible to check each other's research, they now have closer ties ethically. Politically and economically, too, the world's societies are closely bound up with each other. Under these circumstances, outside researchers can no longer feign indifference toward the people they study, for their research may entail adverse consequences. The scientific prerogative of 'detachment,' which ethnologists and anthropologists used to postulate between themselves and their research objects, is no longer tenable. Because of this detachment, researchers have long been able to assume that their observations of foreign people and culture are objective and superior (Kawada 1997:65).

Yanagita argued that when foreign travelers return from their journey to a distant land, 'people accept them as the sole experts on that place and do not question what they have said' (Yanagita 1998b:35). He also wrote, 'The scarcity of research into one region by different scholars has made it difficult to compare their descriptions' (Yanagita 1998b:36). Regarding this as a major deficiency of ethnology, he further commented that he had made it a rule to read Western descriptions of Japan before evaluating the overall credibility of their ethnography. 'The literate Japanese are in a position to work as inspectors,' said Yanagita. Today, these 'inspectors' are native anthropologists or 'natives who talk back.' Despite the persistent inequality in the academic world system, they have finally entered the theater as actors or actresses creating their own performances. In this new situation, Yanagita's global folkloristics provides a model, though far from complete, for creating a worldwide forum for dialogue open to all people as equal partners.

Theoretical problems of global folkloristics

In this section, I will first discuss the 'national' of national folkloristics, which was originally conceptualized as the constituent unit of global folkloristics, and then critically examine Yanagita's assertion that only natives can understand their culture.

On the nation

An important question that must be raised about global folkloristics is whether it is proper to take the nation as the basic unit for ethnographic analysis and knowledge production. Since the 1980s, the homogeneity of a nation, which has long been assumed in the study of culture, has been attacked by so many theorists that no argument that asserts its centrality can avoid addressing this question. The Japanese folklorist Shigenori Iwata, for example, criticized Yanagita for having neglected the internal diversity of Japan, as manifested in ethnicity, region, class, and gender. He called Yanagita's national folkloristics 'a discipline that obliterates the differences and the diversity within Japan' (Iwata 1998:13). Similar criticisms have been raised in other fields. Among the most notable are the historical analyses by Yoshihiko Amino (1990), who has challenged the commonly accepted view that Japan is an agrarian nation with a homogeneous culture. Also notable are the cultural critiques by Naoki Sakai (1997), who has examined how the discourse of Japanese national culture has been constructed. These criticisms are powerful and attractive, but I still contend that 'the nation' has not completely lost significance as a frame for scholarly analysis. Certainly, totalizing discourse such as *nihonjinron* (theory of Japanese culture) is problematic, but is it correct to argue, as some scholars have, that the Japanese nation has been 'fabricated'?

Two things should be noted. First, the nation-state, the dominant political entity that emerged after the mid-sixteenth century, has been, and remains, the political basis of the modern world, and is the primary unit of international relations (Evans and Newnham 1998:343). As a result of globalization, the nation-state's foundation is gradually weakening, but it has neither collapsed nor disappeared. If anything, globalization has triggered nationalistic reactions in many parts of the world. Second, the development of a national culture and that of a nation-state have had a close relationship in modern history. Certainly, as Hobsbawm's and Ranger's *The Invention of Tradition* (1983) reveals, the idea of culture is a product of modern politics, containing many simulated elements that have arbitrarily been instituted or 'invented' by the ruling class. However, we must remember that the resultant national culture has many commonalities that transcend the various differences and ruptures within it. These commonalities are most clearly seen when one national culture is compared with another.[7]

When deconstructing the prevailing discourse of Japan as a homogeneous nation, ethnic minority groups such as the Ainu, Okinawans, and Koreans are often highlighted to show Japan's internal diversity. Very few people would disagree today that Japan is more diverse than it has hitherto been portrayed, but it is often overlooked that these minority groups are themselves quite diverse. Media reports about their internal conflict, most notably the long-standing feud between pro-South and pro-North Koreans, coupled with the generational differences within each group, clearly attest to this point. If, as the deconstructionists have argued, homogenization is a major weakness of the discourse of national culture, the same should also be said of the minority groups they have highlighted to disrupt the monolithic image of Japan. Carried to a logical extreme, their reasoning would end up in a position that denies any kind of generalization, from which would emerge anarchic pictures of the world. We must remember that ethnic minority groups in Japan, or for that matter in any other country, exist within the country's boundary, and their status may only be understood in relation to the larger national community of which they are a part. As Roger Averill has suggested, the deconstruction of homogenized national identities is theoretically important, but many institutional interactions continue to be conducted on the basis of nationhood, and the generalized identity of a nation still has currency for many people living in a particular nation-state. Therefore, for both pragmatic and empirical reasons, it remains viable to posit nationality as a defining identifier (personal communication).

This is, of course, not to glorify the nation. It has become increasingly clear that the traditional thinking based on the idea of national sovereignty has serious limitations in solving contemporary problems affecting all human beings. The ever growing flow of people, goods, capital, and information over the globe has also cast doubt on the viability of the nation-state in ways inconceivable a few decades ago. However, these considerations do not imply that the nation has completely lost its significance. On the contrary, it continues to function as a basic frame for scholarly activities. To appreciate this, consider how academic societies are organized throughout the world. At the Folklore Society of Japan (FSJ), for example, participants in annual meetings are mostly Japanese, who take it for granted that presentations are made in Japanese for a Japanese audience. Almost every utterance made at the meetings acknowledges a debt to Yanagita, about whom there is a national consensus regarding his status as an intellectual giant of modern Japan. No one would ask who Yanagita is.[8] Thus, speaking at the FSJ is a 'national undertaking,' the meaning of which is dependent on the presence of Japan as a single 'imagined community' (Anderson 1991). The situation is more complex in multiethnic nations like the United States, but the difference is in degree, not in kind. Nationality is unequivocally expressed in the very designation of American Folklore Society, and its practice is as national as its name.[9]

Can only natives understand their culture?

In *Minkan Denshōron*, *Kyōdo Seikatsu no Kenkyūhō*, and *Gakumon to Seinen*, Yanagita repeatedly expressed deep misgivings about a foreigner's ability to explore the native mind, arguing that only natives could fully understand their culture. This point of view stemmed partially from his methodology, in which the analysis of folk terminology was considered to be the basis of folklore research. As he remarked, 'The spiritual life of a people is expressed in their art of language...It is inaccessible to foreign travelers who speak different languages. Some people take delight in translating into English the American Indians' verbal art, but can they truly *ajiwau* (literally 'taste,' meaning 'appreciate') it? I think not. The distinctive *aji* (taste) of one's language may only be appreciated by one's compatriots' (Yanagita 1998b:134).

No one would seriously disagree that language is an expression of the folk spirit (*Volksgeist*) and that no cultural understanding would be complete without a mastery of the local language. To argue, however, that only natives can appreciate their culture is tantamount to saying that non-natives, including folklorists, have little or nothing to contribute. Since Yanagita devoted his life to establishing folkloristics in Japan, it is unlikely that he had intentionally made statements that contradicted his mission. I would therefore submit that Yanagita's view was derived from his distinct conception of *wakaru* or 'understanding.' Ironically, he made remarks that seemingly contradicted his mission because he was unaware that his own conception was deeply embedded in the Japanese way of thinking.

In my interpretation, when Yanagita made statements, such as, 'After all, it is impossible for outsiders to know how local people feel,' and 'People brought up under different circumstances will never understand' (Yanagita 1998c:367), he referred to the difficulties of appreciating local life with the *body*, rather than questioning the outsiders' ability to grasp it cognitively. In other words, he was questioning whether non-natives could experience the culture they studied as the natives experienced it. This type of understanding is similar to what is technically known as 'empathy.'[10] Yanagita's use of the word *ajiwau* (taste) clearly attests to this point. Although it was used figuratively, tasting something involves the functioning of a bodily apparatus – the tongue. Indeed, the Japanese concept of *wakaru* suggests something more than cognitive understanding – a full-bodied experience that transcends abstract thinking. For the Japanese, and certainly for Yanagita, it is not sufficient to understand by *atama* (head). More important is the ability to learn something using the entire *karada* (body). The favorite Japanese expression '*minitsuku*' (attaching to the body), as in *Chishiki ga minitsuku* (literally, Knowledge has been attached to the body), illuminates this point.[11] We may say that *wakaru* is analogous to the Zen ideal of 'no dependence on words,' which holds that truth lies in bodily experience, not in words (Suzuki 1940:7).[12]

H. D. Harootunian put it well when he observed that, for Yanagita, understanding meant 'getting inside, beneath the surface' (Harootunian 1998:148).

> For this reason, he and his followers dismissed ethnography: because it consisted of reporting from the perspective of an outsider, it could never hope to reach the interior of folk experience...The discipline of native ethnology [i.e., Japanese folkloristics] put the investigator inside the scene of investigation to become one with it...Despite his celebration of scientific rigor and its implied openness, Yanagita came close to promoting a methodology restricted to those who, like himself, were inside the scene...Understanding the folk required not interpretation but empathy. The study of native ethnology meant probing beneath the surface to locate those deeply embedded unconscious habits of mind that ceaselessly regulated the repetitive rhythms of everyday life. The investigator had to be in a position to recognize what constituted the fund

of spiritual beliefs that the folk took as second nature, which would remain forever beyond the powers of the outsider to grasp (Harootunian 1998:148–154).

By contrast, modern Western thinking generally draws a sharp dividing line between the mind and the body – a reflection of the pervading influence of Cartesian dualism. Representing the domain of reason, the mind is regarded as superior to the body, which is believed to be affected by emotion. For Westerners, understanding something means grasping it by the power of reason, and this conception is central to their notion of rationality. Empathy plays only a minor role because it is mediated by the body, which is considered to be emotional and irrational. This is, of course, not to say that the body has been neglected in Western philosophy. Some scholars have noted the importance of bodily experience in their attempt to overcome the limitations of the mind/body dualism. In the eighteenth century, for example, Immanuel Kant criticized Descartes, noting the duality of human experience (Maxwell 1999:149). By and large, however, Cartesian dualism has exerted a lasting influence on Western thought, so that understanding is identified with a logical analysis clearly articulated by words.

The Enlightenment grew out of this intellectual tradition. Advocating the supremacy of the mind, it successfully developed science by the power of reason to a degree unknown in human history. Significantly, it was against this current of ideas that romanticism emerged. Represented in the writings of the German philosopher Johann Gottfried Herder, romanticism rejected the Enlightenment ideals of rationality and universality, celebrating instead non-rational aspects of human thought (Mautner 1999:488). Herder's 'cultural pluralism,' which came from his admiration of local and national traditions, was an important source of inspiration for the rise of nationalism in developing countries within Europe (Mautner 1999:247). As Mikako Iwatake (1996) pointed out, romanticism contributed to the formation of folkloristics as a 'national discipline' in the less developed parts of the modern world, including Japan.

As mentioned earlier, Yanagita was strongly influenced by British empiricism, but on a deeper level, he was fascinated by German romanticism. Masao Oka, Yanagita's contemporary who helped found Japanese anthropology, made this observation:

The Japan in which Yanagita's scholarship developed was full of nationalism. The Japanese people's view of their country as 'backward' relative to the West had fostered a strong national consciousness among them. Thus, they resisted the influx of Western ideas and goods. It was a period when the search for a distinctively Japanese culture began, and the need to maintain and strengthen the Japanese spirit was emphasized. Japanese folkloristics, therefore, has had some fundamental similarities with its German counterpart (Oka 1979:82).

Kazuhiko Komatsu, a leading folklorist in Japan, maintained that to 'know' something is to 'possess' it, contending that a strong desire to possess one's culture is hidden in the study of folklore (Komatsu 1998:202). Edward Said essentially made the same point when he argued in *Orientalism* (1978) that the study of a foreign culture is a form of domination over that culture. Since Yanagita called his discipline 'a science of introspection,' he was mainly interested in 'knowing' his country. As I see it, the ensuing desire to 'possess' Japan caused Yanagita to develop a strong cultural nationalism, which eventually resulted in the attempt to exclude foreign (especially Western) researchers from studying Japan. He justified this attempt in terms of their alleged inability to *wakaru* the Japanese mind. On the level of cognition, however, understanding is possible for any person intelligent enough to analyze what he or she has seen. Yanagita therefore discounted the foreigners' ability on the grounds that they could not possibly have a full-bodied experience of Japanese culture. I propose to call Yanagita's approach to understanding 'embodied,' as contrasted with the Western approach that emphasizes rational thinking, which is called here 'analytical.'

Lest my arguments become too complex, I will refrain from discussing Yanagita's relationship with his fellow Japanese researchers, notably amateur researchers called '*kyōdoshika*,' who studied the history and culture of their homeland. (Interested readers should refer to Kuwayama 2000:26–27). Two comments are in order, however. First, in terms of *kyōdo kenkyū* (community studies), Yanagita was at a disadvantage because, living in central Tokyo and not being a native of the research community, he was subject to the same criticisms he had made of non-Japanese scholars. Second, Yanagita tried to solve this dilemma, whether consciously or unconsciously, by arguing that natives paid so much attention to the details of everyday life that they frequently overlooked its essence. In other words, contrary to his statement about the alleged inability of non-Japanese people to have a full-bodied experience of the culture, Yanagita here gave priority to the 'analytical understanding' of outsiders over the 'embodied understanding' of natives. In this way, he privileged his own inside/outside position vis-à-vis other researchers of Japan, both foreign and local.

Yanagita's 'arrogance' is not the issue here. Rather, the problem is with his desire to exclude foreigners, which, in my interpretation, endangers the very foundation on which the idea of global folkloristics rests. As explained earlier, in comparative folkloristics, collaboration with foreign researchers is encouraged, whereas in global folkloristics they are excluded until natives have produced tangible research results. However, the study of culture almost inevitably involves comparison, and a folkloristics that lacks the outsiders' perspective is incomplete because, as Yanagita himself argued, natives take for granted and overlook what outsiders can see easily. Thus, even if a distinctive tradition of folkloristics is successfully established in each nation, its deficiencies will soon be revealed when examined against other traditions. Furthermore, the natives' strong desire to 'know' and 'possess' their culture will necessarily clash with the equally strong desire of interested outsiders to study and know it. When this happens, it becomes practically impossible to engage in dialogue without a head-on confrontation. Yanagita's assertion, then, that only natives can understand their culture is inimical to the realization of global folkloristics.

Influenced by romanticism, Yanagita's writings were literary and required empathy on the part of a reader. After Japan's defeat in World War II, he remarked, 'We used to carry out research without having foreign readers in mind. I thought it was demeaning to have them read our works' (Yanagita, Orikuchi, and Ishida 1965:59). Another thing Yanagita failed to anticipate was the spread of Japanese studies throughout the world after the war. The study of Japan is a thriving field, and there are now all sorts of discourses about the country and its people. Under these circumstances, it is important to note that there are different types of understanding, such as 'embodied' and 'analytical,' and that they are complementary, rather than mutually exclusive. The study of one's culture may only be opened to the global community when we remember this.

Summary and conclusions

In this chapter, I have taken up Yanagita's long-neglected idea of global folkloristics, and reinterpreted it by placing his arguments in the contemporary context of postcolonialism. As already discussed, decolonization after World War II has transformed natives in the non-Western world from objects to subjects (active agents) of representation. The impact of this transformation has already been felt in museum exhibits (see Chapter 1 on this point), but the views of native scholars have only rarely been incorporated into the written accounts of culture, as the West's continued neglect of Yanagita illustrates. The idea of global folkloristics as a community of different traditions of national folkloristics was innovative, and has contemporary significance as it has the potential to change the structure of the academic world system. Global folkloristics may best be conceptualized as 'dialogic space,' figuratively understood as the ethnographic *za* (communal theater), open to all scholars around the world. Yet the strong cultural nationalism contained in Yanagita's writings poses a major obstacle to the realization of dialogue across national boundaries. To overcome this problem, I have introduced the distinction between 'embodied understanding' and 'analytical understanding,' arguing that both are necessary for producing balanced pictures of a culture. Concerning the criticism that the nation is merely a social construct or even a 'fabrication,' I have argued that the nation has been, and still is, a verifiable presence, which, despite the growing trend toward globalization, may usefully be regarded as a framework for international scholarship.

In the 1930s, Kunio Yanagita proposed the ambitious project of global folkloristics. His mission was noble, but he abandoned it mid-stream. Moreover, in his later days, he assumed a negative attitude toward his own project, describing it as a 'failure.' This miscarriage resulted from his refusal to broaden his perspective beyond Japan, rather than from any specific theoretical weaknesses. Born in modern Japan, characterized as it was by a strong nationalism, Yanagita was unable to resist the powerful desire to 'know' and 'possess' his culture. Our task, then, is to develop the positive aspects of his intellectual legacy and create a much-needed 'dialogic space' in which people with different national back-grounds can participate on an equal basis.

5 Ethnographic Reading in Reverse: *The Chrysanthemum and the Sword* as a Study of the American Character

If people were asked to choose the single most influential book on Japan, Ruth Benedict's *The Chrysanthemum and the Sword* (1946) would probably be close to the top of most people's list. Not only is it regarded as a landmark in the study of Japan in the United States, but it has also been widely debated among the people described since it was translated into Japanese in 1948. Indeed, some of the prevailing ideas about Japan, such as social indebtedness and a shame culture, originated in this book. Despite Benedict's failure to fully acknowledge the contributions of her wartime colleagues, she skillfully rendered the Japanese, who at that time were considered 'subhuman,' understandable to the American public. Furthermore, her book made a lasting impact on the way the Japanese think about themselves and their culture. There is, therefore, a firm conviction, almost an unquestioned faith, on both sides of the Pacific, and probably elsewhere, that *The Chrysanthemum and the Sword* is a book about Japan.

Clifford Geertz, in *Works and Lives* (1988), proposed an alternative reading. He contended that Benedict's rhetorical strategy is characterized by 'the juxtaposition of the all-too-familiar and the wildly exotic' (Geertz 1988:106). This strategy, said Geertz, had been used throughout her career, but was particularly evident in *The Chrysanthemum and the Sword*. According to him, there is a 'disconcerting twist' in the numerous contrasts Benedict made between the familiar 'us' and the exotic 'them' or the 'in America'/'in Japan' tropes. The cultural scenes are twisted because in Benedict's hands the Japanese begin to look so familiar that in the end an American reader wonders if in fact they are not merely compatriots marooned in a strange and distant land. Put another way, Benedict's text has the curious effect of making the strange familiar, while simultaneously making the familiar strange. As Geertz wrote:

> Japan comes to look, somehow, less and less erratic and arbitrary while the United States comes to look, somehow, more and more so. There is, in fact, nothing 'wrong with the picture,' just with those who look at it upside down; and the enemy who at the beginning of the book is the most alien we have ever fought is, by the end of it, the most reasonable we have ever conquered…What started out as a familiar sort of attempt to unriddle oriental mysteries ends up, only too successfully, as a deconstruction, *avant la lettre*, of occidental clarities. At the close, it is, as it was in *Patterns of Culture*, us that we wonder about. On what, pray tell, do our certainties rest? Not much, apparently, save that they're ours (Geertz 1988:121–122).

For the book's 'subversive effect,' Geertz (1988:122) labeled it as 'one of the most acid ethnographies ever written.' In his view, *The Chrysanthemum and the Sword* should be read not with the works of her wartime colleagues, such as Geoffrey Gorer and Margaret Mead, but with Jonathan Swift's *Gulliver's Travels* and the like.

In this chapter, I go one step further and contend that *The Chrysanthemum and the Sword* presents a self-portrait of Americans by using the radically different culture of Japan as a mirror. As such, it may usefully be read as a study of the American character. Indeed, once the 'in Japan' part of Benedict's text has been peeled away, an eloquent sequence of 'in Americas' will be revealed. An analysis of this sequence demonstrates how the American self has been depicted by one of the most brilliant figures in the history of American anthropology. I therefore propose to read *The Chrysanthemum and the Sword* as a work of native anthropology for America.

Benedict's 'Orientalism'

It should be noted, before examining my thesis, that Benedict's work on Japan contains elements of what today's anthropologists call 'Orientalism.' Not because she presented exotic images of Japan or treated the Japanese as a vanquished people in need of salvation, but rather because she placed herself in the role of a cultural translator, whose job it was to explain Japan on behalf of its people to American readers. In so doing, she emphasized the advantages, if not superiority, of being an outsider to the culture she studied. Consider, for example, the following passage in the opening chapter of *The Chrysanthemum and the Sword*:

> It is not possible to depend entirely upon what each nation says of its own habits of thought and action. Writers in every nation have tried to give an account of themselves. But it is not easy. The lenses through which any nation looks at life are not the ones another nation uses. It is hard to be conscious of the eyes through which one looks…In any matter of spectacles, we do not expect the man who wears them to know the formula for the lenses, and neither can we expect nations to analyze their own outlook upon the world (Benedict 1946:13–14).

This passage recalls Marvin Harris' statement that justified the use of *etic* perspective in his cultural analyses: 'We don't expect dreamers to explain their dreams; no more should we expect lifestyle participants to explain their lifestyles' (Harris 1989:6).

It is important to remember in this context that Benedict's usage of Japanese words is often anomalous. '*Giri* to one's name,' meaning commitment to honor, is a good example. Defined as 'a Japanese version of the German *die Ehre*' (Benedict 1946:116), this concept is regarded throughout as a key to understanding the Japanese sense of obligation. There is, however, no such expression in Japanese, although the word *giri* itself exists and is often used.[1] Benedict in fact stated, 'The Japanese do not have a separate term for what I call here "giri to one's name"' (Benedict 1946:145). This clearly indicates that the expression is Benedict's invention. It is therefore *etic* rather than *emic*. Just because she used indigenous terms does not mean that she described Japan from the inside using the natives' point of view.

In Chapter 2, I maintained that a major task of Orientalists is to render the Orient intelligible to fellow Westerners. To reiterate, their descriptions of the Orient will be appreciated, however different from those of Orientals about themselves, as long as they are useful for the Westerners' understanding of the Orient. Thus, as Edward Said (1978:22) maintained, whether or not 'Orientalism makes sense at all depends more on the West than on the Orient.' This applies to *The Chrysanthemum and the Sword*. Again, in the opening chapter, Benedict remarked:

> The great demand upon [the student of Japan] is to report how [the] accepted practices and judgments [in Japan] become the lenses through

which the Japanese see existence. He has to state the way in which their assumptions affect the focus and perspective in which they view life. *He has to try to make this intelligible to Americans who see existence in very different focus. In this task of analysis the court of authority is not necessarily Tanaka San, the Japanese 'anybody.'* For Tanaka San does not make his assumptions explicit, and interpretations written for Americans will undoubtedly seem to him unduly labored (Benedict 1946:17, emphasis added).

Benedict's accounts of the Japanese emperor amply demonstrate this point. Noting how Westerners misunderstood the idea of emperor as *kami*, she remarked, '*Kami*, the word rendered as 'god,' means literally 'head,' i.e., pinnacle of the hierarchy. The Japanese do not fix a great gulf between human and divine as Occidentals do, and any Japanese becomes kami after death' (Benedict 1946:127). Yet the emperor was regarded as sacred in prewar Japan. To clarify this point, Benedict compared the Japanese with Americans, saying, 'Just as loyalty to the Stars and Stripes is above and beyond all party politics so the Emperor was 'inviolable.' We surround our handling of the flag with a degree of ritual which we regard as completely inappropriate for any human being' (Benedict 1946:128).[2]

Two things should be noted here. First, Benedict anticipated that most of her American readers would respond negatively to viewing the emperor as a living god. This reaction was almost inevitable, she thought, given the strict division between human and divine in Christian theology. She thus pointed out that the god the emperor personifies, *kami*, is different from what the Americans would suppose when they think of the divine – the Almighty. By this way, she effectively communicated to her readers the cultural logic behind the Japanese emperor worship. Furthermore, to help them appreciate the sacredness imparted to the emperor, Benedict chose to compare it with the Americans' attitude toward the Stars and Stripes. This comparison had the magical effect of eventually making Americans wonder about the inviolability of one of their most familiar national symbols.

All this is a skillful rhetorical strategy, but the question we must ask is, 'To whom does it make sense?' To the Japanese who have been described? Or to the American readers who see Japan through Benedict's eyes? The answer is obviously the latter. Here is the genesis of Benedict's 'Orientalism.' For the Japanese at large do not know or even care about the separation between human and divine in the Occident. Even if they do, such knowledge is irrelevant to understanding their own belief. The same is true, probably more so, with the parallel drawn between the emperor worship and the rituals surrounding the Stars and Stripes. By and large, Benedict's interpretations of Japan are tailored for the American readership. They seem to the Japanese 'unduly labored,' as she admitted. And, in so far as she claimed that in evaluating her analyses 'the court of authority' is not Mr. Tanaka (i.e., the Japanese who have been described), *The Chrysanthemum and the Sword* should indeed be considered a classic example of Orientalist writings.

My second point concerns the 'in America' part of the book. As has already been noted, the juxtaposition of the familiar and the exotic characterizes Benedict's writing style. Of particular interest is the fact that, while talking about other peoples, she talked as much about her own people. In cultural representation, one's own culture provides a point of reference, whether the author is aware of it or not, and it is ordinarily hidden backstage. In Benedict's case, the point of reference is made explicit and foregrounded to an exceptional degree. It is, therefore, possible to read *The Chrysanthemum and the Sword* in reverse, as a way of investigating American culture. Much of the rest of this chapter is devoted to an exploration of this possibility.

Two basic themes of *The Chrysanthemum and the Sword*

Although seldom noted, Benedict's descriptions of Japan revolve around two major themes, of which other themes are merely derivatives or variants. These two themes are duality and hierarchy. Duality is here defined as the co-existence of mutually exclusive elements in a single entity. The gentleness of the Japanese, symbolized by the chrysanthemum, and their violence, symbolized by the sword, are the best, most obvious example of this duality. Benedict's poetic characterization of the Japanese reminds us of her characterization of the Zuni and the Kwakiutl as 'Apollonian' and 'Dionysian,' respectively, in *Patterns of Culture* (1934). To my knowledge, no one has ever claimed that Benedict saw in the Japanese both the Zuni and the Kwakiutl, namely, a unique co-existence of what she considered opposite patterns of human character. There are, however, suggestions that this was indeed the case. In an article submitted to the American authorities before Japan's surrender, entitled 'Japanese Behavior Patterns' (exact date of publication unknown), Benedict explained Japan's rural festivals as 'Dionysian,' 'violent,' and 'hysterical' (Benedict n.d. [1]:46). Although not intended as their opposites, Benedict did refer to the beauty of Japanese flower shows, including those of the chrysanthemum, immediately before and after the page in which these terms were used.[3] As noted by Nanako Fukui (1997), who translated and annotated 'Japanese Behavior Patterns,' this article, consisting of 53 single-spaced typewritten pages, was the foundation of Benedict's later work on Japan.

Since it is well known that Benedict explained Japanese hierarchy in terms of such obligations as *chū* (loyalty), *kō* (filial piety), *on* (debt), and *giri* (obligation), it is not necessary here to dwell on this theme. But the question of how hierarchy is related to duality deserves some clarification. A careful reading of Chapters 3 through to 10 of *The Chrysanthemum and the Sword*, in which hierarchy is described in detail, shows that the phrase 'taking one's proper station,' used also as the title of Chapter 3, is the key to answering this question. Simply put, 'taking one's proper station' means that the Japanese individual is properly placed and feels secure when he knows his relative status in the overall social hierarchy. Benedict thought that, in the realm of ethics, this would translate into a situationalism in which proper behavior is determined by a particular position the individual finds himself in at a particular time and place. Bowing is a case in point.

> A bow that is right and proper to one host would be resented as an insult by another who stood in a slightly different relationship to the bower. And bows range all the way from kneeling with forehead lowered to the hands placed flat upon the floor, to the mere inclination of head and shoulders. One must learn, and learn early, how to suit the obeisance to each particular case (Benedict 1946:48).

Though not unique to Japan, such behavioral change as demanded by situational change both puzzled and fascinated Benedict. For example, she often mentioned the 'right-about-face' of Japanese soldiers during World War II. They showed their loyalty to the Emperor by dying a heroic (or, as many people have said, 'tragic') death in the manner of a Kamikaze pilot. Once captured by enemies, however, they became surprisingly cooperative and voluntarily revealed military secrets because they regarded themselves as socially dead. In other words, the situation surrounding them had changed radically, so they tailored their behavior according to the circumstances in which they found themselves. The same may be said of the sudden reversal of attitudes the Japanese showed after the war, when the slogan of 'fighting to death with bamboo spears' was replaced overnight with a warm welcoming of their conquerors. Perhaps the following statement found in a manuscript entitled 'Japanese National Character,' which was apparently prepared for a series of public lectures given after the war, best expresses Benedict's view:

> The Japanese had gone even farther than this in their *exceedingly circumstantial ethics*. Their code of virtue differentiates a whole series of obligations which are incumbent upon a self-respecting man. These obligations are highly specific and the duty of a good man is to identify the debt which is most binding in a particular situation. Their literature and their cinema turn upon the conflict of these obligations. The Japanese are as particularistic in their spheres of obligations as they are in their spheres of aggression and of self-denial (Benedict n.d. [2]:3, emphasis added).

The 'circumstantial ethics' of the Japanese, which Benedict later rephrased as 'situational ethics' (Benedict 1946:308), are emphasized in *The Chrysanthemum and the Sword* as well, especially toward the end. It is very important to note that Japanese situationalism was contrasted with the 'absolute' standard of morality in the West, which in turn was related to the Western belief in unity as opposed to the Japanese belief in duality. 'The contradictions which all Westerners have described in Japanese character,' said Benedict, 'are intelligible from their child rearing. It produces a duality in their outlook on life, neither side of which can be ignored.' She also maintained that since impulses considered in the West to be anti-social or even 'evil' are regarded in Japan as merely 'inappropriate,' they are allowed to be expressed freely under certain circumstances. Unlike the Westerners, Benedict said, the Japanese do not have 'an absolute standard of virtue' (Benedict 1946:286–287).

The logical connection involved becomes clear when we remember that duality allows mutually exclusive elements to co-exist, as in the white and the black of *yin* and *yang*,[4] signifying the lack of something absolute or that which unifies the world by uncompromising either-or principles. The duality Benedict observed in the Japanese character is, therefore, linked through the absence of absolute standards with her definition of Japanese ethics as situational, which she thought stemmed from the importance attached to knowing one's relative place in the social hierarchy or 'taking one's proper station.'

Japanese duality versus American unity

Among the many expressions of Japanese duality, Benedict focused on the existence of opposing traits in the Japanese character. At the very beginning of *The Chrysanthemum and the Sword*, she stated that the Japanese are possessed of 'the most fantastic series of "but also's" ever used for any nation of the world' (Benedict 1946:1). In her mind, the 'but also' that supplemented the cultivation of the chrysanthemum (beauty) was the cult of the sword (violence).

> Both the sword and the chrysanthemum are a part of the picture. The Japanese are, to the highest degree, both aggressive and unaggressive, both militaristic and aesthetic, both insolent and polite, rigid and adaptable, submissive and resentful of being pushed around, loyal and treacherous, brave and timid, conservative and hospitable to new ways (Benedict 1946:2).

Benedict declared that once her cultural bias had been removed, these contradictions no longer looked contradictory and began to make sense:

> Certainly I found that once I had seen where my Occidental assumptions did not fit into their view of life and had got some idea of the categories and symbols they used, many contradictions Westerners are accustomed to see in Japanese behavior were no longer contradictions. I began to see how it was that the Japanese themselves saw certain violent swings of behavior as integral parts of a system consistent within itself (Benedict 1946:19).

What, then, were Benedict's 'Occidental assumptions'? This is one of the basic questions of ethnographic reading in reverse or 'reverse ethnography.'

To answer this question, we must ask first and foremost why the existence of beauty and violence in the same person looked to

Benedict contradictory. This is not presented as a Zen conundrum. In Japan, there are many cases in which two opposite elements occupy the same niche without engaging in mortal combat against each other. So-called '*shinbutsu shūgō*' (rendered as 'amalgamation of Shinto and Buddhism') is a case in point. Conflict has always been part of the history of these different religions with different origins. With some functional differentiation, however, they have co-existed more or less peacefully since the mid-6th century A.D., when Buddhism was introduced to Japan.[5] Another well-known example of Japanese duality is the division of political authority between the emperor and his administrators. Generally, the former has played a 'sacerdotal' role, whereas the latter a 'governmental' role. Benedict compared the Japanese emperor to a Sacred Chief in the pacific islands (Benedict 1946:68–69). There are indeed many other examples, ranging from the custom of wearing Western clothes in public and switching to Japanese clothes in private, to the application of Western or Eastern medicine for different symptoms. From the Japanese viewpoint, there is nothing peculiar about these practices. Nor is duality a special problem deserving of scholarly analysis.

With this in mind, we may surmise that Japanese duality caught Benedict's attention because she thought it violated or conflicted with a basic principle of life in the United States – the importance attached to being consistent in one's thought and behavior across different situations. I would submit that this consistency is central to the American conception of 'integrity,' which extends to the American faith in uniformity or the unity of experience. Thus, an American should be either Protestant or Catholic, liberal or conservative, even male or female, but cannot be both. Put another way, the American faith in uniformity demands a structure of the mind in which double consciousness is prohibited. It therefore surprises Americans to find that the Japanese allow such opposites as *honne* (realism) and *tatemae* (idealism), *ura* (back) and *omote* (front), and *uchi* (inside) and *soto* (outside) to be expressed openly in public life. Here is Benedict's observation of Americans:

> According to our experience, people act 'in character.' We separate the sheep from the goats by whether they are loyal or whether they are treacherous, whether they are cooperative or whether they are stiff-necked. We label people and expect their next behavior to be like their last. They are generous or stingy, willing or suspicious, conservative or

liberal. We expect them to believe in one particular political ideology and consistently to fight the opposite ideology...If individuals move from one side of the fence to the other – as when an unbeliever becomes a Catholic or a 'red' becomes a conservative – such a change has to be duly labeled as a conversion and a new personality built up to fit (Benedict 1946:196).

This 'Western faith in integrated behavior,' according to Benedict, helps the people achieve 'a *Gestalt* in their own characters. It brings order into human existence' (Benedict 1946:196–197).

> Occidentals cannot easily credit the ability of the Japanese to swing from one behavior to another without psychic cost. Such extreme possibilities are not included in our experience. Yet in Japanese life the contradictions, as they seem to us, are as deeply based in their view of life as our uniformities are in ours (Benedict 1946:197).

The famous contrast between shame and guilt should be understood in this context. The idea of Japan as a shame culture has been so popularized that the entire book of *The Chrysanthemum and the Sword* is often identified with it. The fact is, however, that it occupies only a small portion of the book, no more than a few pages of Chapter 10. Moreover, it is too often overlooked that shame is merely one aspect of the situational ethics of the Japanese, while guilt is founded on what Benedict called the 'absolute standards of morality' in the Occident (Benedict 1946:222). Thus, a shame culture requires behavior appropriate to a particular situation, and insofar as the situation changes from time to time and from place to place, there is no consistency of behavior, or so it looks to Western observers. Again, all this contrasts with the American emphasis on integrity, which Benedict expressed as 'our demands for consistency of character and for conflict of good and evil' (Benedict 1946:198). Benedict's well-known passage reads:

> A society that inculcates absolute standards of morality and relies on men's developing a conscience is a guilt culture by definition, but a man in such a society may, as in the United States, suffer in addition from shame when he accuses himself of gaucheries which are in no way sins...True shame cultures rely on external sanctions for good behavior, not, as true guilt cultures do, on an internalized conviction of sin. Shame is a reaction to other people's criticism. A man is shamed either by being

openly ridiculed and rejected or by fantasying to himself that he has been made ridiculous...Shame has the same place of authority in Japanese ethics that 'a clear conscience,' 'being right with God,' and the avoidance of sin have in Western ethics (Benedict 1946:222–224).

At this point, it is interesting to digress slightly and see what Margaret Mead, with whom Benedict had a special relationship in both public and private, had said in her book about America's national character, *And Keep Your Powder Dry* (1943). According to Mead, a guilt culture has developed in the United States because American parents take the responsibility of punishing children. Although this may be taken for granted, she regarded it as relatively uncommon throughout the world. In many societies outside the Judeo-Christian world, Mead maintained, parents resort to external authorities and sanctions when disciplining their children, whether they be scare dancers, as in some Native American tribes or, if I may add my own example, the people of society (*seken*), as among the Japanese.[6] By contrast, American parents take the moral responsibility of facing the child and say, 'I call this wrong, no matter how much it may alienate you from me. It is wrong' (Mead 2000:81). In other words, they present themselves as paragons of virtues, even though they are not the people they say they are. Mead argued that this technique helps the child develop 'a conscience, that inner voice which is able so to admonish the would-be sinner that he pauses and does not sin, or if he has sinned secretly knows no peace until he has atoned or confessed' (Mead 2000:80–81). In the terminology of psychoanalysis, the superego (i.e., the internalized image of parents) is gradually built up in the child as it grows up. In Mead's mind, guilt is closely associated with Puritanism. As she emphatically remarked, '[T]he essence of guilt is that it is relieved by punishment. The sequence: *I sinned, therefore am I punished, if I then endure the punishment, repent and turn towards new ways, then shall I be again blessed* is the essence of the puritan dogma' (Mead 2000:104–105). Mead therefore objected to the introduction of a new child-rearing method in which external sanctions are used. 'It is a method,' she said, 'which might destroy conscience, obliterate any sort of internal moral sanction, and replace it merely by a fear of public disapproval – by shame' (Mead 2000:82).

As is well known, Benedict explained the dual character of the Japanese in terms of child rearing or socialization. According to her, the Japanese go through two opposite patterns of life – that of indulgence and that of restraint. To the former belong childhood and old age, which Benedict called 'free areas,' when people 'know no shame' and are permitted to indulge themselves. By contrast, adulthood is a period of restraint and circumspection. The responsibility of 'knowing shame' falls heavily on the adult's shoulders. Benedict maintained that this discontinuity in socialization creates a dualism in the Japanese character. At the beginning of Chapter 12, 'The Child Learns,' she made these remarks:

> The arc of life in Japan is plotted in opposite fashion to that in the United States. It is a great shallow U-curve with maxim freedom and indulgence allowed to babies and to the old. Restrictions are slowly increased after babyhood till having one's own way reaches a low just before and after marriage. This low line continues many years during the prime of life, but the arc gradually ascends again until after the age of sixty men and women are almost as unhampered by shame as little children are (Benedict 1946:254).

This observation is followed by an observation of life in America:

> In the United States we stand this curve upside down. Firm disciplines are directed toward the infant and these are gradually relaxed as the child grows in strength until a man runs his own life when he gets a self-supporting job and when he sets up a household of his own. The prime of life is with us the high point of freedom and initiative. Restrictions begin to appear as men lose their grip or their energy or become dependent. It is difficult for Americans even to fantasy a life arranged according to the Japanese pattern. It seems to us to fly in the face of reality (Benedict 1946:254).

Again, this demonstrates Benedict's skillful rhetorical strategy that produces by cultural contrast reflexive knowledge of one's own people. I wonder, however, how the discontinuity Benedict observed in American socialization can be connected with her characterization of Americans as a people of integrity.[7] If, as she argued, Japanese duality results from the gap between childhood and adulthood experiences, how can Americans, who also go through a similar gap, though of the opposite pattern from Japan's, escape the same fate?

It is worth mentioning here Benedict's debt to Geoffrey Gorer. Gorer was an Englishman who had come to the United States in the mid-1930s to study anthropology with Benedict and Mead. He received intensive training in the study of culture and personality, known today as 'psychological anthropology.' In 1941, he wrote an article entitled 'Japanese Character Structure and Propaganda: A Preliminary Survey.' This article probably led to his offer of a job at the Office of War Information in 1942. The following year, he took a job at the British embassy and nominated Benedict for his old job at OWI (Caffrey 1989:314). Reading Gorer's articles on Japan (kept in the Ruth Benedict collection at Vassar College), we get the distinct impression that Benedict borrowed many of his ideas without giving him due credit. Consider, for example, the following excerpt from Gorer's 'Japanese Character Structure' (1943):

> The Japanese conceive of the individual life as an arc, starting high in infancy, with every possible indulgence, getting lower and lower until it reaches its nadir just before and just after marriage, and then gradually moving upward until, at the age of 61, the license and indulgence of infancy is again recovered…[T]he Japanese infancy and old age are equated as periods of indulgence, license and happiness; whereas youth and the prime of life are periods of constraint, toil and submission (Gorer 1943:24).

We may well wonder how Benedict avoided the charge of plagiarism.[8] It should be noted, however, that Gorer was himself indebted to Shunkichi Akimoto, whose English book *Family Life in Japan* (1937) was cited in his article.

Gorer's influence on Benedict is evident with regard to the contrast between absolute ethics in the West and situational ethics in Japan. Applying psychoanalytic theory, he maintained that the Japanese are excessively concerned with cleanliness and that this makes them avoid dirt, including excretion, as much as possible. According to him, this explains why the Japanese impose strict toilet training in early infancy. He then contrasted the Japanese avoidance of excretion with the prohibition imposed on infantile sexuality in the West, arguing that the latter is the product of absolute standards of morality.

> Where infantile sexuality is prohibited, it is prohibited absolutely; there are no places and no occasions when a child is allowed to gain whatever

sexual pleasure is physiologically possible to him. Where this prohibition is enforced rigorously, there would appear always to be *moral absolutes* in the value system of the society: *absolute prohibitions, absolute sins, a concept of absolute evil*, a constant contrast between the unreachable ideal (of purity in the first place) and actual mundane practice. Excretion on the other hand cannot, for physiological reasons, be absolutely forbidden; all that can be forbidden is excretion at the wrong time or in the wrong place. If this cleanliness training lies at the base of the value system of the society, it would follow that there would be *no absolutes, no 'right' and 'wrong,'* but instead very strong emphasis on *doing the right thing at the right time*, on the minute following of ritual, on physical and ceremonial cleanliness, on 'correct' or 'suitable' behavior, which would be defined by *context in which the behavior took place* (Gorer 1943:12, emphasis added).

Gorer thus linked the allegedly strict toilet training in Japan with its situational ethics. After the war, his views were discarded because it was found that Japanese toilet training was rather lax. Also, the causality he postulated between child rearing and adult personality was too simplistic, his arguments too far-fetched.[9] It remains, however, that Gorer's insights were incorporated into Benedict's works. There is no question that *The Chrysanthemum and the Sword* is a masterpiece, but it is equally indisputable that this book was a product of Benedict's collaboration with her colleagues during the war. The nature of this collaboration has yet to be thoroughly examined.

Putting that aside, Benedict was convinced that Americans, or for that matter the entire Occidental people, are distinguished from the Japanese in their faith in uniformity. Before offering my analysis of this point, I quote below some of the most telling descriptions of the Western self that I found in Benedict's works, including the paper she wrote prior to the publication of *The Chrysanthemum and the Sword*.

> Occidental ethics are absolute – whether or not we live up to them. According to our tenets, lying is wrong in itself and does not become morally right when it is used benevolently. We have a concept of absolute evil which keeps God and the Devil utterly distinct; we see the world and our own souls as a battlefield between them and are often tragically unable to recognize how small a shift will allow the same power to be used either for good or evil. It is not easy for us, whose moral problem

is whether or not we live up to our principles, to understand the behavior of a people who quite clearly live up to their professed standards with an intensity which shocks us...(Benedict n.d. [1]:51).

When situations change, the Japanese can change their bearings and set themselves on a new course. Changing does not appear to them the moral issue that it does to Westerners. We go in for 'principles,' for convictions on ideological matters. When we lose, we are still of the same mind. Defeated Europeans everywhere banded together in underground movements...[Western students of Japan thus far] confused Japanese ethics of aggression with European forms, according to which any person or nation who fights has first to be convinced of the eternal righteousness of its cause and draw strength from reservoirs of hatred or of moral indignation (Benedict 1946:171–173).

We have many taboos on erotic pleasure which the Japanese do not have. It is an area about which they are not moralistic and we are. Sex, like any other 'human feeling,' they regard as thoroughly good in its minor place in life. There is nothing evil about 'human feelings' and therefore no need to be moralistic about sex pleasures...The Japanese set up no ideal, as we do in the United States, which pictures love and marriage as one and the same thing. We approve of love just in proportion as it is the basis of one's choice of a spouse. 'Being in love' is our most approved reason for marriage. After marriage a husband's physical attraction to another woman is humiliating to his wife because he bestows elsewhere something that rightly belongs to her. The Japanese judge differently (Benedict 1946:183–184).

When it gratifies the men, [Japanese women] are obscene. Likewise, when it gratifies the men, they are asexual. When they are of ripe age, they may throw off taboos, and if they are low-born, be as ribald as any man. The Japanese aim at proper behavior for various ages and occasions rather than at consistent characters like the Occidental 'pure woman' and the 'hussy' (Benedict 1946:285).

These Japanese views on 'human feelings' have several consequences. It cuts the ground out from under the Occidental philosophy of two powers, the flesh and the spirit, continually fighting for supremacy in each human life...Sir George Sansom writes: 'Throughout their history the Japanese seem to have retained in some measure this incapacity to discern, or this reluctance to grapple with, the problem of evil'...In the higher religions, [devilish gods like Susanowo in Japanese mythology] have been excluded because a philosophy of cosmic conflict between good and evil makes it more congenial to separate supernatural beings into groups as different as black and white (Benedict 1946:189–191).

Nothing in Japan is more generally shocking to Westerners than the fact that since the Restoration [of Meiji in 1868] *chu* has been given full religious trappings. The Japanese do not distinguish *human* and *divine* in the Western absolute fashion and the Emperor is fully 'divine' in any sense they recognize...Western churchmen are horrified and even Westerners who are not churchmen repudiate this belief which blurs the distinction between human and divine (Benedict n.d. [1]:27).

This Western emphasis on uniformity may best be analyzed by applying Mary Douglas' theory presented in *Purity and Danger* (1966). In Chapter 3 of this book, 'The Abominations of Leviticus,' she examined various food taboos found in the Old Testament in terms of classification and order. Her basic thesis is that creatures that deviate from the biblical system of classification are regarded as polluted and should not be eaten. Pigs, for example, have cloven hoofs like cattle, but do not chew the cud. This fact violates the Bible's teaching that animals fit to eat should be both cloven-hoofed and ruminant. Being anomalous, pigs defile holy order, and their meat has been tabooed. This taboo is taken all the more seriously because God founded His covenant with His people through the medium of food.

Significantly, Douglas (1966:51) defined holiness as 'wholeness' and 'completeness.' In the biblical context, this means 'the physical perfection that is required of things presented in the temple and of persons approaching it.' Put in a more general context, and seen from the other side, it suggests that an entity with disparate elements within itself will be considered partial and incomplete, thus constituting a breach of holiness.[10] This reasoning makes sense when we consider that tabooed creatures have taken on features that belong to more than one class by cutting across different categories. Douglas (1966:51–53) in fact maintained that 'hybrids and other confusions are abominated' because holiness demands 'rectitude and straight-dealing' and prohibits 'contradiction and double-dealing.'

> Holiness requires that individuals shall conform to the class to which they belong. And holiness requires that different classes of things shall not be

confused...Holiness means keeping distinct the categories of creation. It therefore involves correct definition, discrimination and order...To be holy is to be whole, to be one; holiness is unity, integrity, perfection of the individual and of the kind. The dietary rules merely develop the metaphor of holiness on the same lines (Douglas 1966:53–54).

Seen in this light, it becomes clear why Benedict called attention to Japanese duality as shown in their 'contradictory' character. It breaks a deep-seated assumption in the spiritual life of Westerners, challenging God and the holiness of His order. In a Westerner's mind, the Japanese duality violates a holy taboo and represents a major sin against God. Again, from the Japanese viewpoint, it is no blasphemy to have two opposite traits in one person. As Emiko Ohnuki-Tierney (1987:128–159) demonstrated, Japanese gods are of a dual character, symbolically expressed in the duality of '*nigitama*' (positive power) and '*aratama*' (negative power).[11] Influenced by the Judeo-Christian conception of holiness, Benedict was first astonished to find the dual qualities of the Japanese and then viewed her own people through the lenses the Japanese use to see the world. In so doing, she revealed as much about the Western self as she did the Japanese Other.

Japanese hierarchy versus American equality

Japanese hierarchy, the other major theme of *The Chrysanthemum and the Sword*, is discussed in full detail in the first half of the book. In the opening paragraph of Chapter 3, 'Taking One's Proper Station,' Benedict forcefully remarked:

> Any attempt to understand the Japanese must begin with their version of what it means to 'take one's proper station.' *Their reliance upon order and hierarchy* and *our faith in freedom and equality* are poles apart and it is hard for us to give hierarchy its just due as a possible social mechanism. Japan's confidence in hierarchy is basic in her whole notion of man's relation to his fellow man and of man's relation to the State...(Benedict 1946:43, emphasis added).

Reading Benedict, we are constantly reminded that her work was a product of America's war efforts in the mid-20th century. Not only are there numerous references to the behavior of Japanese soldiers during the Pacific War, but translations of documents relating to Japan's military are also found throughout. They include the preamble to the Tripartite Pact which Japan signed with Germany and Italy, the imperial rescript given on the signing of the Pact, and the proclamation of war handed to Secretary of State, Cordell Hull, after Japan's attack on Pearl Harbor. All these documents emphasized the importance of ordering the world according to each nation 'taking its proper station.' In contrast, in comparable documents, the United States stressed the principle of equality of all nations. Benedict believed this difference separated the two countries decisively – tragically.

> Equality is the highest, most moral American basis for hopes for a better world. It means to us freedom from tyranny, from interference, and from unwanted impositions. It means equality before the law and the right to better one's condition in life. It is the basis for the rights of man as they are organized in the world we know. We uphold the virtue of equality even when we violate it and we fight hierarchy with a righteous indignation (Benedict 1946:45).

According to Benedict, this has always been so since the inception of America as a nation. The American faith in equality is clearly expressed in the Declaration of Independence and the Bill of Rights. It is also a major subject of *Democracy in America* (1835–1840), written by the French aristocrat Alex de Tocqueville (Benedict 1946:45–46).

To investigate Japanese hierarchy, Benedict chose a few familiar words used in Japan and studied their semantic domains. All of them express a sense of indebtedness. *On*, for example, means 'obligations passively incurred' (Benedict 1946:116), and one receives *on* from almost anybody one knows or has had some contact with, ranging from one's parents to the emperor, from one's school teachers to passers-by who did one a favor, etc. In contrast to the diffuse nature of *on*, *kō* and *chū* are directed toward specific categories of people. In Benedict's definition, *kō* refers to one's 'duty to parents and ancestors,' and *chū* to one's 'duty to the Emperor, the law, and Japan' (Benedict 1946:116). In the so-called 'family state' instituted by the prewar Japanese government, *kō* and *chū* were considered identical, and the Japanese were required to serve the emperor as their national father (cf. Kuwayama 2001a). Still another word Benedict examined is *giri*, which she divided into two categories: '*giri*-to-the-world' and '*giri*-to-one's-name.' The former means 'one's obligations to repay *on* to one's fellows,' and the latter, 'the duty of keeping one's name and reputation unspotted by any imputation' (Benedict 1946:134). As mentioned earlier, Benedict's definition here is anomalous, and reflects her lack of proficiency in the language. It remains, however, that she was the first to study these ordinary words and uncover deep cultural meanings buried within them. Even Japanese scholars critical of her have given her credit for this aspect of her work.

Using a variety of materials, including folktales, novels, movies, newspapers, radio broadcasts, interviews with Japanese Americans, and military documents,[12] Benedict vividly described how life in Japan is organized hierarchically from mundane affairs to emperor worship. At the same time, she disclosed how the opposite principle – equality – is central to life in the United States. Below, I present Benedict's portrayals of Americans as contrasted with the Japanese, adding my own interpretations where she left things unsaid.

In anticipation of negative reactions against hierarchy, we should first say that Japanese hierarchy is not a ruthless mechanism of oppression and exploitation; rather it positions each person in society according to his attributes and rewards him on that basis. In the prewar days, ascribed attributes like inherited class, birth order, and gender were taken seriously. People of lower status were expected to obey people of higher status. In return for their loyalty and services, they received rewards in the form of gifts, favors, and protection from possible threats. There is no denying that the system worked in favor of the upper echelons of society, but the reciprocity involved generated a certain sense of indebtedness among the people placed below (beneficiaries) toward the people placed above (benefactors). In the family circle, this feeling was best expressed in the belief that one owed one's whole existence to one's parents. In the family state mentioned above, all Japanese subjects were considered to be the emperor's babes and were required to sacrifice themselves to repay their 'incalculable' debt. The situation has changed dramatically since the end of World War II, but some of the features just explained are still found today in a diluted form. Calling the Japanese 'debtors to the ages,' Benedict remarked:

> Much of what Westerners name ancestor worship is not truly worship and not wholly directed toward ancestors: it is a ritual avowal of man's

> great indebtedness to all that has gone before. Moreover, he is indebted not only to the past; every day-by-day contact with other people increases his indebtedness in the present. From this debt his daily decisions and actions must spring. It is the fundamental starting point (Benedict 1946:98).

The American ideal of equality does just the opposite. Since it rejects the authority of people higher up the social ladder, it instead fosters a spirit of independence and self-reliance.

> Because Westerners pay such extremely slight attention to their debt to the world and what it has given them in care, education, well-being or even in the mere fact of their ever having been born at all, the Japanese feel that our motivations are inadequate. Virtuous men do not say, as they do in America, that they owe nothing to any man (Benedict 1946:98).

As Robert Bellah and his associates pointed out in *Habits of the Heart* (1985), forty years after Benedict made these remarks, successful Americans still tend to claim that they achieved success through their own efforts and seldom acknowledge contributions made by the people who helped them in one way or another along the way.

The diffuse sense of indebtedness in Japan causes the people to return obligations. '*On* is a debt and must be repaid,' said Benedict. 'A man's indebtedness (on) is not virtue; his repayment is. Virtue begins when he dedicates himself actively to the job of gratitude' (Benedict 1946:114). This job finds its pristine expression in the fulfillment of *chū* and *kō-on* (i.e., *on* to the emperor).

> In civil administration chu sanctions everything from death to taxes. The tax collector, the policeman, the local conscription officials are instrumentalities through which a subject renders chu. The Japanese point of view is that obeying the law is repayment upon their highest indebtedness, their ko-on (Benedict 1946:129).

In the United States, by contrast, law is regarded as something that curtails individual freedom and liberty.

> The contrast with folkways in the United States could hardly be more marked. To Americans any new laws, from street stop-lights to income taxes, are resented all over the country as interferences with individual

liberty in one's own affairs. Federal regulations are doubly suspect for they interfere also with the freedom of the individual state to make its own laws. It is felt that they are put over on the people by Washington bureaucrats and many citizens regard the loudest outcry against these laws as less than what is rightly due to their self-respect. The Japanese judge therefore that we are a lawless people. We judge that they are a submissive people with no ideas of democracy (Benedict 1946:129–130).

But what does 'self-respect' mean? Does it mean the same thing to the Japanese and Americans? The answer is, of course, no. Being well aware of the cultural differences in the meaning of self-respect, Benedict defined its Japanese version as 'repaying what [a man] owes to accredited benefactors,' and its American version as 'management of his own affairs' (Benedict 1946:130). This difference is related to the different meanings of 'courage' in the two countries. In the article entitled 'Japanese National Character,' Benedict argued that in Japan courage means 'conforming to conventions,' whereas in the United States people use it in relation to 'revolting against or in modifying the conventions.' She also remarked, 'Around this idea of obligation [the Japanese] organize their moral systems, as the Western democracies have organized theirs around the idea of human rights' (Benedict n.d. [2]:4).

In Benedict's view, in Japan self-respect is associated with '*giri* to one's name.' Japanese people who respect themselves, she said, know the virtue of repaying their debt to the world; they are committed to keeping their names unspotted by imputation. In the egalitarian United States, self-respecting people will not only manage their own affairs, but also fulfill their potential.

> Giri to one's name also requires that one live according to one's proper station in life. If a man fails in this giri he has no right to respect himself. This meant in Tokugawa times that he accepted as part of his self-respect the detailed sumptuary laws which regulated practically everything he wore or had or used. Americans are shocked to the core by laws which define these things by inherited class position. Self-respect in America is bound up with improving one's status and fixed sumptuary laws are a denial of the very basis of our society (Benedict 1946:150).

Benedict went on to say that 'taking one's proper station' is a virtue in hierarchical societies with the inherited class system. In this regard, prewar Japan was allied with pre-Revolutionary France.

In Japan getting rich is under suspicion and maintaining proper station is not. Even today the poor as well as the rich invest their self-respect in observing the conventions of hierarchy. It is a virtue alien to America, and the Frenchman, de Tocqueville, pointed this out in the eighteen-thirties in his book [*Democracy in America*]. Born himself in eighteenth-century France, he knew and loved the aristocratic way of life in spite of his generous comments about the egalitarian United States. America, he said, in spite of its virtues, lacked true dignity. 'True dignity consists in always *taking one's proper station*, neither too high nor too low. And this is as much within the reach of the peasant as of the prince.' De Tocqueville would have understood the Japanese attitude that class differences are not themselves humiliating (Benedict 1946:150, emphasis added).

In February 1948, about six months before her death, Benedict delivered a public lecture entitled 'Patterns of American Culture' at the International House, Columbia University. It was one of the few moments when she talked about America per se. Referring to the inherited class in old Europe, she remarked:

> 'Keeping your place' in such countries had a dignity of its own because it was part of accepted and traditional ways of life but it was not something which fired the imagination of the ordinary man (Benedict 1948:6).

Benedict said that in the United States the meaning of 'class' had changed from something inherited to that which was attained by individual or group efforts. The example she gave was the strong desire to become 'first-class citizens' found among ethnic minority groups and immigrants.

> In our American phrase 'class' has been changed to 'first class citizen.' Our minorities have fought for decades for the right to become first-class citizens instead of second-class citizens. That is something you can fight for. The blot upon being a second-class citizen can be wiped out if you work for it. First-class citizenship, which I may not attain as an immigrant but my children may attain or my grandchildren may attain, has set a kind of pot of gold under the rainbow which one can chase. One can, generation after generation, work toward this position where one will be equal under the law, and in hiring and firing, and in the right to live in particular parts of the city. The history of all our

minorities is the story of how people have, generation after generation, pushed consistently toward this goal (Benedict 1948:6).

It is again interesting to refer here to Mead's *And Keep Your Powder Dry* and see what she had to say about this topic. Like Benedict, she used a rhetorical strategy that explicitly contrasted America with other countries, one of which was England.[13] Mead explained the American conception of class as follows:

> [T]he American system is really a classification based on a ladder, up which people are expected to move, rather than upon orderly stratification or classification of society, within the pigeon-holes of which people are born. What is 'an upper upper'? In England, someone born into the families whose titles confer highest rank in a hierarchy. In America, someone whose only possible social movement is downward (Mead 2000:37).

According to Mead, class is relative and has no fixed content in America. Thus, it is almost impossible to identify a man's class by his bearing and accent, by the food he eats, by the clothes he wears, by the religion he professes, by the political party he supports, etc. The 'fluid moving society which is America' is characterized by 'the lack of any absolute class standards' (Mead 2000:40). Mead argued that in the United States there is no strict correspondence between social action and class, which she considered to be a major contrast between the New World and the Old World.

It is a moot question if such descriptions reflect the social reality or merely social ideals. But that is not important in the context of this discussion. The point is that Benedict, partially influenced by, among others, Mead, underscored America's egalitarianism, to which the emergence of a 'classless society' was often attributed, and presented Japanese hierarchy as *an inverse image of American equality*.

Finally, we should consider Benedict's position on one of America's major postwar policy dilemmas regarding Japan – the question of what to do with the emperor. In December, 1944, the Institute of Pacific Relations held a series of meetings called 'The Conference on Japanese Character Structure.' Benedict, Mead, and Gorer were among those who attended the conference. Benedict played a passive role throughout, but when it came to the question of how the Japanese handled failures, she said, 'In any governmental reorganization of Japan, the phrase explaining the failure has always been that the government "had not carried out the will of the emperor"' (Institute of Pacific Relations n.d.:11). Probably, Benedict thought that the Japanese emperor was more 'sacerdotal' than 'governmental,' and her reluctance to lay responsibility for the war at his feet was revealed in her postwar article, 'What Shall Be Done about the Emperor' (exact date of publication unknown).[14]

In this little known document, Benedict called attention to the negative reactions people exhibit when they witness something 'impossible' in other cultures. According to her, one reason why most Americans loathed Hirohito and attempted to remove him once and for all was that he was accorded a divinity that in the West could only be claimed by God. We may go one step further and say that Hirohito's divinity was not just unthinkable for American Christians, but was a blasphemy. Another reason she gave is the image of the emperor as 'the Good Father,' which conflicted with the American ideal of individualism.

> The Japanese Emperor is the most extreme symbol in the world of the Good Father, and this conflicts with the very basis of an adult American's self-respecting individualism. Growing up means in the United States that one comes to stand on one's own feet and to repudiate dependence not only on the father, but on any father symbol. A nation where dependency is not humiliating is always difficult for Americans to comprehend, because we regard as inevitable this association between dependency and humiliation. Hence most American arguments against the Emperor are backed by statements that only by bombing or removing the Emperor can a beginning of self-respect be made possible for the Japanese. It becomes a moral point based on one of our strongest moral premises (Benedict n.d. [3]:1).

The exact meaning of 'the Good Father' is unclear, but from the context it would be safe to interpret it as meaning the 'great father' – in a negative sense.[15]

As noted earlier, the ideal of equality leads people to reject authority, whether embodied in institutions or personified in actual figures. This hatred of authority generates in turn a spirit of independence and self-reliance – the very opposite of dependence – which constitute the all-embracing American ideal of individualism. This point was amply illustrated by Geoffrey

Gorer in his book *The American People* (1948). He contended that two major characteristics of American culture are 'the emotional egalitarianism which maintains that all (white American) men are equal to the extent that the subordination of one man to another is repugnant and legally forbidden, equal in opportunity and legal position' and 'the belief that authority over people is morally detestable and should be resisted, that the suspicion that others are seeking authority cannot be too vigilant, and that those who occupy the necessary positions of authority within the state should be considered as potential enemies and usurpers' (Gorer 1964:30). Tracing these characteristics to the history of American immigration, to the stories American school children learn about their forefathers' rebellion against English rule, Gorer remarked:

> [T]o reject authority became a praiseworthy and specifically American act, and the sanctions of society were added to the individual motives for rejecting the family authority personified in the father...[T]he making of an American demanded that the father should be rejected both as a model and as a source of authority. Father never knew best. And once the mutation was established, it was maintained; no matter how many generations separate an American from his immigrant ancestors, he rejects his father as authority and exemplar, and expects his sons to reject him (Gorer 1964:31).

Gorer then pointed out that for an authority figure to be accepted in the United States it must be reduced to the level of every mother's son. In the 1940s, three international figures challenged this rule: the Pope, Joseph Stalin, and Hirohito, hence their unpopularity (Gorer 1964:42–43).

Gorer was psychoanalytically oriented and accounted for personality formation in terms of child rearing. He maintained that the greatest crime American parents can commit is to turn their child into a 'sissy,' defined as someone who shows 'more dependence or fear or lack of initiative or passivity than is suitable for the occasion' (Gorer 1964:85). The stigma attached to being a sissy applies to both sexes, Gorer argued, and this is why American parents constant push their children towards independence and adulthood. As he commented, '[T]he successful flouting of authority is a sign of independence, of growing manliness; a boy who never attempted to do so would show grave signs of turning into a sissy' (Gorer 1964:102).

Gorer made these observations soon after the war, and it is difficult to tell how valid they are today. His voice, however, has been echoed in that of many other foreign observers, including Francis Hsu, a one-time president of the American Anthropological Association. In his classic article, 'American Core Value and National Character' (1961), he contended that self-reliance is a core value in the United States, remarking:

> In American society the fear of dependence is so great that an individual who is not self-reliant is an object of hostility and called a misfit. 'Dependent character' is a highly derogatory term, and a person so described is thought to be in need of psychiatric help (Hsu 1970:239).

Although somewhat exaggerated, this statement sheds light on the question of why Takeo Doi's theory of *amae*, usually rendered as 'dependence,' has caught the attention of many American scholars (Doi 1973). Like the dual qualities of the Japanese, it is 'impossible' for Americans to believe that the desire for dependence is not only accepted in Japan as a fact of life, but is also positively nurtured as a sign of social maturity. The great interest shown in Japanese *amae* may be a projection of the forbidden part of the American independent self.[16]

The place of reverse ethnography in the ethnographic triad

In this chapter, I have shown that Benedict's classical work on the Japanese may be read as a work on Americans. I have proposed to call this 'ethnographic reading in reverse.' This reading is not easy. Nor is it always possible because the cultural assumptions on which the original author's writing is based tend to be hidden. *The Chrysanthemum and the Sword* is one of the few major ethnographies ever written in which the describer's culture has been revealed as much as that of the described. However, since comparison with one's culture is almost inevitably involved in the study of foreign cultures, the possibility for this kind of reading always exists.

When I discussed the 'ethnographic triad' in the opening chapter, I mentioned that ethnography as a genre of writing involves three parties – the writer, the described, and the reader. In the present context, the writer is Benedict, and the described are the Japanese. Among the four categories of readers earlier outlined – (1) people who belong to the same linguistic and cultural community as the writer; (2) natives who have been studied and described; (3) native anthropologists; and (4) people who are neither describers nor the described – the second and the third categories are, in Benedict's case, conflated. The fact that she wrote about the Japanese people in general rather than about specific, small communities in part explains the book's enormous impact in Japan. The reverse reading I have given of Benedict's ethnography represents an attempt on the part of the described to 'write back' to the describer (if Benedict were alive) and her assumed readers in a language they understand.[17]

Ethnographic reading in reverse has been made possible by two significant changes in anthropology – the emergence of natives as readers of ethnography and the growing number and influence of native anthropologists. Until quite recently, if they were consulted at all, natives were merely expected to check the accuracy of ethnographic accounts. During fieldwork, of course, they have always played a major role as informants or 'local partners,' but traditionally, once the research results were published, their role was extremely limited and passive. This situation is undergoing a fundamental change today.

In Japan, *The Chrysanthemum and the Sword* has been subjected to many criticisms from many people from many fields. The extensive critiques by Takeyoshi Kawashima and his associates (1950) represent the reactions from the native intellectual community; complaints often heard in the college classroom that Benedict had misunderstood the Japanese are typical reactions from critical readers at large. These criticisms are legitimate, but they are all based on the assumption that Benedict wrote about Japan. In this chapter, I have proposed to put this assumption in parentheses and examine what lies behind Benedict's descriptions of the Japanese. The pictures of Americans I have presented are like the inverse images of photo negatives. To change the metaphor, I have, in more general terms, proposed that ethnographic accounts of other people be regarded as narratives of the describer's self, the Other operating as a cultural mirror. The task of the described, then, is not to examine these ethnographies as faithful pictures of themselves, but rather to reveal the describer's self buried in the ethnographic text.

This is not just another postmodern attempt at deconstruction for its own sake. Rather, it is a genuine attempt to create a dialogic space between the describer and the described as equal partners. The mission of anthropologists is not completed once they have returned from the field and written up their research results. From the moment they set foot on a foreign land, they are engaged in a two-way communication with the people they study that may, as in Benedict's case, live on long after their own death. In this never-ending process, 'we' become objects of inquiry for 'them' as 'they' become the same for 'us.'

6 Representations of Japan in American Anthropology Textbooks: Focusing on the Use of Photographs

In this final chapter, I will examine how Japan has been represented in American anthropology textbooks, paying special attention to the use of visual images.[1] The textbook industry is highly developed in the United States. In the field of anthropology alone, at least 20 major introductory textbooks were available on the market in 2000.[2] Many of these had been regularly revised every 3 to 4 years. Given the impact of textbooks on first-year students, and assuming they reflect views generally accepted in a given scholarly community, their importance should not be underestimated. It is noteworthy, then, that so little has been written about the ways in which textbooks depict other peoples' worlds. Focusing on Japan, the following critical examination begins to redress this oversight.

A personal background to the research

In technical books and articles, authors seldom mention what has motivated their research. Nor do readers expect to read of such things. Yet I feel compelled to discuss at the outset why I became interested in the issue of analyzing introductory textbooks.

I received my degrees from Tokyo University of Foreign Studies, and was trained as an anthropologist at the University of California, Los Angeles (UCLA). My first academic job was at Virginia Commonwealth University (VCU), Richmond. While an assistant professor there from 1989 to 1993, I taught an introductory course in cultural anthropology every semester. The main textbook I used was Serena Nanda's *Cultural Anthropology* (3rd edition, 1987; 4th edition, 1991). Soon after I started teaching, I began to receive sample textbooks from many different publishers. Some companies even dispatched sales staff to my office. At first, I did not pay much attention to these overtures, but as I skimmed through the

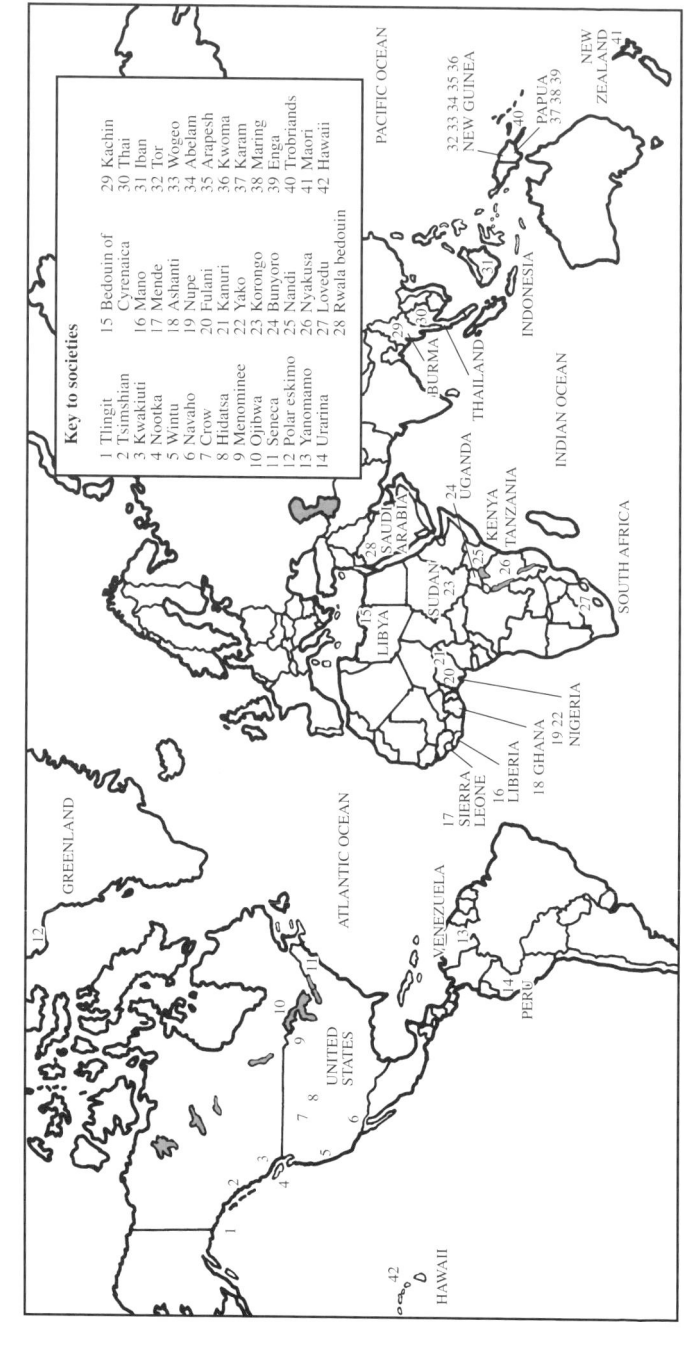

Figure 6.1: Anthropologists' 'world map.' Source: Rosman and Rubel 1998:2–3 (redrawn for Kuwayama 1996b).

complimentary textbooks I noticed two things. First, despite the venerable tradition of Asian studies in America, little attention was paid to Japan and the rest of East Asia. This fact contrasted sharply with the frequent references to Africa, Oceania, Latin American, and Native America. The regional bias of anthropological knowledge was, it seemed, clearly reflected in introductory textbooks.[3] Second, on the rare occasions when Japan was mentioned, it tended to be 'exoticised.' For example, when pictures of Japanese women were shown, they were usually dressed in colorful kimono, which today is only worn on special occasions. Since Japan has produced many internationally renowned fashion designers, I wondered why the textbooks did not show their costumes, instead of, or at least as well as, the traditional clothing. As I thought about such questions, I realized that the stereotypes we often see in anthropology textbooks illustrate, in skeleton form, some of the fundamental problems of cultural representation.

Japan's place in American anthropology

Figure 6.1, taken from Rosman and Rubel (1998:2–3), is symptomatic of the marginal place of Japan, and of East Asia in general, in American anthropology textbooks. A box containing the names of societies mentioned in the book is superimposed on much of the region. In the authors' mind, Japan and its neighbors do not exist. The map in fact testifies to the authors' (and through them, many of their impressionable readers') perception that East Asia is irrelevant to an anthropological understanding of the world. Although this is an extreme case, the situation differs little in other textbooks.

The marginality of East Asia is also observed in the anthropological community at large. This is best shown in the unfavorable time zones to which sessions on Japan are assigned at annual meetings of the American Anthropological Association (AAA). The meetings are ordinarily held for five days toward the end of the year, Wednesday through Sunday, and sessions on Japan are most often given on the first and the last days, when attendances are at their lowest. Also, the rooms allotted are usually small. Another indication of the marginal status of East Asia within the AAA is the belated establishment of a 'section' devoted to its study. In the spring of 2003, the AAA had a total of 35 sections, including the American Ethnological Society, yet it was only in 2000 that the East Asia Section was officially recognized.[4]

A content analysis of American anthropology textbooks

The following findings are based on my analysis of 19 textbooks published in or around the early 1990s (Table 6.1). Many have since been updated, and I will mention the newer editions where appropriate. Differences in edition, however, are not critical because in the United States, where there is a huge market for used textbooks, major changes between editions ordinarily occur in book designs, page layouts, and photo selections. Since these changes are necessitated more for commercial reasons than for academic ones, substantial revisions in the text are uncommon, at least within the span of a decade. There are, of course, exceptions, such as the 6th edition of Nanda's *Cultural Anthropology* (1998), which the new co-author, Richard Warms, revised from a postmodern perspective (See Kuwayama 2001b for the details). On the whole, however, it is sufficient to examine earlier editions in order to establish trends and general features.

The subjects and the frequencies of representation

Table 6.2 classifies representations of Japan, including those of ethnic minorities like the Ainu, in the 19 textbooks represented in Table 6.1. American anthropology textbooks are typically structured according to 16 subject areas: (1) race; (2) prehistory; (3) language; (4) subsistence; (5) economy; (6) marriage and family; (7) kinship; (8) gender; (9) class; (10) politics and law; (11) psychology, socialization, and education; (12) religion; (13) art; (14) culture change; (15) applied; and (16) other.[5] To find out where Japan is mentioned in these textbooks, both the author index (e.g., 'Benedict' and 'Embree') and the subject index (e.g., '*burakumin*,' '*wa*,' and 'Zen') have been used. The classification of materials accords with the authors' own systems. Thus, when the *ie* is discussed in a chapter on 'marriage and family' rather than a chapter on 'kinship,' I have classified it as belonging to the former. There are, however, cases when classification is difficult and arbitrary, so Table 6.2 should be understood as representing a general pattern.

Table 6.1: Introductory Textbooks on Anthropology Selected for Content Analysis

---

(1) Barrett, Richard
   1991 *Culture and Conduct: An Excursion in Anthropology* (2nd ed.). Belmont, California: Wadsworth Publishing.
(2) Bates, Daniel G., and Fred Plog
   1990 *Cultural Anthropology* (3rd ed.). New York: McGraw-Hill.
(3) Bohannan, Paul
   1992 *We, the Alien: An Introduction to Cultural Anthropology*. Prospect Heights, Illinois: Waveland Press.
(4) Crapo, Richley H.
   1993 *Cultural Anthropology: Understanding Ourselves and Others* (3rd ed.). Guilford, Connecticut: Dushkin Publishing.
(5) Ember, Carol R., and Melvin Ember
   1990 *Cultural Anthropology* (6th ed.). Englewood Cliffs, New Jersey: Prentice Hall.
(6) Ferraro, Gary
   1992 *Cultural Anthropology: An Applied Perspective*. St. Paul: West Publishing.
(7) Harris, Marvin
   1991 *Cultural Anthropology* (3rd ed.). New York: Harper Collins.
(8) Harris, Marvin
   1993 *Culture, People, Nature: An Introduction to General Anthropology*. New York: Harper Collins.
(9) Haviland, William
   1993 *Cultural Anthropology* (7th ed.). Fort Worth, Texas: Harcourt Brace Jovanovich.
(10) Howard, Michael C., and Janet Dunaif-Hattis
   1992 *Anthropology: Understanding Human Adaptation*. New York: Harper Collins.
(11) Kottak, Conrad Phillip
   1991 *Cultural Anthropology* (5th ed.). New York: McGraw-Hill.
(12) Nanda, Serena
   1991 *Cultural Anthropology* (4th ed.). Belmont, California: Wadsworth Publishing.
(13) Oswalt, Wendell H.
   1986 *Life Cycles and Lifeways: An Introduction to Cultural Anthropology*. Palo Alto: Mayfield Publishing.
(14) Peoples, James, and Garrick Bailey
   1991 *Humanity: An Introduction to Cultural Anthropology*. St. Paul: West Publishing.
(15) Robbins, Richard H.
   1993 *Cultural Anthropology: A Problem-Based Approach*. Itasca, Illinois: F. E. Peacock Publishers.
(16) Rosman, Abraham, and Paula G. Rubel
   1992 *The Tapestry of Culture: An Introduction to Cultural Anthropology* (4th ed.). New York: McGraw-Hill.
(17) Schultz, Emily A., and Robert H. Lavenda
   1990 *Cultural Anthropology: A Perspective on the Human Condition* (2nd ed.). St. Paul: West Publishing.
(18) Scupin, Raymond, and Christopher R. DeCorse
   1992 *Anthropology: A Global Perspective*. Englewood Cliffs, New Jersey: Prentice Hall.
(19) Schusky, Ernest L., and T. Patrick Culbert
   1987 *Introducing Culture* (4th ed.). Englewood Cliffs, New Jersey: Prentice Hall.

Table 6.2: *Classification of Representations of Japan in 19 American Anthropology Textbooks Used in the Early 1990s*

Subjects	Frequencies (number of times)			
	Textual representations only	Textual representations and photos	Photos only	Total (percentage of each subject in the grand total)
(1) Race	5	2	1	8 (6.0%)
(2) Prehistory	1	1	0	2 (1.5%)
(3) Language	11	1	3	15 (11.3%)
(4) Subsistence	1	0	3	4 (3.0%)
(5) Economy	5	0	6	11 (8.3%)
(6) Marriage and Family	9	1	4	14 (10.5%)
(7) Kinship	0	0	1	1 (0.8%)
(8) Gender	3	0	1	4 (3.0%)
(9) Class	7	1	0	8 (6.0%)
(10) Politics and Law	2	0	1	3 (2.3%)
(11) Psychology, Socialization, and Education	16	2	3	21 (15.8%)
(12) Religion	4	0	3	7 (5.3%)
(13) Art	2	0	2	4 (3.0%)
(14) Culture Change	7	0	3	10 (7.5%)
(15) Applied	4	2	1	7 (5.3%)
(16) Other	13	1	0	14 (10.5%)
Grand total	90 (67.7%)	11 (8.3%)	32 (24.1%)	133 (100%)

Note: Figures are based on an analysis of the 19 textbooks on Table 6.1. 'Representations of Japan' include those of ethnic minorities like the Ainu.

The following three categories are used to assess the frequencies of representation: (i) 'textual representations only,' when there are descriptions of Japan in the text without photographs or other visual images; (ii) 'textual representations and photos,' when descriptions of Japan in the text are juxtaposed with photographs of the country and/or the people; and (iii) 'photos only,' when photographs of Japan are used without any explicit reference to the country in the text. The last category is particularly interesting because even though the text mentions nothing or very little about Japan, photographs relating to Japan are shown to illustrate explanations of a particular subject. Figure 6.2 is a typical example. This fact suggests that for American readers, Japan's Otherness lies more in its appearance than in its reality – a point supported by the frequent appearances of Japan in the popular photo-journal *National*

Figure 6.2: A typical example of 'photos only.' Taken from a chapter on culture change in Ember and Ember (1990), the caption reads, 'These Japanese women have adopted ice cream, but they have not adopted Western clothing.' There is, however, no clear explanation of why the Japanese women in the photograph are wearing kimono, no context given to this cultural change, no indication made as to whether or not this cultural 'mix' is typical in present-day Japan. Source: Ember and Ember 1990:322.

Geographic.[6] Textual representations have been counted each time descriptions of Japan occupy a sizable portion of one or more sequential paragraphs in the text.[7]

As is clear from Table 6.2, of all the 16 subjects, Japan is represented most often in 'Psychology, Socialization, and Education' (15.8%), followed by 'Language' (11.3%), and 'Marriage and Family' (10.5%). Since there is not enough space to analyze all of the subjects, I will discuss these three most popular examples.

Psychology, Socialization, and Education: A major factor in the extensive coverage of Japan on this subject is the lasting influence of Ruth Benedict's *The Chrysanthemum and the Sword* (1946), a psychological study of Japanese national character. In fact, about half of the textual representations in the textbooks relate to Benedict. The following description is typical:

> The search for *national characters* was an important part of the culture-and-personality school of thought. This involved establishing traits that characterized the psyches of different nationalities. National character studies became important around World War II, when the United States government used them to assess the psychological characteristics of people involved in the war. Most influential was Benedict's book *The Chrysanthemum and the Sword* (1946), which played a role in justifying the American restoration of the Japanese emperor (Howard and Dunaif-Hattis 1992:368–369).

Another factor that explains Japan's frequent appearances under this heading is the enormous literature on Japanese personality/self in the culture-and-personality school or what is today more commonly called 'psychological anthropology.' The emphasis here is on the well-known opposition between Western individualism and Japanese collectivism. Different styles of playing baseball in the United States and Japan are sometimes used to illustrate the point:

> Like Americans, the Japanese stress the importance of competition and success, but their emphasis is on competition between groups rather than individuals. Loyalty to the team counts more heavily than the individual's ability to excel. [In 'You've Gotta Have *Wa*,' Robert] Whiting (1979) has compared the Japanese and American approaches to baseball and reports a consistent Japanese willingness to sacrifice outstanding individual team members when their lack of cooperative team spirit threatens the sense of *wa*, or group harmony. Whiting summarizes the different feelings about individualism and cooperation in the two cultures: 'The U.S. is a land where the stubborn individualist is honored and where "doing one's own thing" is a motto of contemporary society. In Japan, *kojinshugi*, the term for individualism, is almost a dirty word. In place of "doing your own thing," the Japanese have a proverb: "The nail that sticks up shall be hammered down." It is practically a national slogan' (Crapo 1993:374–375).

In some acclaimed textbooks, however, cautionary notes are added, which reflects the growing skepticism among Japan specialists about the simple U.S.-Japan binarism. For example, Marvin Harris writes:

Japan's managerial and governing elites have long advocated and extolled the virtues of team spirit, loyalty to firm and state, and peaceful family-style acquiescence to authority. But it is often forgotten that social conflict is also part of Japan's traditions...Dissent often accompanied by violence has been registered by various antipollution and environment movements, the student movement, the consumer movement, the movement against nuclear weapons, the movement against noise pollution, and the decade-long farmers movement to prevent the expansion of Tokyo's Narita airport (Harris 1993:378; repeated in Harris 1997:362).

Language: Three features of Japanese are emphasized: (1) the writing system; (2) the use of *keigo* or honorifics; and (3) a distinctive style of non-verbal communication. Regarding the first feature, the Otherness of *kanji*, or Chinese characters, for Americans is such that photographs of it are often conspicuous in anthropology textbooks. The description below dramatizes the difference between *kanji* and the English alphabet:

Japan may in fact be the only country in the world where the blind have advantages in learning over those with sight. Because blind students learn to read and write by means of a simple phonetic braille, they do not have to invest the enormous amount of time that other Japanese students must in memorizing thousands of characters (*kanji*) (Barrett 1991:108–109).

Curiously, little has been said about *kana*. Being a simplified form of *kanji*, it does not seem as 'exotic' as *kanji* to Americans, which partially explains why it has been neglected. We must remember, however, that *kana* played a vital role in the emergence of women's literature among court ladies in aristocratic times, most notably Shikibu Murasaki, the author of the renowned novel *Genji Monogatari*, which was written at the beginning of the eleventh century. In later periods, the increased use of *hiragana*, a major form of *kana*, was a decisive factor in the attainment of a high literacy rate among commoners (see Amino 1990:317–362 for the details).

Keigo is another feature of Japanese often highlighted. It is usually discussed in relation to speech levels, for which gender differences are also important.

In the Japanese and Korean languages, honorific forms require speakers to distinguish among several different verb forms and address terms that indicate deference, politeness, or everyday speech. Different speech levels reflect age, gender, social person, and outgroupness (the degree to which a person is considered outside of a particular social group) (Scupin and DeCorse 1992:200; repeated in Scupin and DeCorse 1998:261 and in Scupin 2000:111).

In Japanese there are also marked differences between male and female speech, so strong that some observers talk about a 'true' women's language. In contrast to Malagasy, it is the women's speech in Japanese that is characterized by the more frequent use of polite forms (Rosman and Rubel 1992:53; repeated in Rosman and Rubel 1998:59).

Among the Japanese styles of non-verbal communication, bowing has received the greatest attention. This is partially due to the influence of Hollywood movies, in which Japanese actors bow deeply when greeting people, often joining hands Buddhist-style – a practice often imitated by Japanese Major League baseball players. The following is a typical textbook account:

> Nonverbal communication is an important aspect of social interaction. Obvious gestural movements, such as bowing in Japan and shaking hands in the United States, may have a deep symbolic significance in certain contexts. The study of nonverbal communication will enrich our understanding of human behavior and might even improve communication among different societies (Scupin and DeCorse 1992:202; repeated in Scupin and DeCorse 1998:264 and in Scupin 2000:114).

This statement is accompanied by a photograph of three Japanese women engaged in a tea ceremony, wearing kimono and bowing to each other (Figure 6.3).

Marriage and Family: Regarding marriage, *miai*, or arranged marriage, is the focus of attention. Although marriages are arranged in many societies by the new couples' immediate relatives, Japan and China are frequently mentioned as typical examples of this custom. The *miai* is then contrasted with the West's ideal of romantic marriage.

> In an appreciable number of societies, marriages are arranged: negotiations are handled by the immediate families or by go-betweens. Sometimes betrothals are completed while the future partners are still children. This was formerly the custom in much of Hindu India, China, Japan, and

Figure 6.3: Nonverbal communication in Japan. The caption says, 'Japanese bowing to one another. The nonverbal communication is a demonstration of respect.' The kimono, the tea ceremony, the deep bow, and the tatami mat are among the best known 'indexes' of Japanese culture. Source: Scupin and DeCorse 1992:202 (copyright holder unknown).

eastern and southern Europe. Implicit in the arranged marriage is the conviction that the joining together of two kin groups to form new social and economic ties is too important to be left to free choice and romantic love (Ember and Ember 1990:185; repeated in Ember and Ember 1999:168).

While quite a few textbooks note changes in Japan's marriage customs, the overall emphasis remains on the persistence of *miai* as a tradition.

With industrialization in Japanese society, romantic love has had an effect on selecting marital partners, and presently many Japanese individuals choose their own mates. But as anthropologist Joy Hendry (1987) notes [in her book *Understanding Japanese Society*], the 'love marriages' are still held suspect and go up against the serious practical concerns of marital ties and the traditional obligations felt by people toward their parents. In many cases, *miai* are still employed in arranging marriages in this highly modern society (Scupin and DeCorse 1992:362; repeated with a slight revision in Scupin and DeCorse 1998:416 and in Scupin 2000:269).

As for family life, the *ie*, literally meaning 'house,' is described as the traditional form of Japanese family, but receives less attention than does the *miai*. Interestingly, Japan appears quite often in the category of 'Marriage and Family' (10.5%), but is seldom referred to under the heading of kinship (0.8%). This difference is probably related to the arbitrariness of classification mentioned earlier, but may also be explained in terms of the different degrees of Otherness of Japanese customs for Americans. Putting aside the relatively recent origin of the Western family created by romantic love (Shorter 1975), arranged marriages are rare in the United States, at least in the mainstream of society. The *miai*, therefore, looks exotic and attracts attention. By contrast, the Japanese kinship system is in many respects similar to the Western system. For example, in both systems kinship terminology is of the so-called 'Eskimo type' – a favorite topic in American anthropology. Also, descent is bilateral (cognatic) in the two systems, although the *dōzoku*, a hierarchically organized group of *ie*, has a patrilineal bias. Since Japanese kinship has only a low degree of Otherness for American readers, it is probably considered to be of no particular interest. In anthropology textbooks, the different, exotic 'others' tend to be described colorfully and in detail, whereas those people and customs similar to one's own tend to be neglected.

Another subject on Table 6.2 requiring explanation is 'Art.' Given the popularity of the Japanese arts throughout the world, it is curious that there are so few references to Japan (4 out of 133 times or 3.0 percent) in this subject area. This is in stark contrast with tourist books on Japanese culture. In *Introduction to Japanese Culture* (1996), for example, edited by Daniel Sosnoski, a whole section is devoted to this topic, which includes the following entries: *chanoyu* (tea ceremony), *ikebana* (flower arranging), *yakimono* (pottery and ceramics), *nihonga* (Japanese paintings), *shodō* (calligraphy), *hōgaku* (Japanese music), and *kabuki*. These arts are amply illustrated with beautiful color pictures. Indeed, no travel book on Japan would be complete without an introduction to its artistic traditions.

Perhaps a major reason for the relative neglect of Japanese art in anthropology textbooks is the discipline's commitment to the study of ordinary people rather than elites. This commitment derives from the anthropologists' conception of culture as the totality of a people's way of life, which translates in our context into the bias toward folk art as opposed to high art. The arts mentioned above are generally practiced by members of the upper classes, though *chōnin* (townsfolk) did play important roles in the development of those arts in premodern times. It is, however, this present-day elitist status that causes them to be overlooked in introductions to anthropology. There is, however, a curious twist in this neglect, because photographs of Japanese art, especially those of the tea ceremony, are frequently featured.

On the use of photographs

The use of photographs in American anthropology textbooks deserves close examination for two reasons. First, as Table 6.2 shows, Japan is represented a total of 133 times, 32 (24.1%) of which are by 'photos only.' When 'textual representations and photos' (11 times or 8.3%) are added, photographic representations occur 43 times, which accounts for 32.3% of the total.[8] Why are pictures used so often? And how are we to interpret their impact on readers? These questions demand answers. Second, the frequent use of photographs is one of the salient characteristics of anthropology textbooks in the United States. Indeed, the display of photographic images of other peoples in these books is analogous to the exhibition of other cultures' artifacts in ethnological museums – a feature largely absent in British textbooks (e.g., Hendry 1999).

As with the preceding section, examples will be taken from the three most popular subject areas. On the subject of 'Psychology, Socialization, and Education,' it has been mentioned that Benedict's book *The Chrysanthemum and the Sword* has greatly influenced representations of Japan. As discussed in Chapter 5, Benedict's major theme was about the duality of Japanese character, which she summarized as follows: 'The Japanese are, to the highest degree, both aggressive and unaggressive, both militaristic and

Figure 6.4: The duality of Japanese character. Ruth Benedict's theme of Japanese duality is symbolically expressed by juxtaposing photographs of the tea ceremony and the military conquest. Source: Haviland 1987:131.

aesthetic, both insolent and polite, rigid and adaptable, submissive and resentful of being pushed around, loyal and treacherous, brave and timid, conservative and hospitable to new ways' (Benedict 1946:2). This duality is best represented in the two photographs in Figure 6.4. Taken from William Haviland's popular textbook *Cultural Anthropology* (5th edition, 1987, p. 131), the women in kimono performing a tea ceremony signify the 'aesthetic' side of the Japanese, whereas the male warriors in the *banzai* posture point to the 'militaristic' side. It goes without saying that these images correspond to the 'chrysanthemum' and the 'sword,' respectively.

Two things should be noted here. First, there is a gender bifurcation in the photographs: the Japanese aesthetics, politeness, timidity, and submission are associated with women, which contrasts sharply with the men's militarism, insolence, courage, and aggression. In the United States, this bipolar image of the Japanese has a long history, especially in the mass media, with the geisha symbolizing Japan's elegance, and the samurai, its brutality (Ebuchi 1992; Johnson 1988). Second, many of the Japanese people photographed are women. One wonders if this fact reveals an American male fascination with the 'femininity' of Japanese women. Lafcadio Hearn (1850–1904), a Greek-born American writer, who became a naturalized citizen of Japan after he married a Japanese, articulated a sentiment that still appears to be implicit in many of these texts when he said that the best product of Japanese culture is the Japanese woman, and its worst, the Japanese man. Underlying this attitude is a hidden desire to dominate Japan. As will be discussed later, the 'feminization' of the Other is commonly observed when a stronger political power represents the culture of a weaker one. In this context, we should remember that 'Oriental women' have long occupied a central position in the sexual fantasies of modern American and European men.

Returning to Figure 6.3, the photograph, taken from Scupin and DeCorse (1992:202), illustrates the pattern of Japanese non-verbal communication – a major topic in the area of 'Language.' Two women in kimono are ceremoniously bowing to each other. The apparatus placed near the woman in the middle shows that this is part of a performance of the tea ceremony, a tradition originally imported from China, which spread among feudal warriors. To a Japanese viewer, it would be clear that this was a special occasion, one imbued with ritual significance and separated from everyday life. For a non-Japanese viewer unfamiliar with the cultural

Figure 6.5: Arranging marriages in Japan. The use of this kind of fictitious pictures undermines explanations in the text. Source: Ember and Ember 1990:186.

context, however, the image creates the impression that a ritual bow is an ordinary event that can happen anytime, anywhere. This impression accords with the prevailing image of Japan created by Hollywood movies, one further strengthened by the photograph's generalized caption: 'Japanese bowing to one another. This nonverbal form of communication is a demonstration of respect.'[9]

For foreigners, especially Westerners, the kimono, the tea ceremony, the deep bow, and the *tatami* mat contain a high degree of Otherness. Of all the many features of Japanese culture, it is these 'indexes of Japaneseness' that, taken together, most dramatically express the distance between 'us' and 'them.' To the extent that these are Japanese traditions, the scene depicted in the photograph is not a fabrication. When, however, certain features are highlighted without context and are paid disproportionate attention to their everyday practice in the culture, they reinforce cultural stereotypes and deepen the already existing gap between 'us' and 'them.' As a result, the Other becomes more exotic, more strange, and more distant than ever before.

The construction of different 'others' through photographs is also evident in Figure 6.5, which appears in Ember and Ember (1990:186). Intended as a visual 'aid' to the authors' earlier quoted explanation of arranged marriage, this photograph shows two Japanese men in kimono, facing each other across a table on the *tatami*, which is against a paper wall, on which is portrayed court aristocrats at play. The caption says, 'In many societies, people other than the bride and groom may determine important things about a marriage, as, for example, a "go-between" priest in Japan decides on a lucky day for the marriage.' This may only be taken as a jest, for there is no such occupation in Japan as a 'go-between *priest*.' The English word 'go-between' is a translation of the Japanese word '*nakōdo*,' a mediator who works as a bridge between two parties, especially in a marriage. He or she is not a professional priest. Furthermore, the photograph's artificial settings cast doubt on its ethnographic credibility.

Many of the pictures shown in American anthropology textbooks are the work of commercial photographers. Like photographs in *National Geographic*, they have theatrical effect, but are of limited value as ethnographic data. In *Anthropology and Photography 1860–1920* (1992), the editor, Elizabeth Edwards, argued that until the early twentieth century, photography was 'part of the collective endeavour in the production of anthropological data.' With the separation, however, of university-based anthropologists from ethnological museums, coupled with the increasing emphasis on the analysis of invisible, social organization, photography became marginalized within the discipline (Edwards 1992:4). Perhaps this marginalization has resulted in a limited supply of ethnographically reliable photographs and, as such, is responsible for the authors of anthropology textbooks resorting to the use of commercial photographs. This would in turn explain the gap between the generally admirable texts of these books and the dubious quality of their visual representations of other cultures.

This qualitative gap between text and image is amply illustrated in Figure 6.6. The photograph in this figure is juxtaposed with an explanation of the nuclear family in industrial states. According to the authors, Raymond Scupin and Christopher DeCorse:

> During later phases of industrialization (especially since the 1960s), population growth began to decline in societies like England, Western Europe, the United States, and Japan...In contrast to preindustrial societies, in which high birthrates were perceived as beneficial, many people in industrial societies no longer see large families as a benefit. One

Figure 6.6: A modern, nuclear family in Japan. The caption says, 'In industrial societies such as Japan, most couples prefer small families.' How, though, does this depiction of traditional Japanese practices help students understand the modern Japanese family? The same photograph is used in Scupin and DeCorse (1992:353; 1998:407). Source: Scupin 2000:260 (copyright holder unknown).

reason for this view is the higher costs of rearing children in industrial societies. In addition, social factors such as changing gender relations – more women in the work force and the reduction in family size – have contributed to lower fertility rates...Increased knowledge of, and access to, contraceptives helped people to control family size (Scupin and DeCorse 1992:351–353; repeated in Scupin and DeCorse 1998:406–407 and in Scupin 2000:259).

This statement is summed up in the photograph's caption: 'In industrial states such as Japan, most couples prefer small families.'

Despite the sentiments expressed in both the body of the text and the caption, the impression created by Figure 6.6 is that of a traditional Japanese family, not a contemporary one. Given that the figure is intended to illustrate modern, industrial Japan, one feels compelled to ask why the photograph depicts a pre-modern Japanese tradition. People familiar with Japanese fashion will immediately notice that the couple's hairstyles and clothing are both quite dated. Again, it is the cultural features/objects portrayed in the photograph that produce the mismatch of text and image – the woman's kimono in the foreground and a Shinto shrine in the background. Although there is no explanation in the text, there is little doubt that the couple is visiting the shrine for *miyamairi*, reporting the birth of a new child to the local protective deity.

The same disparity is found in the most recent edition of Harris' *Cultural Anthropology* (5th edition, 2000), co-authored with Orna Johnson (Figure 6.7). The photograph in Figure 6.7 is accompanied by the caption: 'Japanese nuclear family at home.' Note that all of the family members are dressed in kimono.[10] Behind the wife/mother is a *butsudan* (Buddhist altar), at the side of which are placed a *kakejiku* (hanging scroll) with an *ukiyoe* image, a Japanese doll in a glass case, and a Japanese-style vase. In front of the doll is a hibachi (brazier), on which you see an iron kettle and iron chopsticks, which are very difficult to find in Japan today. This perfect array of traditional Japanese objects raises the suspicion that the photograph is a set piece, a cultural fiction. Significantly, it appears on the cover page of Harris' chapter on 'domestic life.'[11]

The case of the Japanese nuclear family is particularly interesting in considering some unintended effects of the use of photographs in anthropology textbooks. In the text, Japan is described as an industrial society, in which, unlike pre-industrial societies, large families are no longer considered to be an

Figure 6.7: Another look at the modern, nuclear family in Japan. The caption says, 'The Japanese nuclear family at home.' This photo appears on the cover page of a chapter on domestic life. Its ostensible purpose is to show that the nuclear family is adaptive in industrial societies like Japan, but the objects depicted in the photo emphasize Japan's traditional aspects. Source: Harris and Johnson 2000:125.

advantage, hence the increased numbers of nuclear families. In this regard, Japan is allied with the West. By contrast, the photographs placed side by side with the text illustrate traditional aspects of Japanese culture, thereby underscoring the differences between the two societies. In other words, Japan is at first included in the West as a member of the industrial world – it in fact plays a central role in the Group of Eight (G8), which comprises the world's leading industrial nations (the United States, the United Kingdom, France, Germany, Italy, Canada, Japan, and Russia) – but is instantaneously excluded from the West because of its Asian origin. It is not difficult to detect here an unconscious, Orientalist desire to keep 'them' separate from 'us,' especially in the realm of ethos, which is believed to lie beneath the material surface. As the use of old pictures like Figure 6.6 suggests, this separation works both in time *and* space. Consequently, the different 'others' are denied what Johannes Fabian (1983) called 'coevalness' with the observing Western self. They are condemned to live in a distant past, contained in an exotic 'field' far away from the 'home.'[12]

This denial of coevalness is observable in the visual images used to illustrate other topics. In 'Culture Change,' for example, the focus of the textual representations is on Japan's development into a major economic power. That Japan has retained its tradition, despite the great social transformation since the nineteenth century, is described as a good example of how modernization co-exists with indigenous culture. However, pictures like Figures 6.6 and 6.7 undercut such sensible, balanced descriptions, by representing cultural traditions that stubbornly resist change rather than those that express continuity *in* change.

For textbook writers, this problem is largely unintended, and they may well feel that it is unavoidable because the selection of photographs is usually the task of 'photo editors.' Like photojournalism, the power of editors is strong in textbook production. We must remember, however, that the books have been published in the authors' names. Since the impact of visual images often exceeds that of the written text, careful attention should be paid to the selection of photographs.

Some theoretical issues

I will now explore some of the issues raised in the above section from a theoretical perspective, focusing in particular on the images of kimono in the United States. There are two major reasons for this. First, as the above photographs demonstrate, the kimono is a hidden motif in textbook representations of Japan. Second, by examining one cultural object as a case study, we can understand what kinds of problems are involved in cultural representation in general.

Symbolic significance versus statistical significance

The use of kimono as an index or signifier of Japaneseness suggests that we should distinguish between 'symbolic significance' and 'statistical significance' in the study of culture. By symbolic significance, I mean the value attached to a particular object or phenomenon that is disproportionately greater than that recognized among members of the local community because it possesses a high degree of Otherness in representing that community to the outside world. Symbolic significance is contrasted here with statistical significance, which refers to the value of that object or phenomenon based on the frequencies of its actual occurrence in the local community. These two kinds of significance do not always coincide. If anything, they tend to be in an inverse relationship because things that happen only occasionally in a culture, but do not occur at all in other cultures, inevitably attract attention, whereas things that happen often, but which are observably elsewhere, arouse little interest. The kimono is an archetypal example of objects with a good deal of symbolic significance, but with little statistical significance.

Similar examples abound throughout the world. Yasuko Takezawa, in her article 'Ethnic Stereotypes in the USA' (1988), revealed that whereas the feather headdress of Native Americans was worn only by a small number of tribes (approximately 20 out of 500 tribes in the late nineteenth century), and even though most Native Americans were either farmers or fishermen, the headdress and the horse have long stood for symbols of the entire Native population. Takezawa maintained that ethnic markers are selected arbitrarily, reflecting the perceived distance between the target ethnic group and the dominant society (Takezawa 1988:377–379). Similarly, Kirin Narayan contended that the 'self-torturing holy man' of India who is practicing *tapas* – 'standing on one leg, never lying, keeping an arm aloft, hanging upside-down over fire, and so on' – is an example of partial truths being translated into generalized facts. As she put it, this man has become 'a stock character in the landscape of difference mapped onto India by the Western eye.' Following Arjun Appadurai, Narayan argued that 'the urge to exoticize, to essentialize, and to totalize' underlies Orientalist constructions of the 'others' (Narayan 1993b:480).

This is, of course, not to say that something loaded with symbolic significance is unimportant in the study of culture. When, however, it is magnified so much that it represents the entire culture of which it is only a part, we should not only be cautious, but also ask how it has come to assume such a high profile. Many factors are at work, but the impact of mass media and tourism should be noted. As Shinji Yamashita (1996) and others have shown, tourism has become very popular since the late nineteenth century, and its influence in industrialized society is far greater than commonly thought. Particularly important are the images of other cultures presented in travel books, tourist brochures, picture postcards, and photo journals. For example, in 1911, one year after its first epoch-making color series appeared, *National Geographic* published a photograph of six young Japanese women in bright kimono holding paper umbrellas and fans. Titled 'Dancing Girls,' it was part of a color series called 'Glimpses of Japan' (Bryan 1997:126). In 1995, the same magazine ran a 16-page article entitled 'Geisha.' All of the entertainers depicted were clad in exquisite kimono as they sang, danced, and conversed with their patrons. (This article was deleted from the Japanese edition of *National Geographic*). Images like these have been strengthened and spread by American tourists who have visited a geisha house in Kyoto or elsewhere, and they now form part of what Americans believe they know about Japan. It is this knowledge that interprets the kimono as the essence of an imagined Japaneseness.

A comparison with the notion of 'Italian-ness' in France clarifies this point. Following Roland Barthes' conception of 'myth' as a meta-language, Stuart Hall argued that a photo advertisement showing some products of *Panzani*, a French maker of Italian pasta, placed in a string bag with vegetables becomes, at the level of myth, 'a message about the *essential meaning of Italian-ness as a national culture*' (Hall 1997:41; emphasis in original). Since the advertisement was run in France, this message was obviously directed toward the French, rather than Italians. Put another way, the commodities shown in the photo are signifiers of the French notion of Italian-ness, which the Italians may or may not be aware of. As Barthes remarked, 'It is specifically "French" knowledge (an Italian would barely perceive the connotation of the name [*Panzani*], no more probably than he would the Italianicity of tomato and pepper), based on a familiarity with certain tourist stereotypes' (quoted in Hall 1997:69), that helps identify *Panzani* with Italian-ness in France. By the same token, the kimono as a signifier of Japaneseness makes sense in terms of the American (and more broadly Western) knowledge of Japan, especially that associated with tourism and mass media.

'Conspiracy' between the describer and the described

The role played by the Japanese in making the kimono a signifier of Japaneseness should also be noted. To appreciate this, we should briefly look at the history of kimono. In Japanese, 'kimono' (literally, things to wear) refers to a broad category that includes many different types of clothes. The one identified in the West as the kimono derives from the *kosode* (literally, small sleeves), which was worn as an outer robe among warrior-class women in early feudal times. Having evolved from ancient court attire, the *kosode* became known in Europe through trade with Japan in the late sixteenth century. Later, when Japan virtually withdrew from the outside world, the *kosode* became increasingly extravagant, reflecting the hedonistic culture developing among the townsfolk. This happened despite the sumptuary laws issued by the Tokugawa government. Kabuki actors and courtesans set the fashion trends at that time; *ukiyoe* woodblock prints depicting their images were much sought after. Later still, a type of *kosode*, called '*furisode*,' with long sleeves, became popular among younger women. When Japan re-opened its ports in the middle of the nineteenth century, the extravagant *kosode* and *furisode* fascinated Western visitors. They referred to the dress by one word – 'kimono' (Wada 1996).

The Restoration of Meiji in 1868 began a process of Western-style modernization. At that time the Japanese began to regard their own traditions as 'barbaric,' something to be eliminated on the way to becoming a modern, 'civilized' state. Clothes and appearance were easy targets, and among the upper class *wafuku* (Japanese clothing) was quickly replaced with *yōfuku* (Western clothing). In time, though, there was a backlash to such an excessive project of Westernization, and women's clothing became a national concern. As Yoshiko Wada explained:

> The ensuing critique of the 1890s stressed the problems with Japan's blind rejection of its own cultural heritage. Emphasis was placed on women's clothing, and claims were made that Western corsets were endangering women's health. As a result, women reverted to wearing *wafuku*, and the kimono took on a new symbolic resonance, embodying *the essence of Japanese tradition* – something it would do in Japan and the world for years to come. From this point onward, the kimono became synonymous with *Japanese femininity*, which ironically supported the Western misconception of the kimono as an exotic feminine garment when in fact it had been worn by both sexes and all classes and ages until the Meiji period (1996:153, emphasis added).

At first glance, this history may be read as a story of national resistance, but it in fact reveals how the Japanese 'conspired' with

Westerners in making the kimono Japan's 'national dress.' It is well documented that throughout the world people often return to cultural traditions to preserve their national identity when colonial forces threaten it. In this process of returning to traditions, persons or things that are thought to represent the past become symbols of a collective cultural identity. The above account shows that the kimono was one such symbol in Meiji Japan. This is, however, not to say that it was thoroughly opposed to Western civilization. If anything, the kimono was presented as Japan's proud tradition, in which Westerners could also take delight. Whatever the nationalists' intention might have been, redefining women's kimono as the essence of Japanese culture had the effect of elevating Japan's status in the international community. Had the Westerners regarded the kimono negatively, it might have been banned or discarded like many other Japanese customs and traditions, such as the samurai hairdo and mixed bathing.

Herein lies the paradox of traditions among subjected people. On the one hand, they are compelled to 'invent' a tradition (Hobsbawm and Ranger 1983) to heal their injured pride, to restore their dignity, and possibly to compete against the colonizers. On the other, this invented tradition must be presentable to the wider world, especially in the rulers' eye, because a 'strange' tradition may give the colonizer an excuse for further aggression and control. In this way, the emergence of national traditions inevitably reflects the acquiescence, if not the will, of the colonizer. The result is, ironically, often a collaboration or 'conspiracy' between the two parties.

In today's international relations, so-called 'cultural festivals' give ample space to such conspiracies. Public, including governmental, organizations established to promote friendships, often sponsor these festivals. In Anglo-Japanese relationships, for example, the first such activities were performed by the Japan Society, founded in London in 1892. In the inaugural ceremony, a senior Japanese official gave a lecture on judo, which was enlivened by practical demonstrations. Subsequently, the Society disseminated information on the *Noh* theater, tea ceremony, flower arranging, and so on (Victor Harris 1997:144). This tradition has continued to date, and the one I attended in Oxford, 1998, featured *kyūdō* (archery), *shakuhachi* (bamboo flute), *haiga* (*haiku* or poem painting), *shodō* (calligraphy), in addition to the tea ceremony and flower arranging. Many of the people who demonstrated these arts were Japanese, and they were all clad in kimono. This looked curious to me because the Japanese performers were long-time residents of Great Britain or other places outside of Japan. Also, the tea master's wife, who worked as his assistant throughout, was a Japanese Brazilian. Despite her foreign background, her Japanese appearance and the kimono she was wearing helped authenticate the occasion. Similar to the Japan Society's inaugural ceremony over a century earlier, a senior Japanese diplomat stationed in London gave the opening speech.[13] On the first page of the festival's program was a message from the Japanese ambassador to the United Kingdom. In the United States, the Japanese pavilion at the 1876 Philadelphia Centennial Exhibition is said to have launched a 'Japan Craze,' of which the kimono was a common motif (Stevens 1996:17).

In this context, we must remember that there are many souvenir shops in Japan that make available a variety of goods using the kimono as a main motif. Interestingly, they cater to both foreign tourists *and* Japanese tourists going abroad. For the latter, the kimono, and for that matter any other esteemed Japanese tradition, provides an opportunity to reconsider their cultural identity through foreign eyes. When one's culture is objectified and appropriated in this way, we may speak of a 'conspiracy' between the guest and the host. Many different forces are working in tourist sites, and power does not flow in one direction.[14]

Feminization of the Other

Another issue worthy of attention is the 'feminization' of Japan achieved by the repeated display of pictures of Japanese women dressed in colorful kimono. Concerning Table 6.2, out of the 43 times Japan is represented photographically, the kimono is shown a total of 15 times (34.9 percent), and most of the people wearing it are women. This representation is lopsided because men's kimono are different from women's, and have just as much symbolic significance as the female garment.[15] Although these figures refer exclusively to textbooks, they are suggestive of a general tendency in cultural representation to feminize the foreign 'others,' especially those less powerful than the describer. In feminization, the more powerful culture positions itself as male and views the less powerful culture as female. These women are then subjected to the colonialist gaze, under which they appear as objects of domination, whether political, economic, or sexual.

Feminization of the Other is an insidious form of discrimination that occurs in many cross-cultural encounters. It was classically observed in the relationship between Japan and the United States during the occupation after Japan's defeat in World War II. In John Dower's book, *Embracing Defeat*, which received the Pulitzer Prize in 1999, two photographs of the Japanese are juxtaposed. One of them, shot in late 1944, depicts a naked prisoner of war being 'deloused' on the deck of an American warship, surrounded by hundreds of U. S. sailors, who look both amused and confused to see the captured 'subhuman,' as the caption describes him. The other photo was shot soon after the war. It depicts a young Japanese woman in kimono standing elegantly on the turf of a garden, a scene reminiscent of the 'dancing girls' portrayed in *National Geographic* in 1911. In stark contrast to the POW, this woman is surrounded by GIs who, having been fascinated by her beauty, have flocked to take her picture. As Dower (1999:238) commented, 'The defeated country itself was feminized in the minds of the Americans who poured in...Japan – only yesterday a menacing, masculine threat – had been transformed, almost in the blink of an eye, into a compliant, feminine body, on which the white victors could impose their will.'

If the vanquished were doomed to be feminized, did the opposite – 'masculinization' – happen when the victors and the losers changed places? To answer this question, we need only remember what happened between the two countries' economies four decades after the war. Beginning in the early 1980s, America's trade deficit with Japan soared so high that Lee Iacocca, the CEO of Chrysler Motors at the time, said that a 'trade war' was going on. Contrary to the immediate postwar image of a compliant nation, Japan was now depicted as a fierce competitor who, in the eyes of many Americans, was determined to take over their country by the power of the yen. The cartoon on the front cover of *Business Week* (August 7, 1989) captured the ambience of the time.[16] A Japanese businessman, with stereotypical slanted eyes, is wearing a warrior's helmet. He is placed in a red circle, surrounded by white, a design suggestive of the Japanese flag. Japan is represented here as a masculine figure imbued with the samurai spirit – a trend widely observed in Asian museums.[17]

These examples show that although feminization is the dominant mode of seeing other cultures among colonizers, it is occasionally reversed when the balance of power is perceived to be shifting. Generally, the gender with which a particular culture is associated is determined by the relative strength of that culture at a given time. Thus, images of Japan in the United States have oscillated between geisha and samurai, between chrysanthemum and sword, depending on Japan's relative position in international politics and economics.

From the three issues examined above, we may conclude that American anthropology textbooks, in which visual images of other peoples are abundantly displayed, reflect cultural representations in the wider society of the United States; they cannot be divorced from the ethnic images created by, and circulating in, the mass media and tourism.

The pitfalls of cultural relativism

Finally, as a modern, industrial nation, Japan has many similarities with the United States and Western Europe. As the example of kimono demonstrates, however, it is represented in anthropology textbooks as a culture radically different from the West. Not only different, it is also regarded as opposite, as poles apart, as illustrated by the dichotomy between individualism and collectivism. It is safe to say that few countries represent the radical break between 'us' and 'them,' the West and the rest, more dramatically than does Japan.

A major factor in this dichotomous thinking is cultural relativism. Historically, Franz Boas developed this idea to challenge the unquestioned belief in Western superiority commonly held at that time. The relativists' notion that each culture should be understood and admired in its own terms, that cultural differences should be respected as differences rather than as weaknesses or failings, was directly opposed to the evolutionary view of society, in which the West was placed at the pinnacle of human progress.

On the other hand, the particularism contained in relativism, especially the search for each culture's unique 'configurations' or 'patterns,' as Benedict (1934) called them, has blinded anthropologists to the many similarities that exist across cultures. In cultural representation, one's own culture is ordinarily taken, whether explicitly or implicitly, as a point of reference. Inevitably, the emphasis tends to be placed on those features that distinguish 'them' from 'us,' but this tendency is particularly strong in the relativist tradition. So much so that relativist representations of other peoples often make them look more different than they really are. A major problem of cultural relativism, then, is the maximization of differences *between* cultures, and the concomitant minimization of differences *within* a culture. The construction of different 'others,' such as the exotic Japan, derives in part from this problem.

Another pitfall of relativism is that, contrary to common assumptions, it tends to portray the self in a positive, if not ideal, light. Certainly, a relativist respect for cultural differences generates a sympathetic understanding of people from other cultures, many of whom live in materially and socially deprived conditions. This understanding is, however, easily transformed into an uncritical self-affirmation unless one is prepared to see oneself reflexively and examine one's cultural assumptions by using such people as mirrors for oneself. Consider, for example, the following textbook description of gender:

> Even in male-dominated societies like traditional Japan and China, the eldest female in a household usually had the right to manage household affairs with a fair degree of autonomy. Yet in China, Japan, and many other societies, women were not allowed to participate in public affairs, had hardly any property of their own, had little say over whom they married, and were clearly subordinate to their fathers and husbands socially and even legally (Peoples and Bailey 1991:238; repeated in Peoples and Bailey 2000:173).

The authors have maintained that gender is constructed differently in different cultures. It would be safe to surmise that their intention is not to condemn Japan and China, but rather to warn against the ethnocentrism of judging foreign people by one's own standards. This warning does underscore the moral precepts of cultural relativism, but such descriptions have the unintentional effect of putting students, especially female students who likely experience gender discrimination in their own country, in a state of 'relative deprivation,' by which they find comfort in comparing seemingly less fortunate people with themselves. Furthermore, a sense of relief produced in this way will induce an uncritical affirmation of the self – 'Thank God we are not like them!' When this happens, what at first was a respect for difference is transformed into an easy judgment of, even contempt for, the differences of 'others.'

It should also be noted that an accurate understanding of the status of women is not possible without a careful cross-cultural comparison that utilizes the same time frame. Such a comparison is virtually impossible, however, because the text quoted above just says 'traditional Japan and China,' and the exact time or period to which it refers is unclear. What is implicated, instead, is a 'generic past' (Kahn 1995:328), in which the Eastern Other is deprived of coevalness with the Western self. Thus, students are unable to reflect on their own country's history. After all, it was only in 1920 that the Nineteenth Amendment to the U. S. Constitution gave women the right to vote.

Concluding remarks

By way of conclusion, I wish to offer practical solutions for solving two of the most common problems evident in American anthropology textbooks. Regarding the mismatch between written text and visual images, this drawback may be corrected relatively easily by a closer cooperation between authors and photo editors on the one hand, and between textbook producers and regional specialists on the other. In the formative period of anthropology, taking high-quality photographs needed the skills of trained professionals, but with recent technological advances it is now possible for laypeople to achieve excellent results. Indeed, there is often a large collection of visual data, such as photos, videos, and films, in the anthropologist's office. They may not be as aesthetically pleasing as the photojournalists' works, but are far more valuable ethnographically. Using such visual images in introductory textbooks might diminish their commercial appeal, but it would undoubtedly enhance their academic credibility.

The other problem is the gap in the amount of information given about different aspects of a culture. As we have seen on Table 6.2, Japan is described in detail about such subjects as 'Psychology, Socialization, and Education,' 'Language,' and 'Family,' but is almost ignored about 'Kinship' and 'Politics and Law.' This gap is widened when photographs that exaggerate one particular aspect are used to illustrate the text. Consequently, students are afforded a very lopsided, incomplete picture of a culture. It is not easy to solve this problem, but one possible solution would be to limit the number of cultures discussed in any given textbook. Describing in detail a relatively small selection of cultures might not be ideal in terms of demonstrating the diversity of human culture, but it has the advantage of avoiding lopsided representations that will perpetuate Orientalist stereotypes in textbook descriptions.[18]

Cultural representation has been one of the most important subjects in anthropology since the mid-1980s. In the United States alone, many articles have been published in leading journals, such as *American Anthropologist* and *Cultural Anthropology*. In the former, review essays on museum exhibits and displays, and more recently, on visual anthropology have also regularly appeared. To my knowledge, however, no detailed analysis has ever been conducted of cultural representation in introductory textbooks on anthropology. This is both curious and unfortunate because these texts play a vital role in the 'home' of most anthropologists – the classroom. Hopefully, this chapter will stimulate further analyses of how other peoples' worlds have been described and displayed in textbooks. Hopefully, too, responses from and collaboration with the 'natives' these books describe will be a valued part of such an analysis.

Notes

Chapter 1

1 See M. Nazif Shahrani (1994). A native of Afghanistan, Shahrani remarked that he had worked as a consultant in the production of a prize-winning ethnographic film, *The Kirghiz of Afghanistan* (1975). He was, however, denied any opportunity for input during the editing of the film. As he stated, 'My main grievance was that my consultancy agreement with the producers stipulated my participation in the shooting process in the field as well as in the editing of the final product, but in reality my role was that of an inexpensive native tour guide, facilitator, interviewer, translator, and informant for the real ethnographer, the Western anthropologist filmmaker on their staff' (Shahrani 1994:47).
2 Clifford Geertz, in his book *After the Fact* (1995), wrote about the difficulties he had experienced in collaborating with local scholars when he did fieldwork in postcolonial Indonesia in the 1950s (Geertz 1995:99–109). He then remarked as follows: '[N]ot all ethnographers, by far, now are Western. Not only is there usually a significant contingent of local anthropologists, some of them of international standing – as is the case for both Indonesia and Morocco – but even in the West the profession is no longer a monopoly of Americans and Europeans. Individuals from African, Asian, and Latin American backgrounds, as well as by now Native American, have joined its ranks. The critical gaze from neighboring disciplines is supplemented by a similar gaze, even more searching, from within our own' (Geertz 1995:132).
3 If properly trained, natives can write about their culture and history in ways useful to professional anthropologists. In Japan, in the 1930s, Kunio Yanagita organized a national network of amateur researchers who studied their own community. Called *kyōdo kenkyū* (literally, the study of one's hometown), this tradition has continued to date, playing an important role in the compilation of local histories. For the details, see Chapter 4.
4 Although Trask is an 'activist' native who is not an anthropologist by training, her arguments are directly related to the issue under discussion. The same is true of Asante, who is mentioned later in the text.
5 For criticisms of the dichotomy between the core and the periphery in the academic world system, see van Bremen (1997). His arguments will be examined in Chapter 3.
6 For example, annual meetings of the American Anthropological Association (AAA) are attended by academics from around the world, whereas those of the Japanese Society of Ethnology (JSE) are attended mostly by

the Japanese. With a membership of approximately 2,000 people, JSE is said to be the second largest anthropological organization in the world, but it is no equal of AAA in terms of international influence.
7 In terms of descent, neither Ohtsuka nor Shimizu is a native of Ainu. However, Ohtsuka has long-standing relationships with Ainu people; Shimizu has long been studying the problem under discussion. It is hoped that Kayano, who received a doctorate in anthropology in 2001, will respond to the debate from an Ainu perspective.
8 Niessen's earlier cited description of Umesao is insulting. Umesao is a highly respected scholar, who, in 1994, was awarded *bunka kunshō* (an Order of Cultural Merits), the highest honor bestowed on Japanese academics. Making ill-informed and misleading remarks about someone of his standing is, one would have thought, something to be avoided.

Chapter 2

1 A collection of papers edited by Caroline Brettell, entitled *When They Read What We Write* (1993), has discussed essentially the same issue. However, since most of the contributors did fieldwork in Western cultures, the scope of inquiry does not extend to the relationships between Western and native anthropologists in the non-Western world.
2 It is, however, debatable whether or not Cushing was truly accepted by his host tribe. Recent cartoons of Cushing and his wife Emily by the Zuni artist Phil Hughte, as reproduced in *American Anthropologist* 97(1), 1995, suggest that there was an insurmountable barrier between the Zuni and the Cushings.
3 In her article on African studies in the United States, Deborah Amory (1997:115) pointed out 'the links between broader sociopolitical imbalances of power and scholarly production.' Aidan Southall was quoted as saying that the Westerners' demand for objectivity on the part of African scholars 'is another name for Western ethnocentrism and monopoly of the right to interpret other cultures to the world' (quoted in Amory 1997:116). This statement recalls that of Asante mentioned in Chapter 1. The unequal relations of power in the production and dissemination of knowledge are central to my thesis on the academic world system to be discussed below.
4 Another factor is the shrinking academic market in the United States, which has fostered an inward-looking attitude among young job seekers. Even after they find a job, they will have to go through the stringent tenure system governed, as it is, by the 'publish or perish' principle. Understandably, few junior scholars have the luxury of 'wasting' time making friends with foreigners who are in no position to evaluate their work for promotion. This, though, may be said to be the outcome of anthropological training, which emphasizes the importance of establishing rapport with the people under study, while neglecting the issue of collaboration with local scholars. A look at textbooks on anthropological research methods clarifies this point.
   On the Japanese side, the diminishing number of Japanese anthropologists studying Japan has contributed to the weakening of the ties

between Japanese and American anthropologists. Immediately after the war, when funds for overseas research were scarce, fieldwork at home provided the best, most affordable opportunity to practice anthropology. This situation, however, produced some positive consequences, such as the spread of a better understanding of Japan's folk customs among metropolitan anthropologists. As Japan recovered from the aftermath of the war, funds for overseas research became increasingly available, and fewer and fewer anthropologists studied Japan. As a result, American anthropologists lost interest in collaborating with the Japanese. (This is, however, not the only reason for the American lack of interest in Japanese research, as will be discussed later in the text). For an extensive review of how the geographic focus of Japanese anthropology has changed since 1935, when the first issue of the *Japanese Journal of Ethnology* was published, see Sekimoto's historical analysis (Sekimoto 1995).

5 Regarding Buddhist studies, Noriko Kawahashi (2000:9) remarked that she had heard more than a few American scholars say, 'Japanese teachers are, so to speak, my research assistants,' when, in fact, they are heavily dependent on Japanese research. Like the disparaging comment mentioned earlier, which was made by a leading American anthropologist about Japan's foremost anthropologist, such remarks are usually slips of the tongue made in private. They do reveal, however, what some people positioned at the center of power really think. This is, of course, not to say that every American scholar holds these opinions. Personally, I am indebted to many American people for their professional support and friendship.

6 The social significance of research is often lessened or lost in the process of translation because the same words have different meanings in different social contexts. Translation is difficult because it requires not only superior linguistic skills, but also an appreciation of the local context in which the author's utterances were made.

7 Delmos Jones maintained that anthropology is a Western science based on Western beliefs and values and that the value of a native anthropology lies in its being different from the Western system of thought. Thus, he contended that a fully-fledged native science would liberate the human mind from the constraints of Western civilization. As Jones (1970:258) remarked, 'The emergence of a native anthropology is part of an essential decolonization of anthropological knowledge and requires drastic changes in the recruitment and training of anthropologists.' In Jones' view, the merit of a native anthropology lies in the capacity to offer non-Western perspectives on familiar social phenomena.

8 Many of the Japanese words used in *Crafting Selves* have little or no culturally specific meaning. In this regard, Kondo's rhetorical strategy contrasts with that of Benedict in *The Chrysanthemum and the Sword*. Benedict concentrated on a limited number of words which she thought expressed the *Volksgeist* of the Japanese, such as *on* (obligation), *giri* (debt), and *haji* (shame). Her study compelled the Japanese to rethink their culture because the significance of these words had hitherto escaped their attention. The same can hardly be said of Kondo's extravagant use of local words.

9 For example, in a footnote, Kondo referred to the importance of considering socio-economic differences when examining the *ie* consciousness of the Japanese. As she remarked, 'Socioeconomic status is also likely to make a difference in the degree to which specific *ie* manifest features of hierarchical *ie* organization' (Kondo 1990:318). The fact that this statement was relegated to a footnote suggests that Kondo attached only secondary importance to the multiple experience of *ie*, despite her claim to the contrary.
10 For a comprehensive review of the literature on the *ie*, see Kuwayama (1996a).
11 The following statement by Geertz is suggestive in understanding why natives are excluded from anthropological discourse: 'In itself, Being There is a postcard experience ("I've been to Katmandu – have you?") It is Being Here, a scholar among scholars, that gets your anthropology read…published, reviewed, cited, taught' (Geertz 1988:130).
12 The extent to which 'primitive' society has been isolated from the larger outside world is a moot question. Under the influence of structural functionalism, which regards each society as a complete whole separate from its neighboring societies, 'primitives' have been described as more insulated than the facts warrant. Moreover, the school's emphasis on the here and now has frozen 'primitive' history at the time of observation.
13 Brian Schwimmer (1996) argued that the effective use of the Internet would break down the traditional structure of academic authority, which he predicted would create a new social order marked by 'egalitarianism,' 'collaborative scholarship,' and an 'altruistic sharing of knowledge.'

Chapter 3

1 As Nicholas Dirks, Geoff Eley, and Sherry Ortner (1994:19) stated, 'The difference between competing for access within an already constituted system and transforming the system itself' is familiar to 'subordinate or marginalized groups as they seek to contest the power of hegemonic formations, whether these are constituted within academic disciplines, particular institutional fields, or at the level of whole societies.'
2 In the introduction to *Asian Trajectories* (1998), Kuan-Hsing Chen criticized 'the hegemony of the English language and the controlled circulation of publications' (Chen 1998:5). According to Chen, when the manuscripts of a book he had edited were reviewed by some Western publishers, 'one of the interested publishers responded that if we got rid of the Asian names, then they would do it' (Chen 1998:xvii). This episode suggests that not only is foreign discourse at a disadvantage, but that foreign names, especially unfamiliar Asian names, are considered to be a sort of 'stigma' in the English-language publishing industry.
3 Chapter 1 of John Thompson's *Ideology and Modern Culture* (1990) provides a most useful review of the concept of ideology from a Marxist perspective. Also useful is Terry Eagleton's overview of the subject (Eagleton 1991:1–31). As is often pointed out, one of the best known anthropological formulations of ideology, that of Clifford Geertz, who

defined ideology as a 'cultural system,' overlooks the dimensions of power and of domination, which are critical to an understanding of the world system.
4 Wallerstein (1979:102) has this to say about the bourgeoisie in semi-peripheral countries: 'The degree to which this [semi-peripheral] indigenous bourgeoisie is structurally linked to corporations located in the core countries varies, but the percentage tends to be far larger than is true of the bourgeoisie within any core country; indeed, this is one of the defining characteristics that differentiates a contemporary core and "non-socialist" semiperipheral country.'
5 There is an interesting parallel here to postcolonial studies. Whereas earlier theories assumed irreducible binary oppositions, such as colonizer/colonized, domination/subordination, and center/margin, recent analysis has shifted from this rigid binarism to a more flexible model that accommodates the 'cultural exchange' and 'peculiar intimacy' between the two parties. As Bill Ashcroft, Gareth Griffiths, and Helen Tiffin (1995:86) stated, 'Theorizing this complex "intimacy" without giving away the fact of persisting and historic *inequalities* within those relations and structures [of colonialism] is perhaps *the* major focus of contemporary post-colonial theory' (italics in the original).
6 The 'generalized Asian stereotype' emphasizes those characteristics, usually racial and cultural, that distinguish Asians from white Americans. Thus, the differences between 'us' (white Americans) and 'them' (Asians) are stressed, while neglecting the differences among 'them,' let alone the similarities that exist between 'us' and 'them' as members of the human species.
7 For example, the Asia Pacific Sociological Association, founded in 1997, is seeking the possibility of creating 'multicultural' social science in an attempt to overcome Eurocentrism. Its first annual meeting was held in Kuala Lumpur in Malaysia (Sugimoto 2000:179).
8 Generally, Korean scholars are more concerned with the vestiges of Japan's colonialism than those of Western colonialism, which they experienced only indirectly through Japan. Japan occupies a far greater place in their mind than the Japanese generally realize. This difference in perception often blocks cross-cultural exchanges between the two countries, including scholarly communications.
9 Yanagita was an original thinker who developed a distinctive approach to the study of folklore. His approach was different from that of European scholars in many important respects. It remains, however, that he had read major European works of his time and that he found it necessary to refer to them, whether positively or negatively, to establish his own tradition. Given the power imbalance between the center and the periphery, this was almost inevitable. Indeed, a careful reading of his book *Minkan Denshōron* (*The Science of Popular Tradition*, 1934) shows that Yanagita almost always mentioned European scholars, Charlotte Burne and James Frazer in particular, when discussing theoretically important ideas. Parenthetically, Yanagita did have a degree of international influence. In a Korean textbook on folklore studies, for instance, his theories are introduced briefly (Lee, Chang, and Lee 1991:11–12).

Chapter 4

1. The term 'folkloristics' is used to describe the study of folklore as an academic field. Alternative expressions include 'folklore studies' and 'folklore research' (cf. Georges and Jones 1995:1, 23). Note that in Japanese both ethnology and folkloristics are pronounced *minzokugaku*, although the characters used are different.
2. For useful critiques of Yanagita written in English, see Kawada (1993), Koschmann, Oiwa, and Yamashita (1985), Morse (1990), and Tsurumi (1975).
3. Only the introduction and the first chapter of this book were written by Yanagita himself. The remaining chapters were hand-recorded and transcribed by one of his students who had attended his lectures delivered in his house. This fact is partially responsible for the scant attention paid to global folkloristics. However, the arguments presented in *Minkan Denshōron* are consistent with those in *Seinen to Gakumon* and *Kyōdo Seikatsu no Kenkyūhō* to be mentioned later. Thus, it is safe to regard *Minkan Denshōron* as Yanagita's own work.
4. Unlike Great Britain, where anthropology has been clearly separated from folkloristics, in Japan the two fields have developed as twin disciplines since the late nineteenth century. This history is probably related to the relatively late modernization of Japan. In Japan's countryside, researchers from the cities discovered many old customs and manners comparable to those European scholars had discovered in 'primitive' societies. For Japanese scholars, therefore, the exotic 'others' existed both inside and outside Japan. Chie Nakane (1987:33) remarked that the situation was quite similar in both Korea and China. She argued that folk traditions in these countries had been 'discovered' by urban intellectuals who visited the countryside.
5. For the Annales school, see Burke (1990). Yanagita's model of folklore research is similar to that of Bronislaw Malinowski in *Argonauts of the Western Pacific* (1922). Malinowski classified ethnographic research into three parts, each studying the following subjects in ascending order of complexity: (1) the organization of the tribe and the anatomy of its culture; (2) the 'imponderabilia' of actual life; and (3) the native mind (Malinowski 1984:24). It is a moot question whether Yanagita had read Malinowski before writing *Minkan Denshōron*. Significantly, Yanagita considered it practically impossible for non-natives to understand the native mind, whereas Malinowski had no doubt concerning their ability to grasp it (cf. Kawada 1993:127).
6. In an article in the 1976 edition of *Annual Review of Anthropology*, Gopal Sarana and Dharni Sinha remarked that India had a long tradition of native anthropology, one without parallel in the world. As they stated, 'We do not think that there is any other country in the world where anthropological self-study has been conducted by native-born anthropologists for almost seven decades. Before long, anthropologists of all countries, particularly the developing countries, will have to start studying their own culture. We cannot anticipate the kinds of problems these native anthropologists will face. This new aspect of anthropology in almost every country will

encounter growing pains. The only exception will be India, which has long passed that stage' (Sarana and Dharni 1976:217, quoted in Sinha 2000b:21). If 'India' and 'anthropology' were replaced, respectively, with 'Japan' and 'folkloristics,' we might mistake this for Yanagita's statement.

7 Theoretically, a major weakness of the idea of culture is the assumption that culture constitutes a coherent, homogeneous whole. In today's deconstructionist movement, this assumption has been attacked by many scholars. Among the best known criticisms is Lila Abu-Lughod's article entitled 'Writing against Culture' (1991). Since, however, culture is a collective representation, there is no fundamental solution to this problem unless the idea is discarded altogether. As for the debate on how the nation and nationalism should be understood, see Anthony Smith's critique of the 'modernist' approach as represented by Gellner (Smith 1991).

8 After I gave a paper on Yanagita at an international conference held in Bangalore, India, in early 2000, a Taiwanese scholar approached me, asking if I knew a Japanese folklorist he was interested in. He wrote down the folklorist's name in two Chinese characters, the first meaning 'willow' and the second 'paddy field.' In Japanese, they are pronounced 'Yanagita,' but in Chinese they are read differently. Because of the pronunciation differences, the Taiwanese scholar did not know that the Japanese he was interested in was the same person I had discussed. He continued to ask what I thought were obvious questions until we finally noticed that we were both talking about Yanagita. This episode shows that things taken for granted in one country are often little known or not known at all in another, hence the continued importance of the nation as the basic frame for scholarship.

9 Major characteristics of annual meetings of American academic societies include the following. (1) The meetings are huge. The number of participants often reaches a few thousand, which makes it impossible to hold a plenary session in which all participants can gather at one place at the one time. (2) They are usually held at expensive hotels in urban centers. Little consideration is given to participants with limited economic resources, especially people coming from developing countries. In anthropology, this custom effectively precludes the majority of people who have been studied and described in ethnography. (3) There is a strict time limit to each presentation (15 to 20 minutes). Presenters are more interested in performing than exchanging ideas with the audience. (4) Publishers regard these academic meetings as great opportunities for advertising their products. They pay to obtain the right to exhibit books and other commodities. As a result, an atmosphere of commercialism prevails at certain sections of the meeting venue. (5) Job interviews are given, whether in designated areas for this purpose or in guestrooms. These interviews are typically used as an initial screening of candidates. Those who successfully pass this stage will be invited to the prospective employer's campus for a full interview.

10 A concise explanation of empathy is found in *The Penguin Dictionary of Psychology*. The second definition under the heading of 'empathy' reads: 'A vicarious affective response to the emotional experiences of another person that mirrors or mimics that emotion. In this sense there is the clear

implication that an empathic experience is a sharing of the emotion with the other person' (Reber 1995:249). This sharing is mediated by the body (in contrast to the mind), the realm to which emotion belongs. Johann Gottfried Herder used a similar concept, *Einfühlung*, meaning 'feeling into,' in order to indicate intuitive understanding of a nation's culture (Mautner 1999:165).

11 The characters used for *karada* and '*mi*' in *minitsuku* have the same meaning – the body.

12 For an insightful explanation of the difference between the Japanese and Western conceptions of the mind and the body, see Lebra (1993). She argued that in Japan there is no clear distinction between the two because they partially overlap with each other. Thus, she proposed to express *kokoro* (mind) and *karada* (body) as 'the bodied mind' and 'the minded body,' respectively.

Chapter 5

1 In the Japanese translation, 'giri to one's name' is clumsily rendered as '*na ni taisuru giri*,' a literal translation of Benedict's phrase.

2 Similarly, Benedict explained State Shinto in prewar Japan by likening it to the Stars and Stripes. As she stated, 'Since it was concerned with proper respect to national symbols, as saluting the flag is in the United States, State Shinto was, they said, "no religion." Japan therefore could require it of all citizens without violating the Occidental dogma of religious freedom any more than the United States violates it in requiring a salute to the Stars and Stripes. It was a mere sign of allegiance' (Benedict 1946:87).

3 Benedict's reference here to the chrysanthemum is not so much about the gentle character of the Japanese, but rather the Japanese notion of *jichō* (self-respect), which demands that one should behave carefully to avoid the ridicule of society. As Benedict remarked, '[The Japanese] therefore treat themselves much as they treat their famous dwarf trees whose roots they prune or their chrysanthemum in their popular flower shows, into which they insert tiny wire racks to hold each petal in meticulous place' (Benedict n.d. [1]:45). Similar remarks are found in Chapter 12 of *The Chrysanthemum and the Sword*. It remains, however, that the *jichō* required of Japanese adults is contrasted with the wild behavior allowed to Japanese children. This contrast is a parallel to that between Apollonian and Dionysian impulses.

4 The white of *yang* and the black of *yin* should not be equated with good and evil as conceptualized in the West. Edwin Reischauer (1995:141) eloquently explained the difference when he remarked, 'In the West the division was between good and evil, always in mortal combat with each other. In East Asia the division of *yang* and *yin* was between day and night, male and female, lightness and darkness – that is, between complementary forces that alternate with and balance each other. There was no strict good-bad dichotomy but rather a sense of harmony and a balance of forces.'

5 In the late 6th century A.D., a battle developed between the pro-Buddhist Soga and the anti-Buddhist Mononobe clans, which resulted in victory for

the former. Soon afterwards, the leader of this clan, Umako Soga, murdered his nephew, Emperor Sushun, and thereby monopolized power. He later collaborated with his younger relative, Prince Shōtoku, who played a central role in the spread of Buddhism in Japan. Supported by the imperial house and the court aristocrats, Buddhism (a 'great tradition' in Robert Redfield's terminology) has absorbed much of Shinto (a 'little tradition') without completely eliminating it. Thus the two religions have maintained separate identities. In modern times, State Shinto was concocted as a political device to control the populace, and the emperor was considered to be a living god. Today, among the general public, Shinto ceremonies usually occur at a community level to solicit the protection of local deities, whereas Buddhism is practiced in individual households in order to worship one's ancestors. A major point of contrast between the two religions is that Shinto is mainly concerned with the here and now, while Buddhism is oriented towards the afterlife. This partially explains why the former is associated with auspicious occasions, such as birth and marriage, and the latter with death.

6   Although Benedict did not use the term '*seken*,' she meant it when she discussed the importance of the approval of 'the outside world' in Japanese socialization (Benedict 1946:274). As she acknowledged, this idea originated in Gorer's 'Japanese Character Structure' (Gorer 1943:26–27). In my own work (Kuwayama 1992), I interpreted *seken* as 'reference society,' which, together with *mawari* (immediate reference others) and *hito* (generalized reference others), constitutes concentric circles that extend outwards from *jibun* (self), situated at the center.

7   Another important aspect of Benedict's account concerns the role of gender in Japanese society. When she described the experience of working in the United States, she used the third-person pronoun singular in masculine form – 'he.' This usage suggests the American model she described is gendered. From today's viewpoint, a major problem with *The Chrysanthemum and the Sword*, Chapter 12 in particular, is that Benedict paid little attention to gender differences, whether in Japan or America. This contrasts with Gorer's account of the Japanese. In his article, 'Japanese Character Structure,' (which will be discussed later in the text), he carefully noted how the lives of Japanese men differed from those of Japanese women. Although Benedict borrowed many of Gorer's ideas, she neglected his insights on this matter and presented a generalized picture of the Japanese life cycle.

8   Margaret Mead identified Gorer's work as 'the precursor of [Benedict's] work on national character in general and on Japan in particular,' saying, 'The work of her students and younger contemporaries had become so much a part of her thinking, of the air in which she moved, that it was something for which she could give general but not particular thanks' (Mead 1959:426).

9   Unlike Gorer, Benedict was not uncritical in her approach to psychoanalysis. Its influence on her thinking is much more limited than is commonly thought. Mead (1959:428) remarked that psychoanalytic theories that centered on the functioning of body zones made no sense to Benedict.

10 Like the new Japanese custom of calling children of mixed parentage '*daburu*' (double), instead of '*hāfu*' (half), as had previously been the case, dual entities may be said to have more substance than homogeneous ones because they draw their qualities from both categories. Douglas, however, supported the old Japanese custom and regarded duality as a liability, rather than as an asset.

11 Ohnuki-Tierney critically examined Douglas' theory, remarking, 'As the product of God, the classification [of the universe into culture/humans and nature/animals] or order is good, whereas its absence is blasphemy, a major sin against God, and thus evil. The basic dyad of humans and animals, therefore, is like two boxes, clearly separated by a sharp line of taboos not to be violated. In contrast, a dualistic universe [like Japan's] is characterized by the centrality of ambiguity. In such a universe, order and inverted order are not antithetical to each other...[A] monolithic universe places emphasis on the separation of categories, whereas a dualistic universe emphasizes the synthesis of two opposing principles – yin and yang, the self and other' (Ohnuki-Tierney 1987:158). Ohnuki-Tierney further maintained that the type of taboo typically found in the dualistic universe is 'breakable,' which facilitates 'inter-categorical communication.'

12 The techniques used by Benedict and her associates to study enemy countries are collectively known as 'the study of culture at a distance.' For the details, see Mead and Métraux (1953). This volume has recently been reissued as part of the Berghan Books series called 'Margaret Mead: The Study of Contemporary Western Cultures,' with William O. Beeman as the general editor. According to him, the volume by Mead and Métraux has been welcomed in media studies (personal communication).

13 In 'Bibliographical Note – 1942,' Mead acknowledged that much of the information about England had been supplied by Gregory Bateson, her husband. Also, she mentioned Ruth Benedict as one of the people who had helped her formulate the concept of 'character structure,' and Geoffrey Gorer was credited for his insights into America as a foreign culture.

14 This article has recently been translated into Japanese and appears as part of Benedict (1997).

15 The same phrase is used in *The Chrysanthemum and the Sword*. Benedict wrote, 'The Emperor had to be a Scared Father removed from all secular considerations. A man's fealty to him, chu, the supreme virtue, must become an ecstatic contemplation of a fantasied [sic] Good Father uncontaminated by contacts with the world' (Benedict 1946:125).

16 As I have written elsewhere, a major reason for the unusual attention given to Doi's theory in the United States is that the desire for dependence – the hidden wish to be loved, protected, and embraced by an omnipotent figure or the longing for what Erich Fromm (1980:29) called 'the paradisiacal state' of childhood – is repressed by the cultural ideal of self-reliance and that this forbidden self is conjured up, in the manner of 'the return of the oppressed,' by the theory of *amae*. *Amae* is thus looked upon with a mixed sense of anxiety and curiosity (Kuwayama 1996:173). For a detailed exposition of *amae*, see Frank Johnson (1993).

17 I must add here a personal note that my career as a foreign student in America and later as a professor has made my position betwixt and between.

Chapter 6

1 'Anthropology' refers here primarily to cultural anthropology. A major feature of American anthropology is the so-called 'four-field approach,' which comprises the biological, the archeological, the cultural or sociocultural, and the linguistic.
2 I obtained a total of 21 textbooks. In alphabetical order of the authors, they were: (1) Richard A. Barrett, *Culture and Conduct: An Excursion in Anthropology* (2nd ed.), Belmont, California: Wadsworth Publishing, 1991. (2) Daniel G. Bates and Elliot M. Fratkin, *Cultural Anthropology* (2nd. ed.), Boston: Allyn and Bacon, 1999. (3) Paul Bohannan, *We, the Alien: An Introduction to Cultural Anthropology*, Prospect Heights, Illinois: Waveland Press, 1992. (4) Richley H. Crapo, *Cultural Anthropology: Understanding Ourselves and Others* (4th ed.), Guilford, Connecticut: Brown & Benchmark Publishers, 1996. (5) Carol R. Ember and Melvin Ember, *Cultural Anthropology* (9th ed.), New Jersey: Prentice Hall, 1999. (6) Gary Ferraro, *Cultural Anthropology: An Applied Perspective* (3rd ed.), Belmont, California: Wadsworth Publishing, 1998. (7) Marvin Harris, *Culture, People, Nature: An Introduction to General Anthropology* (7th ed.), New York: Longman, 1997. (8) Marvin Harris and Orna Johnson, *Cultural Anthropology* (5th ed.), Boston: Allyn and Bacon, 2000. (9) William Haviland, *Cultural Anthropology* (9th ed.), Fort Worth, Texas: Harcourt Brace College Publishers, 1999. (10) Roger M. Keesing and Andrew J. Strathern, *Cultural Anthropology: A Contemporary Perspective* (3rd ed.), Fort Worth, Texas: Harcourt Brace College Publishers, 1998. (11) Conrad P. Kottak, *Anthropology: The Exploration of Human Diversity* (7th ed.), New York: McGraw-Hill, 1997. (12) Conrad P. Kottak, *Cultural Anthropology* (8th ed.), New York: McGraw-Hill, 2000. (13) Serena Nanda and Richard L. Warms, *Cultural Anthropology* (6th ed.), Belmont, California: Wadsworth Publishing, 1998. (14) James Peoples and Garrick Bailey, *Humanity: An Introduction to Cultural Anthropology* (5th ed.), Belmont, California: Wadsworth Publishing, 2000. (15) Richard H. Robbins, *Cultural Anthropology: A Problem-Based Approach* (2nd ed.), Itasca, Illinois: F. E. Peacock Publishers, 1997. (16) Abraham Rosman and Paula G. Rubel, *The Tapestry of Culture: An Introduction to Cultural Anthropology* (6th ed.), New York: McGraw-Hill, 1998. (17) Emily A. Schultz and Robert H. Lavenda, *Cultural Anthropology: A Perspective on the Human Condition* (4th ed.), Mountain View, California: Mayfield Publishing, 1998. (18) Raymond Scupin, *Cultural Anthropology: A Global Perspective* (4th ed.), New Jersey: Prentice-Hall, 2000. (19) Raymond Scupin and Christopher R. DeCorse, *Anthropology: A Global Perspective* (3rd ed.), New Jersey: Prentice Hall, 1998. (20) Ernest L. Schusky and T. Patrick Culbert, *Introducing Culture* (4th ed.), New Jersey: Prentice Hall, 1987. (21) Sheldon Smith and Philip D. Young, *Cultural Anthropology: Understanding a World in Transition*, Boston: Allyn and Bacon, 1998.
3 For the situation in Great Britain, see Adam Kuper (1983:206–210). According to a survey conducted in 1981, the geographic areas studied by British anthropologists were, in descending order of interest, sub-Saharan

Africa, Britain, India and Nepal, Continental Europe, Southeast Asia, the Middle East and North Africa, Melanesia and Polynesia, South and Central America, the Arctic and North Atlantic, and the Caribbean. There was no entry on East Asia, although a few scholars, including Joy Hendry and Brian Morean, were studying Japan at that time.

4 Before the establishment of the East Asia Section, the following regions were recognized as sections: Africa, the Middle East, Europe, North America, and Latin America. Melanesia has an 'interest group,' one rank below 'section.' Major areas of the world that are yet to be represented are concentrated in the Asia-Pacific region and Russia. Note that Figure 1 conceals much of Russia, except the areas close to Moscow.

5 This structure is convenient for classroom use because many American universities have adopted the 15-week semester system. Also, textbook chapters are usually arranged in the order mentioned in the text, from the tangible to the intangible, which follows the materialist model, as in Marvin Harris's text, or, more generally, the evolutionary model based on the classification of subsistence patterns. This trend ignores the strong influence of the symbolic/hermeneutic school on professional anthropologists.

6 According to Catherine Lutz and Jane Collins (1993:120), among the countries featured in *National Geographic* from 1950 to 1986, Japan appeared most frequently. Similarly, in terms of the proportion of a country's population to the frequency of its appearances in the same magazine, Japan is second to none.

7 To be statistically precise, words in each textual representation should be counted. The area occupied by each photograph should also be measured, which in turn should be converted into a comparable number of words by a systematic method. I have omitted this complex process, however, because my purpose is to show a general pattern.

8 Percentages are rounded to one decimal.

9 A senior colleague of mine at VCU often bowed in the Hollywood style when exchanging greetings with me. One day, when I reciprocated with a big leap imitating the frog, he laughed and said, 'No, that doesn't work.' But that was exactly the point. He did not know that his deep bow is as strange as my animal jump in the Japanese context.

10 The type of kimono shown in the photograph is called '*yukata*,' which is made of light fabric. Since the end of World War II, the kimono's popularity has declined, but the *yukata* made a comeback among young women in the 1990s, when it became a trendy garment worn to firework shows in the summer. For the details, see Wada (1996:158).

11 The third edition of Harris' *Cultural Anthropology* (1991) shows, on the cover page of Chapter 8 'Domestic Life,' an image similar to Figure 6.6. It depicts a Japanese father, in the Oriental squatting position, taking pictures of his nuclear family on the precinct of Meiji Shrine, Tokyo. The same photograph has been used as a visual aid to the text in Harris' more comprehensive textbook *Culture, People, Nature* (6th edition, 1993, p. 259; 7th edition, 1997, p. 246).

12 For the contrast between 'field' and 'home,' see Gupta and Ferguson (1997). They argued that the 'field,' in which the exotic 'others' studied by anthropologists live, has been radically separated from 'home,' i.e., the

dominant, majority culture of the West. Furthermore, the value of each 'field' is determined by the degree of its Otherness from an archetypal anthropological 'home.' Gupta and Ferguson argued that this practice has brought about 'a hierarchy of purity of field sites' (Gupta and Ferguson 1997:12–15).

13 Impressed with the dazzling display and performance of Japan's traditional arts, which are only occasionally seen in the homeland, this diplomat said to me, 'Japanese culture is shown here in a condensed form!'

14 In the introduction to *Tourists and Tourism* (1997), Simone Abram and Jacqueline Waldren remarked that there is 'interplay between government interests, the tourism industry and the development of concepts of heritage, local identity and perceptions of belonging.' They further argued that the power relation is often 'mutual exploitation,' with hosts biting back, thus blurring the distinction between actors (Abram and Waldren 1997:9).

15 Lutz and Collins (1993:146) reported that, in *National Geographic*, 'women alone populate galleries of portraits.' The only exception is Melanesia, which is known for men's decorative practices. Lutz and Collins also contended that developing countries have customarily been feminized (ibid.:179–180). Until pornographic magazines became widely available in the 1960s, *National Geographic* was known as 'the only mass culture venue where Americans could see women's breasts' (ibid.:172).

16 The original cover page was entitled 'Rethinking Japan,' and the following description appeared at the side of the samurai figure: 'After years of haggling, the U.S. still runs a $52 billion annual trade deficit with Japan, and Japanese society remains closed in crucial ways. As a result, a radical shift in U.S. thinking about Japan is under way. This revisionist view holds that Japan is really different – and that conventional free-trade policies won't work. Once, such view would have been dismissed as "Japan-bashing," but now they have an intellectual base. At a time of political crisis in Japan, America's challenge is to restore economic balance without destroying our broader relationship.'

17 According to Kenji Yoshida (2001:118), at major war memorial museums in China and Korea, the focus of display is on Japan's military aggression during World War II. These museums opened in the mid-1980s, when there was a strong protest against the alleged distortion of history by the Japanese government in the process of inspecting school textbooks. For a detailed report on how Japan is displayed in foreign museums, see Kurita (2001), of which Yoshida's paper is a part.

18 A partial solution to this problem is found in Wendell Oswalt's textbook *Life Cycles and Lifeways* (1986). He selected five ethnic groups that represented different levels of cultural complexity – the Siriono, the Netsilik, the Gusii, the Hopi, and the Qemant. In each chapter, Oswalt gave brief descriptions of these groups about the chapter's main theme, putting them in boxes set apart from the text. This strategy helps students get holistic pictures of the ethnic groups without losing sight of the cultural diversity explained in the text.

References

Abram, Simone, and Jacqueline Waldren (1997), 'Introduction: Tourists and Tourism Identifying with People and Places,' in Simone Abram, Jacqueline Waldren, and Donald V. L. Macleod (eds.), *Tourists and Tourism: Identifying with People and Places,* Oxford: Berg, pp. 1–11.

Abu-Lughod, Lila (1991), 'Writing against Culture,' in Richard G. Fox (ed.), *Recapturing Anthropology: Working in the Present*, Santa Fe, New Mexico: School of American Research Press, pp. 138–162.

Aguilar, John L. (1981), 'Insider Research: An Ethnography of a Debate,' in Donald A. Messerschmidt (ed.), *Anthropologists at Home in North America: Methods and Issues in the Study of One's Own Society*, Cambridge: Cambridge University Press, pp. 15–26.

Alatas, Syed Farid (2001), 'The Study of the Social Sciences in Developing Societies: Towards an Adequate Conceptualization of Relevance,' *Current Sociology* 49(2):1–28.

Amino, Yoshihiko (1990), *Nihonron no Shiza* (*Perspectives on Theories of Japan*), Tokyo: Shōgakkan.

Amory, Deborah (1997), 'African Studies as American Institution,' in Akhil Gupta and James Ferguson (eds.), *Anthropological Locations: Boundaries and Grounds of a Field Science*, Berkeley: University of California Press, pp. 102–116.

Anderson, Benedict (1991), *Imagined Communities: Reflections on the Origin and Spread of Nationalism* (revised ed.), London: Verso, (orig. 1983).

Appadurai, Arjun (1992), 'Putting Hierarchy in Its Place,' in George E. Marcus (ed.), *Rereading Cultural Anthropology*, Durham: Duke University Press, pp. 34–47.

Asad, Talal (1986), 'The Concept of Cultural Translation in British Social Anthropology,' in James Clifford and George E. Marcus (eds.), *Writing Culture: The Poetics and Politics of Ethnography*, Berkeley: University of California Press, pp. 141–164.

Asante, Molefi Kete (1999), *The Painful Demise of Eurocentrism: An Afrocentric Response to Critics*, Trenton, New Jersey: Africa World Press.

Ashcroft, Bill, Gareth Griffiths, and Helen Tiffin (eds.), (1995), *The Post-Colonial Studies Reader*, London: Routledge.

Asquith, Pamela J. (1996), 'Japanese Science and Western Hegemonies: Primatology and the Limits Set to Questions,' in Laura Nader (ed.), *Naked Science: Anthropological Inquiry into Boundaries, Power, and Knowledge*, New York: Routledge, pp. 239–256.

────── (1998), 'The "World System" of Anthropology from a Primatological Perspective: Comments on the Kuwayama – van Bremen Debate,' *Japan Anthropology Workshop Newsletter* 28:16–27.

---------- (1999), 'The "World System" of Anthropology and "Professional Others,"' in E. L. Cerroni-Long (ed.), *Anthropological Theory in North America*, Westport, Connecticut: Bergin & Garvey, pp. 33–53.
Bachnik, Jane M. (1994), 'Introduction: *Uchi/Soto*: Challenging Our Conceptualizations of Self, Social Order, and Language,' in *Situated Meaning: Inside and Outside in Japanese Self, Society, and Language*. Jane M. Bachnik and Charles J. Quinn Jr. (eds.), Princeton: Princeton University Press, pp. 3–37.
Bakalaki, Alexandra (1997), 'Students, Natives, Colleagues: Encounters in Academia and in the Field,' *Cultural Anthropology* 12(4): 502–526.
Beardsley, Richard K., John W. Hall, and Robert E. Ward (1959), *Village Japan*, Chicago: University of Chicago Press.
Befu, Harumi (1989), 'Review. *Health, Illness, and Medical Care in Japan: Cultural and Social Dimensions*' (Edward Norbeck and Margaret Lock (eds.), Honolulu: University of Honolulu Press, 1987), *Journal of Japanese Studies* 15(1): 261–266.
---------- (1992), 'Introduction: Framework of Analysis,' in Harumi Befu and Joseph Kreiner (eds.), *Othernesses of Japan: Historical and Cultural Influences on Japanese Studies in Ten Countries*, München: Iudicium, pp. 15–35.
---------- (1994), 'Japan as Other: Merits and Demerits of Overseas Japanese Studies,' in Josef Kreiner (ed.), *Japan in Global Context*, München: Iudicium, pp. 33–45.
Bellah, Robert N., Richard Madsen, William M. Sullivan, Ann Swidler, and Steven M. Tipton (1985), *Habits of the Heart: Individualism and Commitment in American Life*, Berkeley: University of California Press.
Benedict, Ruth F. (1934) *Patterns of Culture*, Boston: Houghton Mifflin.
---------- (1946), *The Chrysanthemum and the Sword: Patterns of Japanese Culture*, Boston: Houghton Mifflin.
---------- (1948), 'Patterns of American Culture,' Ruth Fulton Benedict Papers, Vassar College Library (Folder 58.17).
---------- (1997), *Nihonjin no Kōdō Patān* (*Japanese Behavior Patterns*), translated and annotated by Nanako Fukui, Tokyo: NHK Books.
---------- n.d. [1] 'Japanese Behavior Patterns,' Ruth Fulton Benedict Papers, Vassar College Library (Folder 102.8).
---------- n.d. [2] 'Japanese National Character,' Ruth Fulton Benedict Papers, Vassar College Library (Folder 50.1).
---------- n.d. [3] 'What Shall Be Done about the Emperor,' Ruth Fulton Benedict Papers, Vassar College Library (Folder 103.7).
Brettell, Caroline B. (ed.), (1993), *When They Read What We Write: The Politics of Ethnography*, Westport, Connecticut: Bergin & Garvey.
Bryan, C. D. B. (1997), *The National Geographic Society: 100 Years of Adventure and Discovery*, New York: Harry N. Abrams.
Burke, Peter (1990), *The French Historical Revolution: The Annales School 1929–1989*, Stanford: Stanford University Press.
Caffrey, Margaret M. (1989), *Ruth Benedict: Strangers in This Land*, Austin: University of Texas Press.
Chen, Kuan-Hsing (ed.), (1998), *Trajectories: Inter-Asia Cultural Studies*, London: Routledge.

References

Clifford, James (1986), 'Introduction: Partial Truths,' in James Clifford and George E. Marcus (eds.), *Writing Culture: The Poetics and Politics of Ethnography*, Berkeley: University of California Press, pp. 1–26.
.... (1988), *The Predicament of Culture: Twentieth-Century Ethnography, Literature, and Art*, Cambridge, Massachusetts: Harvard University Press.
Dale, Peter N. (1986), *The Myth of Japanese Uniqueness*, New York: St. Martin's Press.
Dirks, Nicholas B., Geoff Eley, and Sherry B. Ortner (1994), 'Introduction,' in Nicholas B. Dirks, Geoff Eley, and Sherry B. Ortner (eds.), *Culture/Power/History: A Reader in Contemporary Social Theory*, Princeton: Princeton University Press, pp. 3–45.
Doi, Takeo (1973), *The Anatomy of Dependence* (translated by John Bester), Tokyo: Kodansha International.
Douglas, Mary (1966), *Purity and Danger: An Analysis of the Concepts of Pollution and Taboo*, London: Routledge.
Dower, John W. (1999), *Embracing Defeat: Japan in the Wake of World War II*, New York: W. W. Norton.
Dundes, Alan (ed.), (1999), *International Folkloristics: Classic Contributions by the Founders of Folklore*, Lanham, Maryland: Rowman & Littlefield Publishers.
Eades, J.S. (1994), '*Gaikoku kara Mita Nihon no Bunka Jinruigaku*' (Japanese Cultural Anthropology as Seen from Foreign Countries), *Newsletter Bunka Jinruigaku* (*Newsletter, Cultural Anthropology*) 1: 12–13.
Eagleton, Terry (1991), *Ideology: An Introduction*, London: Verso.
Ebuchi, Kazukimi (1992), '*Amerikajin no Tainichi Imēji*' (Images of Japan among Americans), in Tsuneo Ayabe (ed.), *Soto kara Mita Nihon* (*Japan as Seen from the Outside*), Tokyo: Asahi Shinbunsha, pp. 31–64.
Edgerton, Robert B. (1985), *Rules, Exceptions, and Social Order*, Berkeley: University of California Press.
Edwards, Elizabeth (1992), 'Introduction,' in Elizabeth Edwards (ed.), *Anthropology and Photography 1860–1920*, New Haven and London: Yale University Press, pp. 3–17.
Ember, Carol R., and Melvin Ember (1999), *Cultural Anthropology* (9th ed.), Upper Saddle River, New Jersey: Prentice Hall.
Embree, John F. (1939), *Suye Mura: A Japanese Village*, Chicago: University of Chicago Press.
Evans, Graham, and Jeffrey Newnham (1998), *The Penguin Dictionary of International Relations*, Harmondsworth: Penguin Books.
Evans-Pritchard, E. E. (1940), *The Nuer: A Description of the Modes of Livelihood and Political Institutions of a Nilotic People*, New York: Oxford University Press.
Fabian, Johannes (1983), *Time and the Other: How Anthropology Makes Its Object*, New York: Columbia University Press.
Fahim, Hussein (ed.), (1982), *Indigenous Anthropology in Non-Western Countries: Proceedings of a Burg Wartenstein Symposium*, Durham, North Carolina: Carolina Academic Press.
Freeman, Derek (1983), *Margaret Mead and Samoa: The Making and*

Unmaking of an Anthropological Myth, Cambridge, Massachusetts: Harvard University Press.

Fromm, Eric (1980), *Greatness and Limitations of Freud's Thought*, New York: Harper and Row.

Fukui, Nanako (1997), '*Kaisetsu 1: 'Nihonjin no Kōdō Patān' kara Kiku to Katana e*' (Annotation 1: From 'Japanese Behavior Patterns' to *The Chrysanthemum and the Sword*), in Ruth Benedict, *Nihonjin no Kōdō Patān (Japanese Behavior Patterns)*, Tokyo: NHK Books, pp. 139–172.

Geertz, Clifford (1983), *Local Knowledge: Further Essays in Interpretive Anthropology*, New York: Basic Books.

—— (1988), *Works and Lives: The Anthropologist as Author*, Stanford: Stanford University Press.

—— (1995), *After the Fact: Two Countries, Four Decades, One Anthropologist*, Cambridge, Massachusetts: Harvard University Press.

Gellner, Earnest (1983), *Nations and Nationalism*, Oxford: Blackwell.

Georges, Robert A. and Michael Owen Jones (1995) *Folkloristics: An Introduction*, Bloomington and Indianapolis: Indiana University Press.

Gerholm, Tomas (1995), 'Sweden: Central Ethnology, Peripheral Anthropology,' in Han. F. Vermeulen and Arturo A. Roldán (eds.), *Fieldwork and Footnotes: Studies in the History of European Anthropology*, London: Routledge, pp. 159–170.

Gerholm, Tomas, and Ulf Hannerz (1982), 'Introduction: The Shaping of National Anthropologies,' *Ethnos* 47(I–II): 5–35.

Gluck, Carol (1995), '*Sengo Shigaku no Metahisutori*' (A Meta-History of Postwar Historiography), in *Iwanami Kōza Nihon Tsūshi (Bekkan 1): Rekishi Ishiki no Genzai* (*Iwanami's Complete History of Japan, Annexed Volume 1: The Present of Historical Consciousness*), Tokyo: Iwanami Shoten, pp. 3–43.

Gorer, Geoffrey (1943), 'Japanese Character Structure,' New York: Institute for Intercultural Studies (Ruth Fulton Benedict Papers, Vassar College, Folder 103.3).

—— (1964), *The American People: A Study in National Character* (revised ed.), New York: W. W. Norton, (orig. 1948).

Gupta, Akhil, and James Ferguson (1997), 'Discipline and Practice: "The Field" as Site, Method, and Location in Anthropology,' in Akhil Gupta and James Ferguson (eds.), *Anthropological Locations: Boundaries and Grounds of a Field Science*, Berkeley: University of California Press, pp. 1–46.

Hall, Stuart (ed.), (1997), *Representation: Cultural Representations and Signifying Practices*, London: Sage.

Harris, Marvin (1989), *Cows, Pigs, Wars, and Witches: The Riddles of Culture*, New York: Vintage Books, (orig. 1974).

—— (1997), *Culture, People, Nature: An Introduction to General Anthropology* (7th ed.), New York: Longman.

Harris, Marvin, and Orna Johnson (2000), *Cultural Anthropology* (5th ed.), Boston: Allyn and Bacon.

Harris, Victor (1997), 'Some Images of Japan Held by the West in the Meiji Period,' in Kenji Yoshida and John Mack (eds.), *Ibunka no Manazashi:*

Images of Other Cultures (bilingual publication), Tokyo: NHK Service Center, pp. 142–145.
Haviland, William A. (1987), *Cultural Anthropology* (5th ed.), New York: Holt, Rinehart and Winston.
Hendry, Joy (1998), 'Introduction: The Contributions of Social Anthropology to Japanese Studies,' in Joy Hendry (ed.), *Interpreting Japanese Society: Anthropological Approaches* (2nd ed.), London: Routledge, pp. 1–12.
.... (1999), *An Introduction to Social Anthropology: Other People's Worlds*, London: Macmillan.
Hobsbawm, Eric, and Terence Ranger (eds.), (1983), *The Invention of Tradition*, Cambridge: Cambridge University Press.
Hsu, Francis, L. K. (1970), 'American Core Value and National Character' (orig. 1961), in Michael McGiffert (ed.), *The Character of Americans: A Book of Readings* (revised ed.), Homewood, Illinois: The Dorsey Press, pp. 231–249.
Hymes, Dell (1972), 'The Use of Anthropology: Critical, Political, Personal,' in Dell Hymes (ed.), *Reinventing Anthropology*, New York: Random House, pp. 3–79.
Institute of Pacific Relations (1944), 'Provisional Analytical Summary of Institute of Pacific Relations Conference on Japanese Character Structure, December 16–17, 1944,' Ruth Fulton Benedict Papers, Vassar College Library (Folder 103.4).
Ito, Abito (1996), *Kankoku* (*Korea*), Tokyo: Kawade Shobō Shinsha.
Iwata, Shigenori (1998), '*Minzokugaku to Gendai*' (Folkloristics and the Present), *Nihon Minzokugaku* (*Bulletin of the Folklore Society of Japan*) 215: 6–16.
Iwatake, Mikako (1996), *Minzokugaku no Seijisei* (*The Politics of Folklore*), Tokyo: Miraisha.
Johnson, Frank A. (1993), *Dependency and Japanese Socialization: Psychoanalytic and Anthropological Investigations into Amae*, New York: New York University Press.
Johnson, Sheila K. (1988), *The Japanese through American Eyes*, Tokyo: Kodansha International.
Jones, Delmos J. (1970), 'Towards a Native Anthropology,' *Human Organization* 29(4): 251–259.
JSE (Japanese Society of Ethnology) (1995a), *Gakkai Meishō Henkō Teian Kanren Shiryō* (*Documents Relating to the Proposal for Changing the Name of the JSE*), Tokyo: Japanese Society of Ethnology.
.... (1995b), *Fōramu* (*Forum*), Tokyo: Japanese Society of Ethnology.
.... (1996), *Fōramu* (*Forum*), Tokyo: Japanese Society of Ethnology.
.... (1997), *Gakkai Meishō Mondai nado Kentō Iinkai Hōkoku* (*A Report by the Investigative Committee on the Name Change of the JSE and Other Matters*), Tokyo: Japanese Society of Ethnology.
Kahn, Miriam (1995), 'Heterotopic Dissonance in the Museum Representation of Pacific Islands Culture,' *American Anthropologist* 97(2): 324–328.
Kawada, Junzo (1997), '*Nichiō Kindaishi no naka no Yanagita Kunio*' (Kunio Yanagita in the Modern History of Japan and Europe), *Seijo Daigaku*

Minzokugaku Kenkjūjo Kiyō (*Bulletin of the Center for Folklore Studies, Seijo University*) 21: 37–66.

Kawada, Minoru (1993), *The Origin of Ethnography in Japan: Yanagita Kunio and His Times* (translated by Toshiko Kishida-Ellis), London: Kegan Paul International.

Kawahashi, Noriko (2000), '*Posuto Koroniaru Jōkyō ni okeru Shūkyō to Jendā no Katari*' (Gender and Religion: A Postcolonial Narrative,' *Chiiki Kenkyū Ronshū* (*Bulletin of Area Studies*) 3(2):7–19.

Kawashima, Takeyoshi, Hiroshi Minami, Kizaemon Ariga, Tetsuro Watsuji, and Kunio Yanagita (1950), '*Rūsu Benedikuto "Kiku to Katana" no Ataeru Mono* (The Gift from Ruth Benedict, the Author of *The Chrysanthemum and the Sword*), *Minzokugaku Kenkyū* (*Japanese Journal of Ethnology*), 14(4):263–297.

Kelly, William (1988), 'Japan bashing,' *American Ethnologist* 15(2): 365–368.

.... (1991), 'Directions in the Anthropology of Contemporary Japan,' *Annual Review of Anthropology* 20: 395–431.

Kohn, Hans (1995), 'Western and Eastern Nationalisms,' in John Hutchinson and Anthony D. Smith (eds.), *Nationalism*, Oxford: Oxford University Press, pp. 162–165.

Komatsu, Kazuhiko (1998), '*Minzoku Chōsa no Niruikei*' (Two Types of Folklore Research), in Ajio Fukuta (ed.), *Minzokugaku no Hōhō* (*Methods in Folkloristics*), Tokyo: Yūzankaku, pp. 199–212.

Kondo, Dorinne K. (1990), *Crafting Selves: Power, Gender, and Discourses in a Japanese Workplace*, Chicago: University of Chicago Press.

Koschmann, J. Victor, Keibo Oiwa, and Shinji Yamashita (eds.), (1985), *International Perspectives on Yanagita Kunio and Japanese Folklore Studies* (Cornell East Asia Series 37), Ithaca: Cornell University East Asia Program.

Kuper, Adam (1983), *Anthropology and Anthropologists: The Modern British School* (revised ed.), London: Routledge & Kegan Paul.

Kurita, Yasuyuki (ed.), (2001), *Kaigai no Hakubutsukan Bijutsukan ni okeru Nihon Tenji no Kiso Kenkyū* (*Basic Research on the Display of Japan in Foreign Museums*), Research Report, Grant-in-Aid for Scientific Research (Basic Research A-2), 1998–2001, the Ministry of Education, Science, Sports and Culture, Japan.

Kuwayama, Takami (1991), 'Japanese Individuality: The Group Model Reconsidered through Native Eyes,' *Anthropology Newsletter,* April, 1991.

.... (1992), 'The Reference Other Orientation,' in Nancy R. Rosenberger (ed.), *Japanese Sense of Self*, Cambridge: Cambridge University Press, pp. 121–151.

.... (1994), 'Japan's Place in the Global Community: Is Japan Eastern or Western?' *Virginia Geographer* 26: 1–10.

.... (1996a), 'The Familial (*Ie*) Model of Japanese Society,' in Josef Kreiner and Hans D. Ölschleger (eds.), *Japanese Culture and Society: Models of Interpretation*, München: Iudicium, pp. 143–188.

.... (1996b), '*Amerika no Jinruigaku no Kyōkasho to Nihonjinzō*' (Images of the Japanese in American Anthropology Textbooks), *Newsletter Bunka Jinruigaku* (*Newsletter, Cultural Anthropology*) 3:14–15.

.... (1997a), '*"Genchi" no Jinrui Gakusha*' ('Native' Anthropologists), *Minzokugaku Kenkyū (Japanese Journal of Ethnology)* 61(4): 517–542.
.... (1997b), 'Native Anthropologists: With Special Reference to Japanese Studies Inside and Outside Japan,' *Japan Anthropology Workshop Newsletter* 26 and 27: 52–56.
.... (1997c), 'Response to Jan van Bremen,' *Japan Anthropology Workshop Newsletter* 26 and 27: 66–69.
.... (1999), '*Sōtaishugi to Fuhenshugi no Hazama de*' (Between Relativism and Universalism), in Tsuyoshi Nakano (ed.), *Hikaku Bunka towa Nani ka* (*What is Comparative Culture?*), Tokyo: Daisanbunmei-sha, pp. 200–236.
.... (2000), '*Yanagita Kunio no "Sekai Minzokugaku" Saikō*' (A Reconsideration of Kunio Yanagita's 'Global Folkloristics'), *Nihon Minzokugaku (Bulletin of the Folklore Society of Japan)* 222: 1–32.
.... (2001a), 'The Discourse of *Ie* (Family) in Japan's Cultural Nationalism: A Critique,' *Japanese Review of Cultural Anthropology* 2:3–37.
.... (2001b), '*Amerika no Bunka Jinruigaku Kyōkasho no Naiyō Bunsekii*' (A Content Analysis of American Textbooks on Cultural Anthropology), *Kokuritsu Minzokugaku Hakubutsukan Kenkyū Hōkoku (Bulletin of the National Museum of Ethnology)* 25(3): 355–384.
Lebra, Takie Sugiyama (1993), 'Culture, Self, and Communication in Japan and the United States,' in William B. Gudykunst (ed.), *Communication in Japan and the United States*, New York: State University of New York Press, pp. 51–87.
Lee, O-Young (1984), *The Compact Culture: The Japanese Tradition of 'Smaller is Better,'* Tokyo: Kodansha International.
Lee, Sa-Hyun, Su-Kun Chang, and Kwang-Kyu Lee (1991), *An Introduction to Korean Folklore Studies: A New Edition* (in Korean), Seoul: Ilchokak.
Lévi-Strauss, Claude (1992), *The View from Afar*, Chicago: University of Chicago Press.
Lewis, Oscar (1951), *Life in a Mexican Village: Tepoztlán Restudied*. Urbana, Illinois: University of Illinois Press.
.... (1961), *The Children of Sanchez: Autobiography of a Mexican Family*, New York: Vintage Books.
Linnekin, Jocelyn S. (1983), 'Defining Tradition,' *American Ethnologist* 10: 241–252.
Lutz, Catherine A., and Jane L. Collins (1993), *Reading National Geographic*, Chicago: University of Chicago Press.
Mabuchi, Toichi (1964), 'Spiritual Predominance of the Sister,' in Alan H. Smith (ed.), *Ryukyuan Culture and Society: A Survey*, Honolulu: University of Hawaii Press, pp. 79–91.
Malinowski, Bronislaw (1984), *Argonauts of the Western Pacific: An Account of Native Enterprise and Adventure in the Archipelagoes of Melanesian New Guinea*, Prospect Heights, Illinois: Waveland Press, (Orig. 1922).
Marcus, George E. and Michael M. J. Fischer (1986), *Anthropology as Cultural Critique: An Experimental Moment in the Human Sciences*, Chicago: University of Chicago Press.
Maquet, Jacques J. (1964), 'Objectivity in Anthropology,' *Current Anthropology* 5(1): 47–55.

Mautner, Thomas (ed.), (1999), *The Penguin Dictionary of Philosophy*, Harmondsworth: Penguin Books.
Maxwell, Joseph A. (1999), 'A Realist/Postmodern Concept of Culture,' in E. L. Cerroni-Long (ed.), *Anthropological Theory in North America*, Westport, Connecticut: Bergin & Garvey, pp. 142–173.
Mead, Margaret (1928), *Coming of Age in Samoa: A Psychological Study of Primitive Youth for Western Civilization*, New York: William Morrow.
.... (1959), *An Anthropologist at Work: Writings of Ruth Benedict*, Boston: Houghton Mifflin.
.... (2000), *And Keep Your Powder Dry: An Anthropologist Looks at America* (with an introduction by Hervé Varenne), New York: Berghahn Books, (orig. 1943).
Mead, Margaret and Rhoda Métraux (eds.), (1953), *The Study of Culture at a Distance*, Chicago: University of Chicago Press.
Medicine, Beatrice (2001), *Learning to Be an Anthropologist and Remaining 'Native': Selected Writings*, Urbana and Chicago: University of Illinois Press.
Messenger, John (1969), *Inis Beag: Isle of Ireland*, New York: Holt, Rinehart and Winston.
Messerschmidt, Donald A. (1981), 'On Anthropology "at home,"' in Donald A. Messerschmidt (ed.), *Anthropologists at Home in North America: Methods and Issues in the Study of One's Own Society*, Cambridge: Cambridge University Press, pp. 3–14.
Messerschmidt, Donald A. (ed.), (1981), *Anthropologists at Home in North America: Methods and Issues in the Study of One's Own Society*, Cambridge: Cambridge University Press.
Miyoshi, Masao (1991), *Off Center: Power and Culture Relations between Japan and the United States*, Cambridge, Massachusetts: Harvard University Press.
Moore, Henrietta L. (1996), 'The Changing Nature of Anthropological Knowledge: An Introduction,' in Henrietta L. Moore (ed.), *The Future of Anthropological Knowledge*, London: Routledge, pp. 1–15.
Morgan, Lewis Henry (1877), *Ancient Society: Researches in the Lines of Human Progress from Savagery, through Barbarism to Civilization*, New York: Henry Holt.
Morse, Ronald A. (1990), *Yanagita Kunio and the Folklore Movement: The Search for Japan's National Character and Distinctiveness*, New York: Garland Publishers.
Nakane, Chie (1967), *Garo and Khasi: A Comparative Study in Matrilineal Systems*, The Hague: Mouton.
.... (1970), *Japanese Society*, Berkeley: University of California Press.
.... (1987), *Shakai Jinruigaku (Social Anthropology)*, Tokyo: University of Tokyo Press.
Nanda, Serena, and Richard L. Warms (1998), *Cultural Anthropology* (6th ed.), Belmont, California: Wadsworth.
Narayan, Kirin (1993a), 'How Native is a "Native" Anthropologist?' *American Anthropologist* 95(3): 671–686.
.... (1993b), 'Refractions of the Field at Home: American Represent-

ations of Hindu Holy Men in the 19th and 20th Centuries,' *Cultural Anthropology* 8(4): 476–509.
Niessen, Sandra A. (1994), 'The Ainu in Mimpaku: A Representation of Japan's Indigenous People at the National Museum of Ethnology,' *Museum Anthropology* 18(3): 18–25.
.... (1997), 'Representing the Ainu Reconsidered,' *Museum Anthropology* 20(3): 132–144.
Nishikawa, Nagao (1992), *Kokkyō no Koekata (Beyond National Boundaries)*, Tokyo: Chikuma Shobō.
Norbeck, Edward, and Margaret Lock (eds.), (1987), *Health, Illness, and Medical Care in Japan: Cultural and Social Dimensions*, Honolulu: University of Hawaii Press.
Oboler, Suzanne (1995), *Ethnic Labels, Latino Lives: Identity and the Politics of (Re)Presentation in the United States*, Minneapolis: University of Minnesota Press.
Ohnuki-Tierney, Emiko (1987), *The Monkey as Mirror: Symbolic Transformations in Japanese History and Ritual*, Princeton: Princeton University Press.
Ohtsuka, Kazuyoshi (1997), 'Exhibiting Ainu Culture at Minpaku: A Reply to Sandra A. Niessen,' *Museum Anthropology* 20(3): 108–119.
Oka, Masao (1979), *Ijin Sonota (Strangers and Others)*. Tokyo: Gensōsha.
Ota, Yoshinobu (1993), '*Orientarizumu Hihan to Bunka Jinruigaku*' (Anthropology and Postcolonial Criticism), *Kokuritsu Minzokugaku Hakubutsukan Kenkyū Hōkoku (Bulletin of the National Museum of Ethnology)* 18(3): 453–494.
Peoples, James, and Garrick Bailey (2000), *Humanity: An Introduction to Cultural Anthropology* (5th ed.), Belmont, California: Wadsworth.
Reber, Arthur S. (ed.) (1995), *The Penguin Dictionary of Psychology* (2nd ed.), Harmondsworth: Penguin Books.
Redfield, Robert (1930), *Tepoztlán: A Mexican Village*, Chicago: University of Chicago Press.
Reischauer, Edwin O. (and Marius B. Jansen) (1995), *The Japanese Today: Change and Continuity* (enlarged ed.), Cambridge, Massachusetts: Harvard University Press.
Rosaldo, Renato (1989), *Culture and Truth: The Remaking of Social Analysis*, Boston: Beacon Press.
Roscoe, Paul B. (1995), 'The Perils of "Positivism" in Cultural Anthropology,' *American Anthropologist* 97(3): 492–504.
Rosman, Abraham, and Paul G. Rubel (1998), *The Tapestry of Culture: An Introduction to Cultural Anthropology* (6th ed.), New York: McGraw-Hill.
Sahlins, Marshall D. (1976), *Culture and Practical Reason*, Chicago: University of Chicago Press.
Said, Edward (1978), *Orientalism*, New York: Vintage Books.
Sakai, Naoki (1997), *Translation and Subjectivity: On 'Japan' and Cultural Nationalism*, Minneapolis: University of Minnesota Press.
Sano, Kenji (1998), '*Hikaku Kenkyū*' (Comparative Research), in Ajio Fukuta (ed.), *Minzokugaku no Hōhō (Methods in Folkloristics)*, Tokyo: Yūzankaku, pp. 115–131.

Sato, Ikuya (1992), *Fīrudo Wāku* (*Fieldwork*), Tokyo: Shinyōsha.
Scheper-Hughes, Nancy (1979), *Saints, Scholars, and Schizophrenics: Mental Illness in Rural Ireland*, Berkeley: University of California Press.
Schneider, David M. (1968), *American Kinship: A Cultural Account*, Chicago: University of Chicago Press.
Schwimmer, Brian (1996), 'Anthropology on the Internet: A Review and Evaluation of Networked Resources,' *Current Anthropology* 37(3): 561–568.
Scupin, Raymond (2000), *Cultural Anthropology: A Global Perspective* (4th ed.), Upper Saddle River, New Jersey: Prentice Hall.
Scupin, Raymond, and Christopher R. DeCorse (1998), *Anthropology: A Global Perspective* (3rd ed.), Upper Saddle River, New Jersey: Prentice Hall.
Sekimoto, Teruo (1995), '*Nihon no Jinruigaku to Nihon Shigaku*' (Japanese Anthropology and Japanese Historiography), in *Iwanami Kōza Nihon Tsūshi* (*Bekkan 1*)*: Rekishi Ishiki no Genzai* (*Iwanami's Complete History of Japan, Annexed Volume 1: The Present of Historical Consciousness*), Tokyo: Iwanami Shoten, pp. 123–147.
Shahrani, M. Nazif (1994), 'Honored Guest and Marginal Man: Long-Term Field Research and Predicaments of a Native Anthropologist,' in Don D. Fowler and Donald L. Hardesty (eds.), *Others Knowing Others: Perspectives on Ethnographic Careers*, Washington: Smithsonian Institute Press, p. 15–67.
Shimizu, Akitoshi (1997), 'Cooperation, not Domination: A Rejoinder to Niessen on the Ainu Exhibition at Minpaku,' *Museum Anthropology* 20(3): 120–131.
Shorter, Edward (1977), *The Making of Modern Family*. New York: Basic Books.
Sinha, Vineeta (2000a), 'Moving beyond Critique: Practising the Social Sciences in the Context of Globalization, Postmodernity and Post-coloniality,' *Southeast Asian Journal of Social Science* 28(1): 67–104.
.... (2000b), 'Socio-Cultural Theory and Colonial Encounters: The Discourse on Indigenizing Anthropology in India,' Working Papers No. 148, Department of Sociology, National University of Singapore.
Smith, Anthony D. (1991), *National Identity*, Harmondsworth: Penguin Books.
Smith, Robert J. (1989), '*Beikoku ni okeru Nihon Kenkyū*' (Japanese Studies in the United States), *Minzokugaku Kenkyū* (*Japanese Journal of Ethnology*) 54(3): 360–374.
Sofue, Takao, S. Wang, and Michio Suenari (1989), '*Zadankai: Nihon Kenkyū o dō Kangaeruka*' (Forum: Perspectives on Japanese Studies), *Minzokugaku Kenkyū* (*Japanese Journal of Ethnology*) 54(3): 410–419.
Sorokin, Pitirim, Carl Zimmerman, and Charles Gaplin (1965), 'The Family as the Basic Institution and Familism as the Fundamental Relationship of Rural Social Organization,' in Pitirim Sorokin, Carl Zimmerman, and Charles Gaplin (eds.), *A Systematic Source Book in Rural Sociology* (*Vol.2*), New York: Russel & Russel, pp. 3–123.
Sosnoski, Daniel (ed.), (1996), *Introduction to Japanese Culture*, Rutland, Vermont & Tokyo: Charles E. Tuttle Company.

References

Srinivas, M. N. (1966), *Social Change in Modern India*, Berkeley: University of California Press.

.... (1976), *The Remembered Village*. Berkeley: University of California Press.

Stevens, Rebecca A. T. (1996), 'Introduction,' in Rebecca A. T. Stevens and Yoshiko Iwamoto Wada (eds.), *The Kimono Inspiration: Art and Art-To-Wear in America*, San Francisco: Pomegranate Artbooks, pp. 15–19.

Sugimoto, Yoshio (2000), *Ōsutoraria* (*Australia*), Tokyo: Iwanami Shoten.

Suzuki, Daisetz T. (1940), *Zen to Nihon Bunka* (*Zen and Japanese Culture*) (translated from English by Momoo Kitagawa), Tokyo: Iwanami Shoten.

Suzuki, Eitaro (1940), *Nihon Nōson Shakaigaku Genri* (*Principles of Japanese Rural Sociology*), Tokyo: Jichōsha.

Takezawa, Yasuko (1988), '*Amerika Gasshūkoku ni okeru Sutereotaipu to Esunishiti*' (Ethnic Stereotypes in the U.S.A.), *Minzokugaku Kenkyū* (*Japanese Journal of Ethnology*) 52(4): 363–390.

Tanabe, Shigeharu (1994), *Ecology and Practical Technology: Peasant Farming Systems in Thailand*, Bangkok: White Lotus.

Thompson, John B. (1990), *Ideology and Modern Culture: Critical Social Theory in the Era of Mass Communication*, Stanford: Stanford University Press.

Trask, Haunani-Kay (1999), *From a Native Daughter: Colonialism and Sovereignty in Hawai'i* (revised ed.), Honolulu: University of Honolulu Press.

Tsurumi, Kazuko (1975), 'Yanagita Kunio's Work as a Model of Endogenous Development,' *Japan Quarterly* 22 (3).

van Bremen, Jan (1997), 'Prompters who do not Appear on the Stage: Japanese Anthropology and Japanese Studies in American and European Anthropology,' *Japan Anthropology Workshop Newsletter* 26/27: 57–65.

Wada, Yoshiko I. (1996), 'The History of the Kimono: Japan's National Dress,' in Rebecca A. T. Stevens and Yoshiko Iwamoto Wada (eds.), *The Kimono Inspiration: Art and Art-To-Wear in America*, San Francisco: Pomegranate Artbooks, pp. 131–160.

Wallerstein, Immanuel (1979), *The Capitalist World-Economy*, Cambridge: Cambridge University Press.

Yamamoto, Matori (1994), '*Han-Shokuminchishugi no Sekushuariti*' (Sexuality in Anti-Colonialism), *Shakai Jinruigaku Nenpō* (*Annals of Social Anthropology*) 20:111–130.

Yamashita, Shinji (ed.), (1996), *Kankō Jinruigaku* (*The Anthropology of Tourism*), Tokyo: Shinyōsha.

Yanagita, Kunio (1957), *Japanese Manners and Customs in the Meiji Era* (translated and adapted by Charles S. Terry), Tokyo: Ōbunsha.

.... (1964), '*Hikaku Minzokugaku no Mondai*' (Problems in Comparative Folkloristics), in *Teihon Yanagita Kunio-shū* (*The Works of Kunio Yanagita, Standard Edition*), Volume 30, Tokyo: Chikuma Shobō.

.... (1970), *About Our Ancestors* (translated by Fanny H. Mayer and Yasuyo Ishiwara), Tokyo: Japan Society for the Promotion of Science.

.... (1972), *Japanese Folk Tales* (translated by Fanny H. Mayer), Taipei: Orient Cultural Service.

.... (1975), *The Legends of Tōno* (translated, with an introduction, by Ronald A. Morse), Tokyo: Japan Foundation.
.... (1998a), *Seinen to Gakumon* (*Youth and Scholarship*), in *Yanagita Kunio Zenshū* (*The Complete Works of Kunio Yanagita*), Volume 4, Tokyo: Chikuma Shobō, (orig. 1928).
.... (1998b), *Minkan Denshōron* (*The Science of Popular Tradition*), in *Yanagita Kunio Zenshū* (*The Complete Works of Kunio Yanagita*), Volume 8, Tokyo: Chikuma Shobō, (orig. 1934).
.... (1998c), *Kyōdo Seikatsu no Kenkyūhō* (*Methods in the Study of Community Life*), in *Yanagita Kunio Zenshū* (*The Complete Works of Kunio Yanagita*), Volume 8, Tokyo: Chikuma Shobō, (orig. 1935).
Yanagita, Kunio, Shinobu Orikuchi, and Eiichiro Ishida (1965), '*Minzokugaku kara Minzokugaku e*' (From Folkloristics to Ethnology), in Kunio Yanagita et al., *Minzokugaku ni tsuite* (*On Folkloristics*), Tokyo: Chikuma Shobō, pp. 49–86.
Yoshida, Kenji (1999), *Bunka no Hakken* (*The Discovery of Culture*), Tokyo: Iwanami Shoten.
.... (2001), '*Kioku to Bōkyaku no Sōchi*' (Devices for Remembering and Forgetting), in *Kaigai no Hakubutsukan Bijutsukan ni okeru Nihon Tenji no Kiso Kenkyū (Basic Research on the Display of Japan in Foreign Museums)*, Research Report, Grant-in-Aid for Scientific Research (Basic Research A-2), 1998–2001, the Ministry of Education, Science, Sports and Culture, Japan, pp. 112–120.

Index

Abram, Simone, 158
absolute standards of morality, 93
Abu-Lughod, Lila, 152
academic hegemony, 1, 25, 30, 73 *See also* hegemony
academic world system, 9–10, 28–29, 36, 45–46, 48, 50–51, 55–56, 60–61, 63–64, 74–75, 78, 86, 146–147 *See also* world system
Africa, 1, 8, 28, 38, 78, 117, 157
African social science, 13
Africanists, 8
Africans, 8, 28
Afrocentrism, 8
Aguilar, John L., 20
Ainu, 10–12, 80, 118, 120, 147
aji (taste), 81
ajiwau (taste; appreciate), 81–82
Akimoto, Shunkichi, 99
Alatas, Syed Farid, 2
aloha 'āina, 7–8
alternative discourse, 2
amae (dependence), 112, 155
ambiguity, 155
American Anthropological Association (AAA), 24, 112, 117, 146–147
American Anthropologist, 145, 147
American anthropology, North, 10, 39, 51, 88, 115, 117–118, 120, 126–127, 131, 142, 144, 156
American character, 87–88
American Ethnological Society (AES), 43, 118
American Folklore Society, 81
Amino, Yoshihiko, 79, 123
Amory, Deborah, 147
analytical understanding, 65, 84–86 *See also* embodied understanding
Anderson, Benedict, 81
Anglo-Americanization, 53
Anglophone world, 6
Annales school, the, 71, 151
anonymity, 41, 43
anthropological knowledge, 35, 38, 117, 148; as partial, 38, 55; regional bias of, 117; structure of, 3, 25–26, 30
anthropological self, 38, 62
anthropologists' world maps, 116
anthropology at home, 4
apartheid, 52
Apollonian, 91, 153
Appadurai, Arjun, 21, 136
aratama (negative power), 103
arcs of life, 98
Asad, Talal, 29, 52
Asante, Molefi Kete, 8, 146–147
Ashcroft, Bill, 150

171

Asia Pacific Sociological Association, 150
Asia, 1, 38, 48–49, 52, 56–57, 59–62, 72, 76, 157
Asian anthropology, 59
Asian social science, 61, 63
Asia-Pacific region, 38, 74, 157
Asquith, Pamela J., 30
atama (head), 82
audience, 19, 21, 30, 35, 41–42, 46, 62, 81, 152 See also readership
Averill, Roger, 80

Bachnik, Jane M., 18
Bailey, Garrick, 119, 156
Bakalaki, Alexandra, 21
Barrett, Richard A., 119, 123, 156
Barthes, Roland, 137
baseball, 122, 124
Bates, Daniel G., 119, 156
Bateson, Gregory, 155
Beardsley, Richard K., 22
Befu, Harumi, 22–23, 39–40, 45, 50
Bellah, Robert, 106
Benedict, Ruth F., 15, 17, 21, 38, 46, 87–114, 118, 121–122, 127–129, 142, 148, 153–155
Bhabha, Homi, 59
binarism, 49–50, 58, 122, 150
binary opposition, 56, 150
Boas, Franz, 69–70, 142
Bohannan, Paul, 119, 153
bow/bowing, 92, 124–125, 129–130, 157
brainwashing, 11–12

Brettell, Caroline B., 2, 16, 147
Bryan, C. D. B., 137
Buddhism, 95, 154
Burke, Peter, 151
Burne, Charlotte, 150

Caffrey, Margaret M., 99
calligraphy, 126, 139
Canada/Canadian, 11–12, 134
Cartesian dualism, 83
Chen, Kuan-Hsing, 59, 149
child rearing, 93, 97, 100, 111 See also socialization
China, 52, 67, 124, 129, 143–144, 151, 158
Chinese, 57, 123, 152
Chrysanthemum and the Sword, The, 15, 46, 87–114, 121–122, 127, 148, 153–155
chū (loyalty), 92, 102, 104, 106, 155
class, 18, 31–32, 58, 79–80, 102, 105, 107–109, 118, 120, 138
Clifford, James, 5, 38–40, 42–43
co-authorship, 41
coevalness, 134, 144
collectivism, 35–36, 122, 142 See also group orientation
Collins, Jane L., 157–158
colonial roots of anthropology, 3, 21, 38, 48, 73
colonialism, 21, 28, 58–59, 150; internal, 25; scientific, 27–28, 36
colonization, 57–59

counter-hegemonic discourse, 73–74, 77
Crapo, Richard H., 119, 122, 156
critical knowledge, 20
Culbert, T. Patrick, 119, 156
cultural, comparison, 36, 66, 70, 143; contrast, 36, 98; essentialism, 18; festivals, 139; identity, 18, 139–140; mirror, 113; nationalism, 8, 13–14, 61, 65, 84, 86 See also nationalism; pluralism, 83; purity, 18; relativism, 24, 53, 142–143; revival, 7; unconscious, 20
Cultural Anthropology, 145
cultural representation, 2, 5, 11, 14–15, 20, 38–40, 91, 117, 135, 140, 142, 145; points of reference in, 19, 91, 143
culture-and-personality, *See* psychological anthropology
Cushing, Frank Hamilton, 18–19, 147

Dale, Peter N., 24
de Tocqueville, Alex, 104, 108
decolonization, 86, 148
deconstruction, 55, 76, 80, 88, 113, 152
DeCorse, Christopher R., 119, 124–126, 129, 131–133, 156
dependence/dependency, 110, 111–112, 155

Descartes, René, 83
describer – described, 1–2, 5–6, 17, 35, 37–44, 45, 48, 75, 112–114; conspiracy between, 137, 139–140; power differences between, 2, 21, 41, 48
dialogic, circle of ethnography, 7; Other/others, 6, 36; partners, 1, 14, 37; space, 45, 64, 75–76, 86, 113
dialogue, 5–6, 15, 22, 25–26, 36, 41, 43, 46–47, 85–86; forum for, 41, 45, 75, 78
digital divide, 75
Dionysian, 91–92, 153
Dirks, Nicholas B., 51, 149
displayed, the, 5
displayers, 4–5
Doi, Takeo, 112, 155
domination, 8, 21, 55–56, 61–62, 74, 84, 141, 150
double consciousness, 95
double dealing, 102
Douglas, Mary, 102–103, 155
Dower, John W., 141
dōzoku (federation of *ie*), 126 *See also* ie
dualistic universe, 155
duality, 74, 83, 91–95, 98, 103, 127–129, 155
Dunaif-Hattis, Janet, 119, 122
Dundes, Alan, 74–75

Eades, J. S., 28
Eagleton, Terry, 149
East Asia Section within AAA, 118, 157

East Asia, 57, 67, 72, 117–118, 153, 157
East, the, 50–51, 57 *See also* the Orient
Ebuchi, Kazukimi, 129
Edgerton, Robert B., 34
Edwards, Elizabeth, 131
egalitarianism, 109, 111, 149
Einfühlung, 153
Eley, Geoff, 51, 149
Ember, Carol R., 119, 121, 125, 130, 156
Ember, Melvin, 119, 121, 125, 130, 156
embodied understanding, 65, 84–86 *See also* analytical understanding
Embree, John F., 21
emic – etic, 89
empathy, 82–83, 85, 152
Emperor, 61, 90–92, 95, 102, 104–106, 109–110, 122, 154–155; as Good Father, 110, 155; as Sacred Chief, 95
English, 19, 30–31, 39, 46, 52–54, 57–58, 75, 81, 123, 149, 151
Enlightenment, the, 83
equality, 103–105, 109–110
Eskimo-type kinship, 126
ethnic groups, 66, 69–70, 136, 158
ethnic minority, 11, 20, 44, 80, 108, 118, 120
ethnographic reading, and writing, 1, 15, 30; in reverse, 87, 94, 112–113, 153
ethnographic triad, 4–6, 112

ethnography, 2, 5, 7, 30, 33, 41, 64, 77–78, 82, 112–113, 152; as homemade, 5, 35; Orientalist, 37; postmodern, 35; reflexive, 35–36, 41; reverse, 94, 112
ethnology, 10, 22, 25, 49, 52, 59, 69–71, 73, 77–78, 82, 146, 148, 151
Eurocentrism, 1, 60–61, 150
Evans, Graham, 79
Evans-Pritchard, E., E., 18, 62
exotic others, 48
experimental writing, 6
Fabian, Johannes, 7, 36, 134
Fahim, Hussein, 1, 4
familism, 36
family state, 32, 61, 104–105
feather headdress, 136
feminization, 129, 140–142
Ferguson, James, 21, 55–56, 157–158
Ferraro, Gary, 119, 156
field, 5, 15–16, 19, 21, 39, 53, 114, 146
fieldwork, 4–7, 12–13, 21, 23–24, 28, 33, 37, 43, 53, 73, 113, 146–148
First Nation, 11
first-class citizens, 108
Fischer, Michael M. J., 6
five blind men and the elephant, 38, 72
flower arranging, 42, 126, 140
flower shows, 92, 153
Folklore Society of Japan, 81

folklore, 13–14, 64–65, 69, 71–75, 77, 81, 84, 150–151
folkloristics (folklore studies), 64, 67–72, 74, 76, 81, 83, 85, 150–152; comparative, 66–67, 85; global, 14, 64–70, 72, 74–76, 78–79, 85–86, 151; Japanese, 14, 64, 74, 82, 84; national, 14, 65–66, 68–71, 78–79, 86
Foucault, Michel, 36
four-field approach, 156
France, 9, 25–26, 45, 50, 55, 62, 107–108, 134, 137
Fratkin, Elliot M., 156
Frazer, James, 14, 74–75, 150
free areas of life, 98
Freeman, Derek, 38
Fromm, Eric, 155
Fukui, Nanako, 92
full-bodied experience, 82, 84

gaze, 48, 141, 146
Geertz, Clifford, 5, 20, 26, 35, 53, 87–88, 146, 149
geisha, 129, 137, 142
Gellner, Earnest, 24, 152
gender, 18, 79, 105, 118, 120, 123–124, 129, 133, 142–143, 154
generalization, 80
generic past, 144
Genji Monogatari, 123
Georges, Robert A., 151
Gerholm, Tomas, 9, 26–27, 49–51
German romanticism, *See* romanticism

Germany, 61, 104, 134
Gestalt, 96
giri (obligation), 89, 92, 104, 148; to one's name, 89, 104, 107, 153; to the world, 104
global folkloristics, *See* folkloristics
globalization, 37, 57, 62–63, 77, 79, 86
Gluck, Carol, 60
going native, 18
Gorer, Geoffrey, 88, 99–100, 109, 111–112, 154–155
Great Britain, 9, 25–26, 45, 50, 56, 58, 62, 140, 151, 156
Griffiths, Gareth, 150
Grimm, Jacob, 74
Group of Eight (G8), 134
group orientation, 34 *See also* collectivism
guilt, 96–97
guilt culture, 96–97
Gupta, Akhil, 21, 55–56, 157–158

Hall, John W., 22
Hall, Stuart, 137
Han, Kyung-Koo, 60
Hannerz, Ulf, 26–27, 50
Harris, Marvin, 89, 119, 122–123, 133–134, 156–157
Harris, Victor, 139
Haviland, William A., 119, 128–129, 156
Hawaii, 7–8
Hearn, Lafcadio, 129
hegemony, 12, 29, 45, 54, 56, 149 *See also* academic hegemony

Hendry, Joy, 50, 125, 127, 157
Herder, Johann Gottfried, 83, 153
heritage, concepts of, 158
hierarchy, 90–92, 94, 103–105, 108–109, 158
hikaku minzokugaku, 66 *See also* comparative folkloristics
hiragana, 123 *See also* kana
Hirohito, 110–11
Hispanic, 57
historiography, 60, 68, 73
Hobsbawm, Eric, 79, 139
holiness, 102–103
Hollywood, 124, 130, 157
home, anthropological notion of, 135, 145, 148, 157–158
homemade, anthropology as, 5, 35
homogeneity, 79
homogenization, 51, 80
honne (truth) – *tatemae* (principle), 95
Howard, Michael C., 119, 122
Hsu, Francis L. K., 112
Hughte, Phil, 147
Hull, Cordell, 104
hybridity, 59
hybrids, 102
Hymes, Dell, 28

ideology, 55, 96, 149–150
ie (family), 31–34, 36–37, 118, 126; consciousness, 149
ikkoku minzokugaku, 65 *See also* national folkloristics

India, 58, 76, 124, 136, 151–152, 157
Indian/Indians, 18, 58–59
indigenous, 3
indigenous, people's rights, 2, 48. *See also* native rights movement; social science, 1; system of thought, 13, 61
individual freedom, 34, 106
individualism, 34–36, 110, 122, 142
Indonesia, 146
indulgence, 98–99
industrialization, 125, 131
infantile sexuality, 99
insider research, 3–4, 21
Institute of Pacific Relations, 109–110
Institute of Social and Cultural Anthropology, Oxford, 62
integrity, 95–96, 98, 103 *See also* uniformity; unity
International Research Center for Japanese Studies, Kyoto, 23
internationalization, 57
Internet, 41, 43, 75, 149
inter-subjective reality, 40
Irish, 16
Ishida, Eiichiro, 85
Italianness, 137
Italy/Italian, 104, 134, 137
Ito, Abito, 58
Iwata, Shigenori, 79
Iwatake, Mikako, 83

Japan, and colonialism, 38, 52, 57–59, 74, 76, 139, 150; and its Asian

neighbors, 52, 57, 76; as betwixt and between, 38; as homogeneous nation, 79–80, 155; as semi-periphery in world system, 52; exotic, 143
Japan Anthropology Workshop (JAWS), 46
Japan Society, 139–140
Japanese, anthropologists, 4, 10–11, 19, 22, 25–26, 35, 46, 51, 57, 60, 147; anthropology, 25, 28, 51–52, 54, 83, 148; art, 126–127; character, 93–94, 98–99, 107, 109, 121, 127–128, 154; collectivism, 35–36, 122, 142; ethics, 94, 97, 101; ethnography, 77; femininity, 129, 138; historiography, 60; individuality, 24; primatology, 30; scholarship, 10, 23, 29, 73–74; soldiers, 92, 103; spirit, 84; women, 101, 117, 121, 124, 129, 137, 140, 154
Japanese, the, as group-oriented people, 24, 34; as debtors to the ages, 105; as honorary whites, 52; as natives, 3; brainwashing of, 11–12; collaboration with, 23
Japanese Journal of Ethnology, 22, 25, 148
Japanese Society of Cultural Anthropology, 59
Japanese Society of Ethnology (JSE), 22, 52, 59, 146–147
Japanese studies, 15, 23, 39, 45–46, 50, 85
Japaneseness, 130, 135, 137
jichō (self-respect), 153
jiko shōsatsu no gaku (science of introspection), 76, 84
Johnson, Frank A., 155
Johnson, Orna, 133, 156
Johnson, Sheila K., 57, 129
jōmin (plebeian), 73
Jones, Delmos J., 19, 29, 148
Jones, Michael Owen, 151
Judeo-Christian, 97, 103
judo, 139

kabuki, 42, 126, 138
Kahn, Miriam, 144
Kaho'olawe, 7–8
kami (god), 90
Kamikaze, 92
kana (syllabic letters), 123
kanji (Chinese characters), 123
Kant, Immanuel, 83
karada (minded body), 82, 153
Kawada, Junzo, 77–78
Kawada, Minoru, 69, 151
Kawahashi, Noriko, 148
Kawashima, Takeyoshi, 15, 113
Kayano, Shigeru, 10–11, 147
Keesing, Roger M., 153
keigo (honorifics), 123
Kelly, William, 21, 24
kimono, 117, 121, 124–125, 129–131, 133, 135–142, 157

177

kō (filial piety), 92, 104, 106
Kohn, Hans, 61
kokoro (bodied mind), 153
Komatsu, Kazuhiko, 84
Kondo, Dorinne K., 31–37, 41, 148–149
Korea, 52, 58, 60, 67, 151, 158
Korean, 57, 123, 150
Korean Cultural Anthropology, 60
Korean Society for Cultural Anthropology (KSCA), 60
Koreans, 39, 58, 80
Koschmann, J. Victor, 151
Kottak, Conrad Philip, 119, 156
Kreiner, Josef, 39
Krohn, Kaarle, 74
Kuper, Adam, 156
Kurita, Yasuyuki, 158
Kuwayama, Takami, 24, 34, 36, 49, 54, 56, 65, 84, 104, 116, 118, 149, 154–155
Kwakiutl, 91
kyōdo kenkyū (community studies), 68, 77, 84, 146
Kyōdo Seikatsu no Kenkyūhō, 68, 71, 73, 81, 151
kyōdoshika (local historians), 84

language, barrier, 29, 71; local, 6, 12, 20, 81; problems, 4, 29; social construction of, 29, 52; use of non-native, 52; women's, 124
Latin America, 27, 117, 146, 157

Lavenda, Robert H., 119, 156
Lebra, Takie Sugiyama, 22, 153
Lee, Iacocca, 141
Lee, O-Young, 42
Lévi-Strauss, Claude, 26, 52
Leviticus, 102
Lewis, Oscar, 2, 16, 38
Linnekin, Jocelyn, S., 7–8
local, 3
local knowledge, 26, 53
Lock, Margaret, 39
Lutz, Catherine A., 157–158

Mabuchi, Toichi, 51–52, 54
Malaysia, 150
Malinowski, Bronislaw, 16–17, 20, 77, 151
Maquet, Jacques J., 28, 38
Marcus, George E., 5–6, 38
marginalization, 13, 51, 131
Marx, Karl, 17, 149
masculinization, 141
mass media, 129, 136–137, 142
Mathews, Gordon, 49
Mautner, Thomas, 83, 153
Maxwell, Joseph A., 83
Mead, Margaret, 6, 38, 88, 97, 99, 109, 154–155
Medicine, Beatrice, 7
Meiji, 75, 102, 138–139, 157; Restoration of, 138
Melanesia, 157–158
mentality, 71
Messenger, John, 16
Messerschmidt, Donald A., 4, 21
Métraux, Rhoda, 155
metropolitan West, the, 9, 21
Mexico/Mexicans, 2, 16

miai (arranged marriage), 124–126, 130
mind – body, 83, 153
Minkan Denshōron, 64–67, 71, 73, 81, 150–151
Minpaku, 10–12
minzokugaku (ethnology), 59, 151
minzokugaku (folkloristics), 65–66, 151
miyamairi, 133
Miyoshi, Masao, 23, 29, 54
modernity, 13
monolithic universe, 155
Mononobe clan, 153
Moore, Henrietta L., 55–56
Morean, Brian, 157
Morgan, Lewis Henry, 2
Morse, Ronald A., 151
Murasaki, Shikibu, 123
museums, 5, 10–12, 141, 158; ethnological, 4, 127, 131; exhibits at, 86, 145; the study of, 4, 12; war memorial, 158

Nakane, Chie, 33, 51–52, 54, 57–58, 151
nakōdo (go-between), 124, 131
Nanda, Serena, 115, 118–119, 156
Narayan, Kirin, 18, 29–30, 136
narratives, 6, 31, 33, 35, 55, 113
nation, 34, 57, 59, 62, 64, 66, 69, 72–73, 79–81, 85–86, 89, 94, 101, 104, 110, 134, 141–142, 152; as unit of scholarship, 66, 76, 79, 152; modernist approach to the study of, 152
national character, 93, 97, 107, 112, 121–122, 154
national culture, 79–80, 137
national folkloristics, *See* folkloristics
National Geographic, 131, 137, 141, 157–158
National Museum of Ethnology, Osaka, *See* Minpaku
nationalism, 7–8, 13–14, 24, 61, 65, 73, 83–84, 86, 152
nationalistic sentiments, 20, 62, 72, 79
nationalization of culture, 61
nation-state, 24, 79–80
native, 3
native, as relational concept, 4; claims, 13, 48; discourse, 2, 9–10, 13; intellectuals/academics, 2, 4, 9, 12–13, 17, 20, 113; scholarship, 24, 27; points of view, 2, 19–20, 89; protest, 2, 7–8, 11, 16, 19, 37; rights movement, 13, 16. *See also* indigenous people's rights; texts, 12; voices as noise, 2, 9, 44
Native America/Americans, 7, 97, 117, 136, 146
native anthropologists, 1, 5, 15, 21, 45–46, 77, 113, 147, 151; and postcolonialism, 1;

Anglo-Americanization of, 53; as informants/travel guides, 25; as inspectors of Western ethnography, 78; as professional others, 15, 38; as rivals in trade, 5; definitions of, 3, 17; merits and demerits of, 4
native anthropology, 1–2, 4, 29, 44, 48; and decolonization, 148; and *The Chrysanthemum and the Sword*, 88; as attempt to overcome Eurocentrism, 1; as challenge to existing scholarship, 1; as epistemological issue, 4; definitions of, 1, 37; factors behind current interest in, 2; India as pioneer in, 151
natives, as active agents of research, 1, 68, 77, 86; as co-authors, 1; as collaborators, 1, 43; as critics of Western scholarship, 8, 15, 17; as dialogic partners, 1, 14, 37, 146; as ethnographic readers, 15, 113; as objects of representation, 1–2, 5, 15, 37; as objects of thought, 7, 30; as outsiders in anthropological discourse, 6, 30; exploitation of, 7–8, 113; who talk back, 78
Needham, Rodney, 51
Newnham, Jeffrey, 79

Niessen, Sandra A., 10–12, 147
nigitama (positive power), 103
nihonjinron (theories of the Japanese), 24, 79
Niiike village, 22
Nishida, Kitaro, 54
Nishikawa, Nagao, 24
non-verbal communication, 123–124, 129
Norbeck, Edward, 39
nuclear family, 131–134, 157

objectivity, 4, 20–21, 38–39, 41, 45, 147
Oboler, Suzanne, 57
Occident, the, 43, 57, 91, 96 *See also* the West
Occidentalism, 13
Oceania, 117
Office of War Information, 99
Ohnuki-Tierney, Emiko, 22, 103, 155
Ohtsuka, Kazuyoshi, 11–12, 147
Oiwa, Keibo, 151
Oka, Masao, 83–84
on (indebtedness; benevolence), 92, 104, 105–106, 148
open discourse, 41
open text, 41, 45
Orient, the, 36, 43, 51, 56, 89 *See also* the East
Orientalism, 2, 17, 84
Orientalism, 13, 24, 36–37, 41, 58, 88–91, 134, 136, 145
Orikuchi, Shinobu, 85

Ortner, Sherry B., 51, 149
Oswalt, Wendell, 119, 158
Ota, Yoshinobu, 41
Otherness, 59, 120, 123, 126, 130, 135, 158

Pacific War, 103
partial truths, 40, 136
particularism, 142
Pearl Harbor, 104
peculiar customs, 24, 30
peculiar intimacy, 58, 150
peer review, 10, 29
Peoples, James, 119, 156
Philadelphia Centennial Exhibition, 140
photographic representation, 127, 140
photography, 131
photojournalism, 135
photos/photographs, 33, 113, 115–145, 157
Plog, Fred, 119
plural authorship, 41–43
Pope, the 111
postcolonial, 1, 17, 146; studies, 59, 150
postcolonialism, 86
postmodern, 37, 39–40; critique, 5, 15, 40; ethnography, 35–36
postmodernism, 15, 40
power and knowledge, 2
practical knowledge, 20
primitive/primitives, 2–3, 16, 21, 37, 70, 72, 77, 149, 151
professional others, 4, 15, 38
Project Camelot, 27
psychoanalysis, 97, 154
psychoanalytic, 40, 99, 111, 154

psychological anthropology, 99, 122
psycho-semantic phenomena 67, 71
Puritanism, 97

racism, 8
Radcliffe-Brown, A. R., 18
Ranger, Terrence, 79, 139
readership, 5–6, 91 *See also* audience
Reber, Arthur S., 153
Redfield, Robert, 38, 154
reflexive anthropology, 34
Reischauer, Edwin O., 53, 153
relative deprivation, 143
relevance of Western thinking, 2
renga (linked verse), 41–42
restraint, 98
Robbins, Richard H., 119, 156
romanticism, 83, 85; German, 83
Rosaldo, Michelle, 43
Rosaldo, Renato, 37, 43
Roscoe, Paul B., 40
Rosman, Abraham, 116–117, 119, 124, 156
Rubel, Paul G., 116–117, 119, 124, 156
Russia, 74, 134, 157

Sahlins, Marshall D., 20
Said, Edward, 2, 17, 36–37, 41, 89
Sakai, Naoki, 79
salvage anthropology, 10
Samoa, 6
Samoans, 6–7

samurai (warriors), 129, 139, 141–142, 158
Sano, Kenji, 67
Sarana, Gopal, 151
Sato, Ikuya, 20
Scheper-Hughes, Nancy, 16
Schneider, David M., 20
Schultz, Emily A., 119, 156
Schusky, Ernest L., 119, 156
Schwimmer, Brian, 43, 149
science, 3, 28, 37–38, 64, 67–69, 76, 83–84, 164; Asian, 61, 63; multicultural social, 150; native, 148; social, 1, 13, 55, 60–61, 63, 150; Western, 48, 55, 61, 148; Western social, 55
Scupin, Raymond, 119, 124–126, 129, 131–133, 156
segmentary system, 18
Seinen to Gakumon, 70, 73, 151
sekai minzokugaku, 65 See also global folkloristics
seken (reference society), 97, 154
Sekimoto, Teruo, 148
self-reliance, 106, 110, 112, 155
self-respect, 93, 107–108, 110, 153
Shahrani, M. Nazif, 146
shame, 30, 87, 96–98, 148
shame culture, 87, 96
Shimizu, Akitoshi, 11–12, 147
shinbutsu shūgō (amalgamation of Shinto and Buddhism), 95
shin'i genshō, See psycho-semantic phenomena

Shinto, 95, 133, 153–154
Shorter, Edward, 126
Shotoku, Prince, 154
Sinha, Dharni, 151
Sinha, Vineeta, 13, 151–152
sissy, 111
situational ethics, 93, 96, 99–100
situationalism, 92–93
Smith, Anthony D., 152
Smith, Robert J., 22, 25–27
Smith, Sheldon, 153
social evolution, 2, 142
socialization, 20, 97–98, 118, 120–121, 127, 144, 154 See also child rearing
Sofue, Takao, 22, 35
Soga clan, 153
Soga, Umako, 154
Sorokin, Pitirim, 36
Sosnoski, Daniel, 126
Southeast Asia, 51, 58–59, 157
souvenir shops, 140
Spirit Sings, The, 11
Srinivas, M. N., 17–18, 39
Stalin, Joseph, 111
Stars and Stripes, the, 90–91, 153
statistical significance, 135–137 See also symbolic significance
Stevens, Rebecca A. T., 140
Strathern, Andrew J., 153
study of culture at a distance, 155
subjectivity, 15, 20, 38–41, 45
Suenari, Michio, 35
Sugimoto, Yoshio, 150
Suzuki, Daisetz T., 82

Index

Suzuki, Eitaro, 36
Swift, Jonathan, 88
symbolic significance, 124, 135–137, 140 See also statistical significance
sympathy, 19, 21, 47

Takezawa, Yasuko, 136
taking one's proper station, 92, 94, 103–104, 107–108
Tanabe, Shigeharu, 51–52, 54
tapas, 136
tatami (mat), 125, 130
tea ceremony, 42, 124–130, 139
textbooks, introductory anthropology, 60, 115–145, 147, 150, 156–158
Third World, the, 1–4, 16, 28, 37–38, 54
Thompson, John B., 55, 149
Tiffin, Helen, 150
toilet training, 99–100
token localism, 36
totalizing discourse, 33, 79
tourism, 136–137, 142, 158
trade war, 141
tradition, 7–8, 34, 42, 48, 50–51, 55, 59, 69, 85–86, 117, 123, 125, 127, 129–130, 133, 135, 138–140, 143, 146, 150–151; academic, intellectual, and scholarly, 13, 53, 66–67, 69, 83; folk and popular, 64, 67, 150, 151; invented, 139; invention of, 7, 79; little/great, 154; national, 28, 55–56, 72, 75, 83, 139

translation, 5, 16, 29, 35, 57, 60, 65, 73, 103, 131, 148; cultural, 30
Trask, Haunani-Kay, 7–8, 146
Tripartite Pact, 104
Tsurumi, Kazuko, 151

uchi (inside) – *soto* (outside), 18, 32, 95
ukiyoe, 133, 138
Umehara, Takeshi, 23
Umesao, Tadao, 11, 57, 147
uniformity, 95, 100, 102
United States of America, the, 3, 9–10, 20–22, 24–26, 28, 33–34, 44–46, 50–51, 55–57, 62, 70, 75, 81, 87–88, 95–99, 101, 104–112, 115–116, 118, 122, 124, 126–127, 129, 131, 134–135, 140–142, 145, 147, 153–155
unity, 42, 57–58, 68, 94, 103; of experience, 93, 95 See also integrity; uniformity
University of California, Los Angeles (UCLA), 115
ura (back) – *omote* (front), 95
us – them, 36, 50, 87, 114, 130, 134, 143, 150

van Bremen, Jan, 49, 51–52, 54, 146
Van Gennep, Arnold, 74
viewers, 5, 42, 129
Virginia Commonwealth University (VCU), 115, 157
Völkerkunde, 70
Volksgeist, 81, 148

Volkskunde, 70

wa (harmony), 118, 122
Wada, Yoshiko I., 138, 157
wakaru (understand), 81–82, 84
Waldren, Jacqueline, 158
Wallerstein, Immanuel, 9, 56, 150
Ward, Robert E., 22
Warms, Richard L., 118, 156
Well, H. G., 73
West, the, 3, 8–9, 13, 15, 20–21, 25, 29–30, 36–38, 44, 50–51, 55, 57, 60–62, 73, 84, 89, 93, 99, 110, 134, 138, 142, 146, 153, 158
See also the Occident
Western Europe, 57, 59, 70, 72, 131, 142
Westernization, 138
wholeness, 102
World Association of Japanese Studies, 45
world system, center/core of, 9–10, 25–29, 36, 44–46, 49–53, 55–56, 58, 60–63, 75, 148, 150; central scholars in, 9, 27–29, 46, 56, 62, 75; ferry traffic in, 27, 60; mainland/island in, 9, 26–27, 60; of anthropology, 9, 25, 48–50, 52, 149; of anthropology defined, 9; peripheral scholars in, 10, 27–29, 46, 51–52, 56, 60, 62, 65, 75; periphery/margin of, 9–10, 26–29, 45–46, 49–53, 56, 60, 63, 146, 150; power differences in, 56, 63; power imbalance in, 26, 53, 150; power inequality in, 9, 46, 56; power structure of, 51; semi-periphery of, 9, 52, 150; symbiotic relationships in, 56
World War II, 16, 22, 32, 37, 58–59, 61, 85–86, 92, 105, 122, 141, 157–158

Yamaguchi, Masao, 57
Yamamoto, Matori, 6
Yamashita, Shinji, 136, 151
Yanagita, Kunio, 14, 61, 64–86, 146, 150, 151–152
yin – yang, 93, 153, 155
Yoshida, Kenji, 5, 158
Young, Philip D., 153
yukata (light-fabric kimono), 157

za (communal theater), 42, 76, 86
Zen, 54, 82, 95, 118
Zuni, 18–19, 91, 147